The Doorbell
of Forgiveness

Dedicated to Don E. Stevens
(January 14, 1919 - April 26, 2011)

My Beautiful Big Bear and an elder brother
in Avatar Meher Baba's love.

In the language of Rwanda, known as Kinyarwanda there are two words: "imbabazi" which means (ask for) forgiveness, and "kubabarira" which means to forgive.

On May 19, 2011 in London, Jean-Paul Samputu, a survivor of the Rwandan genocide wrote for Laurent about forgiveness:

"In life we must find creative (or constructive) ways to negotiate conflicts. We cannot change the past but we can change how we approach it, or how we carry our feelings about it into the future, and forgiveness is the key.

"Forgiveness is the most powerful weapon against terrorism and atrocities. To break these cycles of violence, wars, conflicts, is to preach forgiveness. We live in the world where revenge is the culture. Only the culture of forgiveness will stop the cycle (of war, genocide, etc.).

"My real enemy was not the one who wronged me, my real enemy was my hatred, bitterness, my anger which came alive in me. We become what we don't forgive. Forgiveness means to liberate from bondage, to release from the prison of our desire for revenge, of our anger, our bitterness, and hatred.

"Life is not changed by knowing the word of the truth but by living the truth."

☙

The Doorbell of Forgiveness

Don E. Stevens with his Young People's Group

(October 20 & 21, 2007)

Compiled and Edited by
Laurent Weichberger with Karl Moeller

COMPANION BOOKS
PUBLISHERS

Published by
Companion Books
228 Hammersmith Grove· London
W6 7HG· UK

Copyright © 2011 by Companion Enterprises Limited
All rights reserved

First Printing: July 10, 2011
ISBN: 978-0-9525097-5-2

All quotations from Avatar Meher Baba
Copyright © 2011 by Avatar Meher Baba Perpetual Public Charitable Trust
Post Bag No. 31, Kings Road· Ahmednagar, MS 414 001 India
[Unless noted otherwise.]

Printed in the United States of America

Cover photo of doorbell on Paige Springs Road in Sedona, Arizona
Copyright © 2011 by Laurent Weichberger.

Frontispiece photo of the YPG in
Rancho Palos Verdes, California
Copyright © 2007 by Douglas Frank.

Photo of Avatar Meher Baba (circa 1926) at Meherabad, India Copyright © Meher Nazar
Publications, Ahmednagar. Used by permission. This photo was taken by S. S. Deen.

This book was designed and set into type
by Ralph Schmid.

Back cover photo of Don Stevens in Neskowin, Oregon
Copyright © 2004 by Douglas Frank.

꽃

Contents

Preface by Payam Ajang, Ph.D
12

Introduction by Marnie Frank
15

Prologue by Don Stevens
20

Part I

Saturday Morning
23

Saturday Afternoon
60

Photo Section
110

Sunday Morning
114

Sunday Afternoon
164

Part II

Forgiveness Intuitions from Don Stevens
192

Forgiveness at Meherabad by Laurent Weichberger
251

Epilogue by Nicola Masciandaro
268

Don Stevens' Young People's Group (October 2007) in Rancho Palos Verdes, California. L to R (back): Jamshid, Glenn, Payam, Don, Ellie, and Danny. Front: Doug, Laurent, Marnie, Sevn, and Sam. Nasrin and Mahmoud are not shown.

Young People's Group Gatherings

by Laurent Weichberger and Daniel Sanders

During November 2003, in London, Don and Laurent discussed and planned what Don began to refer to as a new "Carry the Torch" seminar to be held repeatedly in America for the youth. At Don's request, an invitation was sent specifically to select representatives from the younger generation, to join Don at the first seminar in Los Angeles. To quote Don from that invitation, "For some years I have been concerned not only with the Avatar's 'bridges' to the reality of God, but also the key matter of the individuals who would 'carry the torch' after the first (and even second generation) of those who had been personally in the presence of Avatar Meher Baba passed away." More than twenty young people have been repeatedly involved in these seminars with Don, who shared the wisdom of his spiritual (and practical) experiences accumulated over decades in direct service to Meher Baba. Before the first seminar, Don had indicated his wish to have four sets of "God-parents" who would effectively host the seminars over time (and participate), in four locations: Los Angeles, Oregon, Massachusetts, and Atlanta. We gathered with Don as planned, and there were ten such gatherings all told, known as the Young People's Group (YPG) as follows:

1. February 27 through March 1, 2004, near Los Angeles. The original YPG meeting. Much wisdom which Avatar Meher Baba gave to Don was shared with us for the succeeding generations.

2. Middle of May, 2005, Neskowin, Oregon. Special guests, the Tyler family.

3. December 2005, Myrtle Beach, South Carolina at Meher Spiritual Center.

4. March 2006, near Los Angeles. Don also gave a talk at the Avatar Meher Baba Center of Southern California.

5. Late September 2006, Salem, MA. On the Friday night before the YPG meeting, about thirty New England Baba lovers came to Cynthia and Richard Griffin's home for a talk by Don. This was the weekend gathering we had just finished when Don had congestive heart failure.

[Don had heart surgery in Salem and recovered fully, "in record time" according to his doctors.]

6. End of April 2007, Myrtle Beach. Don also gave a talk at the Meeting Place at the Meher Center to a packed house which was videotaped. He talked about his congestive heart failure and recovery. He called the Griffins, and Sevn McAuley up on the stage, as well as Danny Sanders, briefly. Don accredited Sevn with "saving his life."

7. October 20 – 21, 2007, near Los Angeles, and which forms the major content of this book.

8. April 19 – 20, 2008, near Atlanta, Georgia.

9. September 13 – 14 , 2009, near Los Angeles, CA.

10. June 25 – 26, 2010, North Conway, New Hampshire.

[November 2010, Don falls in Paris (at age 91) and breaks his leg badly requiring surgery. He recovers and, after physical therapy, is able to walk again with help. Don recuperates in London.]

Preface

Avatar Meher Baba Ki Jai

The moment I read the title of this book *The Doorbell of Forgiveness*, my heart opened. I immediately saw the image in my mind's eye: me ringing a doorbell, then waiting, as if to say "will you let me in?" I've struggled so many times to ring that bell when I've known I've been wrong about something and needed to make my peace. I've also had a hard time being the one to open the door. Could this ringing of a doorbell be a beginning to unimaginable expressions of love — even in the midst of deep seeded anger, hatred, deceit, or any other wrongs in the world?

As you may have suspected, what you are about to read is about forgiveness. But you may be surprised by the many turns and twists in conversation — some of which seem to have absolutely nothing to do with forgiveness! A little background may be helpful in anchoring what you're about to read. In October 2007, on a sunny weekend in Los Angeles, a group of Meher Baba devotees (including myself), from different parts of the country came together to meet with Don Stevens.

I will digress for a moment to tell you about Don. I met Don Stevens in the mid 1990s. I had just graduated from my doctoral program in psychology and my oral board exams were a week or so away. I was full of angst and nervous energy, at times unable to fall asleep for sheer fear of what I was about to face. Don happened to be in San Francisco, where I was studying, and a mutual friend suggested I go and see Don at his hotel, the Holiday Lodge (where Meher Baba had actually stayed in 1956).

Don immediately had a calming effect. We had a lovely conversation and he gave me a very specific strategy to use during my examination, which was essentially to see

> On August 3, 1956: "Baba was driven to ... a new motel, the Holiday Lodge at 119 Van Ness Avenue. (Nearly every other hotel was booked, because the Republican National Convention was being held at this time.)"
> - See Lord Meher, p. 5069]

Meher Baba sitting next to me during the whole exam – To know that I was not alone in the process. This helped me tremendously in easing my fears and giving me some iota of confidence to get through it.

I waited six months on pins and needles to find out the results. I felt I had done poorly and that I had likely failed. I found out I had passed. Don's help and loving concern for me – who was a total stranger to him at the time – of course affected me deeply. Over the years, we have come to know each other well. Don is such a mix of so many things that it is difficult for me to encapsulate him in a few words. I can say simply that I feel God's love much more when I'm around him. Other matters of life just don't seem to matter as much when I'm in his company.

Of course his experiences in meeting Meher Baba, working under His direct guidance in editing *God Speaks* and *Discourses*, leading a spiritual life while living a worldly life as an executive in the oil industry, his humor, sensitive nature, and gifted intelligence add much more color. But really speaking, hearing about his beautiful remembrances of Meher Baba and his personal journey in coming closer to Him have been the most poignant for me.

So now, going back to our weekend in Los Angeles during October 2007. By this time, we were somewhat accustomed to these wonderful gatherings as we had met as a group several times before. Our focus was always on Meher Baba and Don Stevens lead the way. Somehow, unbeknownst to us, a process of simply being in the company of one another began to have a deeper effect. We didn't know necessarily why we were coming together, but over the years, for me personally, a strong inner connection has taken form. After our first meeting, in February 2004, I quickly looked forward to more of these warm, intimate, sometimes provocative, sometimes intense, and more often beautiful exchanges. Meher Baba's love seemed to permeate the atmosphere so much so that at times I could not contain myself and tears kept coming. This was particularly true on this forgiveness-weekend, especially when Don began to share about

Beloved Baba's *tenderness*. I had, until then, never heard it expressed in such a way.

So what is forgiveness? So many have written about it, and talked about it, but for most of us it's a personal experience that may or may not fit any particular way. A group of us Baba devotees came together to talk about it and here is what transpired. I Hope you will take away something from it, and I really hope it prompts you to ring that doorbell to see what may happen ... you never know, it just might be that ripple of love that will touch the heart of countless others.

Here's what Don said during our wonderful weekend exchange, just in case you needed a little more prompting **"...if you've got the courage to touch the Doorbell of Forgiveness, by God you link into a circuit where things happen that are incredible. End of story."**

Payam Ajang Russ, Ph.D., San Pedro, California,
February 25, 2010

Introduction

In 2004 Don Stevens gathered together a group of spiritual seekers devoted to Avatar Meher Baba. We ranged in age roughly from 25 to 70, and Don called us the Young People's Group (YPG). Perhaps he called us that because he was in his mid-80's at the time and we were younger than he. I think we earned that name because, although sincere, we were young in our understanding of the spiritual path and devotion to God. By His Grace, we were given a most loving and skilled teacher in Don, a true mystic who abundantly shared his experiences with Meher Baba, the living God-Man, and his deep understanding of what it means to devote one's life to love for God.

A very down-to-earth person whom Meher Baba described as **"an almost perfect balance of mind and heart,"**[1] Don has shared his knowledge of how to remember God while living in the world, a state which he refers to as practical mysticism. For those of us in the "YPG," Don's insights and experiences are extremely informative, as each of us also lives a worldly life with demands and responsibilities yet our hearts long for His Knowledge, Truth, and Love.

Initially our meetings with Don focused on his sharing his mystical knowledge and experience learned from our mutual master Meher Baba. I think Don intentionally spoon fed this thrilling information to us and allowed that early teacher-student relationship to develop so we would be hooked to the idea of the YPG and to each other. For me, and for most of us, it worked. As I write this, it is six years later, and I realize how deeply my life and my love for God have been affected by our many gatherings. The members of the YPG are my true companions on this spiritual path. Through the sharing of our own experiences, understanding, and insights, we have forged strong inner links which are of great support as we continue in our individual search for God.

Over the years we have explored many subjects, and Don increasingly has relinquished the role of professor to one of initiator. He offers ideas for exploration, ideas usually based on his intuitions, which the group considers in depth, digging into our own experience and thinking. This process has been an opportunity for tremendous spiritual growth. In the safety of the group, with trusted companions and a wise and experienced leader, we have shared very personal and revealing aspects of ourselves, some of which are embarrassing and humbling, others of which are surprisingly wise and insightful. In either case, we are learning more and more and more about self-effacement, surrender to the will of God, and remembrance of Him.

To give a taste of the YPG's endeavors I will share some of the subjects we have explored. Early on, we scrutinized Meher Baba's New Life and what that means for us now and for the future. The New Life was a period in which Meher Baba and a group of His closest disciples known as mandali wandered throughout India without food or shelter. Although God in human form, Meher Baba lived as an equal, as a companion with his mandali. During this nearly two year period of helplessness and hopelessness, they begged for food, lived in the open, and were dependent entirely on God for survival. The meaning of this phase of His work remains a mystery, although we know intuitively it is profoundly important, Within the YPG, individuals have their own understanding of what that work may be but collectively we believe that it will have enormous significance in the years to come.

We have also studied sanskaras, the impressions created by any action good or bad, which determine the karma of each lifetime and which affect the thoughts, words, and deeds of the individual ego. Don has shared his understanding of the creation and removal of sanskaras and his conviction that in this Advent, Meher Baba has given us the tools to deal with the ego in the most efficient manner possible, helping us to hasten our journey back to Him. These tools are the Avatar's gifts for the New Age. At various gatherings the

YPG has explored the meaning of these tools, which Don intuitively believes are available to all of humanity.

One tool is the gift of intuition. Meher Baba describes intuition as follows: **"The voice that is heard deep within the soul is my voice – the voice of inspiration, of intuition, of guidance. Through those who are receptive to this voice, I speak."**[2]

Another tool is the understanding that all religions share Universal Truth. Don refers to this tool as Beads-on-One-String, a concept which Meher Baba introduced at a 1932 news conference in England. He said,

"True religion consists in developing that attitude of mind, which would ultimately result in seeing one Infinite Existence prevailing throughout the universe; when one could live in the world and yet be not of it, and at the same time, be in harmony with everyone and everything; when one could attend to all worldly duties and affairs, and yet feel completely detached from all their results; when one could see the same divinity in art and science, and experience the highest consciousness and indivisible bliss in everyday life. ...

I intend bringing together all religions and cults like beads on one string and revitalize them for individual and collective needs. This is my mission to the West. The peace and harmony that I shall talk of and that will settle on the face of this worried world is not far off."[3]

Don explained to the YPG, that during His physical lifetime, Meher Baba sent Don throughout India to film holy sites of various religions, including Hinduism, Jainism, Buddhism, and Islam. Don later learned that these were places which Meher Baba had visited often, always incognito, spending significant time in deep meditation doing important spiritual work. Based on Don's own experiences and those of companions he has traveled with to these sites, Don believes that Meher Baba left stores of spiritual energy for humanity in general and spiritual seekers individually to help them on their journey to God. In our YPG discussion it was thrilling to think that such a palpable physical link to the Avatar is available to all who seek Him, no matter what name of God they use. This is the essence of the Avataric gift of Beads-on-One-String

Other subjects the YPG has explored include Meher Baba's words, especially those in His major work *God Speaks*, one more Avataric gift. Another subject we studied is companionship as lived in the New Life. Don explained his belief that Meher Baba's companionship with His mandali forged a model which revealed the inner link between the limited individual self and God Himself, the one true Reality. This companionship with God is available to all humanity and does not require a third person to explain or interpret the Mystery for others. Rather, God is directly linked to each soul, and through remembrance of and surrender to Him, His loving companionship is constantly possible. Related to this, Don has shared his experience of God's tenderness for the individual souls in Creation living the dream of separateness. This stimulated very powerful and personal reflections among the YPG about our own limited expressions of tenderness and our yearning to expand our capacity for such.

There are many more themes which we have considered in our six years together, one of which is forgiveness, the subject of this book. The words on forgiveness stand for themselves and give you, the reader, a taste of the YPG.

I will conclude by sharing the essential lesson of what I have learned from the remarkable journey with my companions in this group. That is: the love we of the YPG have received from Beloved God is constantly given to all of humanity and Creation every moment of everyday. We simply don't know it because the sanskaras of separation distract our minds and hearts from the Reality of His absolute Presence and Love. Nonetheless, He is helping us constantly, no matter how deeply we feel we are suffering. His is the Hand which is holding ours, leading us back to Him with all Love and Compassion. If we do our best in every moment of the day and in every situation He places us, if we try to remember Him continuously, surrendering everything, all the good and all the bad, to Him, we will make Him our constant Companion. He desires this companionship more than we can possibly imagine and for each step we take toward Him, He takes ten toward us. As Meher Baba has said, we do not have to be perfect to come to Him. What He wants from us is our imperfections so that He can cleanse us of our ignorance and bring us home to Union with Him. That is the Treasure which awaits every single one of us.

Marnie Frank, Portland, Oregon, June 2010

Endnotes:

1. From *Meher Baba's Word & His Three Bridges*, by Don E. Stevens, with Norah Moore and Laurent Weichberger (London: Companion Books, 2003), p.42.
2. *Lord Meher*, by V.S. Bhau Kalchuri (Myrtle Beach: Manifestation Inc.), p. 2122.
3. Ibid., p. 1554.

PROLOGUE

The first time I read a very thoughtful editorial, in the *International Herald Tribune*, on the most recent acts of terrorism associated with another flare-up between two Balkan countries, I found a suggested mode of approaching this bane of civilization. It was the not obvious suggestion to try to apply absolute forgiveness to each other for all the acts of cruelty committed during the centuries. Almost at once, I tried a simple act of forgiveness for a happening quite recent in my own life and found it was perhaps the toughest goal I had ever adopted. Nevertheless, I was deeply convinced that here was something important to be explored much further, and I kept it in mind, even talking to members of different study groups in which I have long been involved.

At a meeting of what Laurent and I called the "Young Peoples' Group" (YPG) in the USA, I suggested that my own experiences in exploring the intent of Meher Baba having given me the job of filming several sacred sites in India (without explaining his intent for those films), I had slowly discovered whole chapters of meaning which were very exciting to me. Also involved in all this process of discovery was the modern problem of terrorism, and I was now confident that Meher Baba, and undoubtedly an entire team of experts in the spiritual hierarchy, were far along in evolving a method of resolving these ancient antagonisms. Moreover, I had a great suspicion that absolute forgiveness was the final goal to be reached, but this being so difficult to accomplish in reality, the experts working on the problem had amassed stores of energy and archetypes for attack, and these were now all available to those who were inclined to carry the problem into an active stage of approach. So, I suggested that the YPG might well do some careful thinking and experimenting, and I was convinced that if they just touched the doorbell of forgiveness, which was right in front of them, they would have an instant and astonishing approach opened to them.

We spent much of the weekend together discussing this and the closely related subject of sanskaras, which, after all, is what cruelty is in the long run.

The Young Peoples' Group have done, I feel, a very fine work of opening up the subject to the modern seeker of Truth, and I believe that here is an important arena of modern social problems which desperately needs attack. These bright young minds, which have already spent years wrestling with the goals of inner development and the challenges of the Spiritual Path, will intrigue and encourage further efforts. I know several already who have done so and had fascinating and important results in their own lives.

Don E. Stevens, London, England, June 4, 2010

Part I

Don Stevens' Young People's Group Weekend Seminar

The following is a transcript of the seventh "Young People's Group" (YPG) as so called by Don Stevens. Present that weekend were, Marnie & Doug Frank, Elham & Jamshid Ebrahimzadeh, Payam & Glenn Russ, Laurent Weichberger, Don Stevens, Sevn McAuley, Daniel Sanders, Sam Clayton (from England), and Nasrin & Mahmoud Ajang.

The seminar took place at the home of Nasrin and Mahmoud in Rancho Palos Verdes, California, near Los Angeles, on October 20 and 21, 2007. The theme set by Don for the weekend was "forgiveness." The audio tracks were transcribed by Danny Sanders, and Laurent Weichberger. We have included as many direct quotes as possible to give as accurate a picture we can of this seminar. We use an ellipsis " ... " for words left out, or long pauses, or when the audiotape is inaudible. We use square brackets "[like this]" when words are added to the transcript by the editors for clarity. We use curly braces "{for a description of the setting}" or environment. Parentheses follow their natural usage.

Saturday Morning: The Dream of Creation

*D*on: Shall we be silent with Baba for a few moments?
{The group observes a moment of silence.}

¶ Don: Dearly Beloved Baba. Here we are, gathered together, in your love, in one of the most wonderful homes of Baba lovers I've ever known. We're so grateful to you, taking time off from your duties to enjoy life with us for a couple days. Bless you, Baba.

Now I'd like to suggest we spring to the attack with the most important outstanding subject that we have on the list. That is the continuation of the intuition project. Suggest and invite anybody who's been having some intuitions, if they feel like so doing, to share their project with us, if you've got them ...

Doug Frank: It's not a project but I do have an intuition I'd like to run past everybody. I was thinking the other day about, Baba talks about the time, well, that one — that we always incarnate, we always progress spiritually, we never go backwards, okay? And then I was thinking about the idea of the way we all— the only way any of us can experience time is linear ... the past and future.

So I had this thought that: isn't it possible then, that we could reincarnate in the past? Into our next incarnation and progress spiritually, but who's to say that we can't reincarnate in 500 A.D. and advance in spirit, not just in the future? Because if time doesn't matter, then linearity isn't the only way would ... then we always think in terms of where we're going to incarnate in the future. Always in the future. That comes from the way we view time. But why wouldn't we then be able to reincarnate into the past as well? That was my idea.

Danny: Laurent and I were just discussing this yesterday morning while we were waiting for Glenn to pick us up from the train station.

Doug: This same thing?

Danny: Yeah.

Doug: That must be floating around in the ... {Laughter.}

Danny: Yeah, although we didn't necessarily agree in our perspective on the matter — or I mean with each other. {Laughs.} My feeling is the same as yours, that if your sanskaras match a point in the past, then why wouldn't you just

> Mani S. Irani, Meher Baba's sister, once told how she had complained to Baba, while he was still alive, that she did not want to have to find him all over again in her next lifetime, as that would be a step backward and a losing of ground already covered. Baba gently corrected her with the following comment about staying connected with him through lifetimes: " ... it's always a going forward ... you pick up from where you leave off ... never a going backwards." (From *Meher Baba's Gift of Intuition*, p. 86). Mani's comments are from the video, *Eternal Beloved* (Meher Prasad, 1995). See also *Discourses*, "Reincarnation and Karma VI : The Destiny of the Reincarnated Individual." Regarding Meher Baba's statement about picking up from where you leave off in a previous lifetime, see also *Discourses*, "The Dynamics of Spiritual Advancement." - LW

incarnate in the past?

Sevn: Well, I disagree with that, because I think if you're trying to look outside of linearity, then saying you're going to reincarnate in the past or in the next lifetime, is linear thinking. You know, linear goes forward and back. I think if you're looking outside of the linear structure then it's not about reincarnating in the past, having a realization of a past incarnation, or even embodying past impressions in a current form. Perhaps if you become enlightened during this lifetime, you realize that you were also enlightened in all past incarnations simultaneously.

Doug: Well did Baba ever ... he simply said that when we reincarnate we ...

¶ Don: No, I certainly never, when he was discussing anything that Eruch and I were discussing with him on either *God Speaks* or *Discourses* did he go into that. Incidentally just to toss another little pebble into the works here, but if all Creation is sucked into linearity, then there is no available Creation anywhere accessible which is anywhere but in this linearity, which was set up by the Whim. In other words, it is perhaps a completely meaningless possibility because isn't all of Creation involved in the dream itself and can't, let's say, exist two or a thousand places at the same time. No, I say what if that is impossible, because of the very manner of the structure and the origin of Creation, when the Whim created — when let's say the Whim of God manifested Creation from the Om Point. The linearity and the absolute fact of linearity in the dream itself is prevalent in all of Creation. All of Creation is involved in linearity. Excuse me Doug, go ahead.

Doug: All of linearity is part of ...

¶ Don But I'm saying it can be a controlling — there's no logic which says it can't be a controlling part which cannot be divorced from any part of the dream.

Doug: But if Baba said that time doesn't exist in ...

¶ Don: Then it's all in the dream.

Doug: It's all in the dream.

¶ Don: But I'm talking about, let's say, the laws of the dream itself.

Doug: So in other words we incarnate in the dream, and therefore we incarnate in linear [time] ...

¶ Don: And there's no way to bust that.

Danny: But if it's all happening at once then — I mean, I know we don't perceive it as all happening at once, but if all of time is really happening at once ...

¶ Don: Well, to me it's always been a fascinating concept that — at one point — that God was totally unconscious and then the Whim surged, and then the next point, actually in reality all consciousness and all time had already been elapsed. But it's a property of the dream.

Doug: It's a property of God ... and we reincarnate in the dream, or we have to keep going forward in our ...

¶ Don: In actuality. It doesn't mean that you can't — somewhere or another — tap things that have already been lived through in that linearity, or you can't — somewhere or another — even tap into future things. I've even done that myself. So I know it exists; quite a few people do. But nevertheless when you come out of the dream — within the dream — then you're trapped back into the laws of the linearity of the original Whim.

Sevn: Isn't the dream saying — it's just a dream — broad? I would say it's more specific as gross consciousness, whereas subtle or mental conscious beings would probably be able to transcend that time.

Laurent: I don't think Baba indicated that. I think he indicated that there's "subtle time" and "mental time."

Sevn: Oh, really?

Laurent: Mm-hmm.

¶ Don: Yeah.

Sevn: Ah. It's just different.

Glenn Russ: I recall a quote where Baba actually said that, "God is time and I am God." To me the meaning of time is illusory change or transition, and that perspective of

Glenn videotaped a talk by Dr. Moorty at Meher Mount (near Ojai, CA) on May 8, 2004, in which Moorty tells a story about Baba explaining to him, "God is time, and I am God. So you must learn to honor time. If you don't know how to honor time, you can't honor God."

transition is different for each individual. So I think we have this group hallucination, is what I feel, in the gross. But we have an idea of what we've been taught that time means, relative to objects ... moving forward in time and backward in time. And that was the other thing, moving forward in time backward in consciousness. That in reality — about the timelessness of God — I feel that everything that we perceive is happening (or not happening, or already happened) and it's all existing in God. I don't know even that the Whim exists in that kind of a time, or not.

¶ Don: Well, the Whim certainly follows the drop-soul into the dream of Creation. Baba certainly puts enough in words so that's an inevitable conclusion, because each individual drop-soul certainly has the properties of the Whim. The drop-soul, in fact — is God — Baba says, and that means it has all of the properties of the original latencies and manifested latencies are all there in the Whim, your own personal Whim. I think that's glorious.

Glenn: I had an intuition ... still been fermenting and I shared it with Sevn last night, and I'll try to put it in the simplest terms, but it comes down to consciousness. That really the only thing that's real is consciousness, and I don't know why, in *God Speaks*, that started me thinking, that — I believe it's that, I don't have my *God Speaks* with me — individual conscious ... the human form is the byproduct of the evolution of consciousness. And so I have this sense, and I also remember Baba saying — someone asked him if he'd ever fallen in love, and he said [something like] — "Yes, once a long time ago I fell in love with humanity." So there's this sense, okay, that if God is love, and love is this eternal and complete and whole thing ...

Mehera said, "Someone, perhaps it was a reporter in the early days when Baba visited England, asked Baba whether He had ever been in love. 'Yes,' Baba replied, 'I am always in love with humanity.'" From the book *Mehera*, by Mehera J. Irani (Princeton: Beloved Books) pp. 188-189. -LW

¶ Don: Wait a minute. You're getting on dangerous ground. *I'll just quickly say that Baba certainly did not say God is only love.* God is a lot of other things. But go ahead.

Glenn: Well, that love — the essential — whatever that is — this can be ...

¶ Don: It can't even be the essential thing of God.

Glenn: Well, this is what I'm feeling. That the lover, the Beloved, and the love itself — and I would associate the Whim with the love itself — are really the same thing. It's only a matter of your point of view of experience that they're different things. So you have this wholeness, this completeness, this infinity. And the experience of that, whatever you would call it in multiplicity is really only a matter of expression. So there's, depending upon your point of view and experience, from the finite point there's a sense of time. But all of it probably really exists in timeless whatever. I mean it is all part of a complete whole somehow. And the only thing that really matters, from our point of view, is this concept of the individual whole consciousness. There's this thing that continues beyond Liberation — whatever that is. I don't know what that is. I've been pondering it for quite a bit — it feels very incomplete to me. But I also had an image — I had a thought from a Native American story about the first experience of the ocean. Where the person looks in the ocean and sees his ancestors in the ocean, by the moonlight reflected in the ocean. And I thought — well, you have this infinite ocean, and there are ripples, just like the Whim on the ocean. You have the completeness of the entire — if you focus in on the reflection of one movement in the ocean, you could see the entire sun or the moon in that one reflection, in that one ripple. And so you have this experience of multiplicity that's beautiful in the wholeness of, just the fullness of just that — of infinity. So I don't know. It's kind of a revolving around what really matters. Because there's this whole sense of consciousness, that seems to me is what really matters in this game that we're playing. Anyways ... it's a pot with kind of a big stew.

¶ Don: Somebody like to comment on your ...

Participant: Stew?

¶ Don: ... intuition?

Sevn {to Glenn}: What do you mean by consciousness as opposed to — what? Are you saying *love* as opposed to *lover* and *Beloved*, in the way you're saying consciousness as being the most important aspect?

Glenn: The thing is, in the real state of God, when the Whim is involved, you have essentially a lover and a Beloved in essence, whether you look at it from Creation or from Illusion, the way that energy moves, whether it's the Creation or destruction (or whatever), it seems to me that there's this tri-part movement of infinity that involves the moving aspect, an objective and a subjective aspect. So, I mean that's taking it even more abstract. But depending upon how you view that which is real — beyond illusion, beyond the Creation point, beyond the most finite reality that is still God, that there's this nature that cannot be conceived of, apparently, by our minds as anything but these different perspectives, when in reality there's this timeless whole that doesn't really include ... And somehow the individual consciousness, that's still part of the universal consciousness (whatever it is), when somebody receives "Mukti," Liberation or becomes God-realized or a Perfect Master (or whatever), is part of that complete experience which may have happened in an instantaneous moment, or some timeless (whatever that is).

> Mukti is a Hindi word which means liberation from the cycle of reincarnation and karma. It is a spiritual goal in Hinduism, to be eternally free. -LW

And like, you know past, present, future all exist in the same moment is something that I've often contemplated as well. And I would think that even if you could go backward in time, forward in time, are you really going back in your conscious linearity? I would say no. I would say you're not really going back in your own conscious linearity. You're only ...

Doug: You're not conscious of it. You wouldn't be conscious of it.

Glenn: Because your consciousness is still progressing forward. So there is still a linearity.

Payam {Glenn's wife}: I have to say, I don't understand any of this! {Group laughter.}

Payam: I'm really trying. But I don't know how I can even contemplate ...

Marnie: It seems to me like where it gets confusing is the boundary between — we're talking about two things. We're talking about Creation, and we're talking about God and Reality. And where we get confused is when the boundaries — because of our lack of understanding, but when we mix the two. And it seems like that's what happens when we try to think about ourselves as being drop-souls and part of being God. But we're drop-souls caught in illusion so we can't really compare the two, and that's where we get into trouble.

Doug: Well, God in reality, where everything is happening at the same time ...

Marnie: Right.

Doug: But once you become a drop-soul, then you're trapped in constraints of the ...

Marnie: Exactly. And so we can't compare ourselves to Him, because even though we are Him unconsciously, consciously we're these drop-souls struggling, so we have to keep — in my mind — we kind of have to keep those boundaries clear.

¶ Don: Can I have Laurent put his drop in here? {Laughter}

Laurent: Yeah, my drop. I want to piggyback on what Marnie's saying because I love where you're going with that, Marnie. For me, I think where it gets confusing is if we start talking about anything other than our own direct experience. Because, if we have the experience of it, then we have some clarity about what we experience. If we're talking about what we're conjecturing based on something Baba said, then we should be clear about the distinction — "Well, Baba said this, what does it mean?" When we mingle our experience with conjecture, it can be confusing what we're talking about.

Glenn: Well, I used the experience of love. I mean when we experience, depending upon where the object of experience, particularly with a human being, in those peak moments of experience, there is a sense that this is through the love, the lover and the Beloved and that experience — that this is not separate objects. That somehow there's a whole. There's a whole, real — there's something less apart, and something complete, there's some kind of complete wholeness, timeless something that transcends your ordinary experience. And I think that's true in everyday life even.

Laurent: But isn't Don's experience of love, and my experience of love, and your experience of love individual? And we can share about that, and compare notes, but it may not be one experience of love. It may be ... and Don [himself] may have three different experiences of love.

Glenn: And this is a curious thing, because God creates everything completely fresh and new in every moment. No human being is alike ever from the beginning of time, and so forth. Why would God do the same thing and be bored?

¶ Don: Why would He repeat Himself? He would be a hell of a boring God.

Glenn: And God apparently has something — there's some part of, whatever, Creation aside, there's something that persists that is not only — that is not a byproduct. See, this is where it all started. There's something — you have the fullness of Creation of the full consciousness in a human being — the whole human form. Baba uses the word "byproduct," or at least that's how he came at it in *God Speaks* ...

Laurent: You can borrow this one if you want. {He hands *God Speaks* to Glenn}.

Glenn: And I don't have the page number here, I have it in mine at home. There's something obviously, if you take the word "byproduct," there's something that's not a byproduct — and something that persists, that even Baba says there's a persistence of something — whatever that is ...

¶ Don: Can we be precise about that, because it's an important point, and Baba certainly does give clarity on it. And that is that, for instance, the perhaps most important thing that we're aware of is the material associated with the word "sanskara." And Baba is terribly clear that a sanskara has two primary components — an energy component and a form component. And he was terribly clear in this final collection of *Discourses* that Deshmukh printed, and which I had a copy and somebody stole it (and also the photocopy that I made up) — in that Baba was very clear in his words. He says, now talking about the erasing of sanskaras — this is not a completely accurate concept of what goes on. It is the loss, the elimination, the complete annihilation of the energy aspect of the sanskara, and the retention of form, which is eternal. Now, this was a terribly, terribly important differentiation, and let's say, clarification.

So in other words, your form of your experiences is immortal. It becomes part of God's infinite, individualized consciousness. And infinite, individualized consciousness is, let's say, the reason the whole-damn-thing of Creation floated out of [the OmPoint], and God so loved that — "I want to experience consciously my Godhood" — and so the universe comes out. And to satisfy that, the permanence of the form part is brought from a latency — Baba is clear on that also — latent consciousness is all originally in the Beyond Beyond state of God, God in existence.

For more on the Beyond Beyond state of God, read *God Speaks* by Meher Baba. In that book, Baba compares the experience of Creation with a dream. - LW

And what we're simply doing through Creation is taking the latency and manifesting it and living. And, apparently then, this business of the living aspect has to do with the form which each drop-soul contributes within the dream. And so the dream may be a dream, but it is a hell of an important dream, and it contributes what was lacking in God when He said "Who the hell am I?" {Group laughter.}

Sevn: The edited Whim.

Laurent: That was the original word: "Who the hell am I?" {More laughter.}

¶ Don: I'm sorry that I disrupted the whole ... but I had to toss my ... forgive me for putting this in as you were talking, Glenn. {Laughter persists.} Say, that ripple goes on rippling. {Still yet more laughing.}

Sevn: That was a good one.

¶ Don: Can we divorce ourselves from that part of the dream for a bit now? As you were talking, Glenn, I kept thinking of something that was one of the first, you might say, natural, creative, esoteric things that I did in my life. I was toying with some of these things that we're dealing with right now, and all of sudden (for some reason or another) an apple came to my mind. An apple sitting here, it is a unit. It is a thing. It is an entire unit. But I also know from my own experience that sometimes the color of that apple is important to me ... And yet it is part of a unitary, whole thing. That apple, when you start to think of it, is also substance, it has taste. It has smell. It has all of these various different aspects to its unitary reality. And we can break it down into interesting things to compare. And we say — well, this apple is golden, and that cranberry over there is another color. And so we can compare from one unit to another unit, and break down in the analytical form things that are important. And why shouldn't Reality, why shouldn't God Himself — Baba makes it clear that God has various different eternal aspects? Certain latent aspects, and they're all of God, and some of them are finally brought to a living form by the whole dream of Creation. They're brought from a dormant situation, from the latency, into the manifest — Baba uses these words. He uses "latent" a great deal in *God Speaks*. And he uses the word "manifesting." We just don't concentrate enough on what is going on in manifesting. Was it — unreal — before? Baba says it was latent before. But it exists. It was part of the original — original state of God — but not in a living condition. And so, when God said, "Who am I?" the latency had to wake up, amongst the other things that happened. And it woke up through a dream process.

So there are terribly important things. Baba says the universe was created for love. So a lot of people who are absolutely hipped and hogtied about love, say that's the only thing that's any — excuse me, I'm letting Stevens come in too much again. But Baba doesn't say that love is the only thing in Creation. So we've got to be careful about our own way of wanting to give certain significance, and cast other things out as being really someway or another unreal. So very, very few people have even bothered to read in the *Discourses* where Baba says that actually there are two things about a human being that are terribly important: his head qualities and his heart qualities. And strangely enough Baba then goes on to say in words you cannot argue with, an equilibrium — a balance between those two is absolutely necessary in the process before supra-consciousness can be born. Apparently super-consciousness is what is really God-realization. And he says if there's too much love, things go wrong. If there's too much head, things go wrong. And it calls for eventually an absolute balance between the two before super-consciousness can be born.

> "It is for love that the whole universe sprang into existence and it is for the sake of love that it is kept going."
> ~ Meher Baba, from *Discourses* (6th edition), Volume I, p. 163.

And yet he also says at the end of that same discourse on love, the universe was created for love.

But does that mean love is the only important thing? We just haven't done our homework and read all of the part about the absolute equilibrium that is necessary. It all gets somewhere or another blended into, let's say, the infinitude of God Himself, and what Reality and God is. Well, it's infinitude, and there's no part of it that can be lacking because He wouldn't be infinite if any part turned up missing. That's why no drop-soul can ever get destroyed and lost overboard in the process of it — it all has to go through the process of manifesting whatever it was born for, and then it can go back into the infinite whole.

And along comes the professor from Delhi and asks Baba, "Well, how do I meet God finally? Do I meet Him as a professor from Delhi? Or have I been dissolved and I'm really just God meeting God?" (Something of that general sort). Baba said — No, the whole process of Creation would be futile and useless if you just went back there and met God as God, and that all of the individuality that you had developed was wiped out in the process. He says no. When Jesus Christ goes back to God, after he's done his work, he comes back as Jesus Christ. And all of the God-realized souls, they meet God as their manifest, individualized, impermanent selves. So, there is no part of the latent consciousness, the individualized latent consciousness, that is born, that is ever lost. It's eternal. It's immortal. You know, so the fairy story is real — we are immortal — we don't just get evaporated.

Doug: So what you're saying is, once the energy of these sanskaras has been reduced to zero, the sanskaras go back. And so, you know, you're not meeting God as God. You're meeting God as an individual — with those sanskaric forms still intact.

¶ Don: Intact.

Danny: But with the compulsion gone.

Doug: Yeah.

¶ Don: The compulsion component, which was unreal, was the part that got out. Laurent, what were you saying?

Laurent: If it's okay, I'd like to do my little intuition thing ...

¶ Don: Go ahead, please.

Laurent: ... because this is a good segue way for it. I had heard — somebody may know — but I think it was in either Seattle or Portland, maybe once a year, or they had tried it once (or whatever), they sat down in the morning as a group, and their goal was to finish *God Speaks* by the evening.

Marnie: That's Portland. Yeah, we do it every year.

Doug: That was our group.

"Sometimes human love manifests itself as a force which is divorced from reason and runs parallel to it. Sometimes it manifests itself as a force which gets mixed up with reason and comes into conflict with it. Lastly, it expresses itself as a constituent of the harmonized whole where love and reason have been balanced and fused into an integral unity ... Complete separation between these two aspects of the spirit is of course never possible, but when there is an alternate functioning of love and reason (oscillating in their predominance) we have a love which is unillumined by reason or a reason which is unenlivened by love. In the second type, love and reason are both simultaneously operative but they do not work in harmony with each other. Though this conflict creates confusion, it is a necessary phase in the evolution of the higher state where there is a real synthesis of love and reason. In the third type of love this synthesis between love and reason is an accomplished fact with the result that both love as well as reason are so completely transformed that they precipitate the emergence of a new level of consciousness which, compared to the normal human consciousness, is best described as super-consciousness."
~ Meher Baba, from *Discourses* (6th edition], Volume I, p. 157-158)

Laurent: You guys inspired me.

Sevn: You've got to let us know the next time you guys do it.

Marnie: November 10th.

Laurent: So I heard this story, and I said — if they can do it as a group, I can do it. So I went in my backyard, we have a tree house in the backyard. We rented a house in Flagstaff, and I'd made a deal with [my daughter] Aspen that she could have a different part of the house if I could use the tree house. So I brought my *God Speaks* up in the tree house, and something to sit on. I started in the morning.

¶ Don: Oh, you have sit-down room in the tree house? Wow.

Laurent: And I read *God Speaks* until I was finished. And it didn't take me as long as I'd thought. I'd read all the words from Baba, you know, chapters one through eight. I didn't read the "Supplement" because I've read it before — but something happened. I didn't know quite what had happened. One thing that happened for sure, and I wanted to tell you this, there's no doubt that after reading it straight through from beginning to end, that Baba says [God-realization] is an individual attainment, and that the individuality is definitely persisted. Individual consciousness.

Danny: That part has always confused me.

Laurent: But it's totally clear when you read it — if you read it in succession like that, there is no way to come away from it without realizing that — that is for sure. But the thing that was an intuitive understanding, which kind of surprised me — it took me a couple days to get a handle on it, but I felt less fear. This was a wild experience. It was almost as if, like, as an individual, I'm some sort of spiritual container that contains various different forces, psychic forces — impressions, love, fear, all these different things, you know? Thoughts, concerns, worries, and whatever. And that, somehow, by sitting with *God Speaks* like that for an intensive session, it was almost like Baba had pulled some drain-plug, or something like that, and the fear in particular had drained out. Not completely, but to such an extent that it was like a palpable, tangible-fear-difference. And I was just like — "Wow! What is this?" — and I couldn't understand what I was feeling. And it was the feeling of not being afraid on a very core, primal level — like fear had lessened. That's my intuition.

Sevn: Wow.

Doug: Something that, you know — God Himself laid out ... this amazing plan ... it gives a person a sense of security ... He's really in charge. And I think that can result in a reduction of fear, which we all have — look at the newspapers. But you know when you experience something like that ... I mean I think I felt the same thing ... it is amazing to read it aloud with a group ...

Laurent: Well, thanks for the inspiration you guys.

Payam: Well, I want to piggyback on what you said, because for a year I've been feeling this pull to shift my practice, in the way I've been doing my work, and fear was the biggest obstacle. And every time I would put a step forward towards that direction, there was this huge fear of — what if this, what if that? You know. And it almost stopped me from something — that I felt this intuition — that I wasn't trusting. Or maybe, I was trusting it, but the fear was getting in the way. So, for me, it seems like trusting the intuition has to do with letting go of the fear. And then that also means my trust in Baba. Because, even if I'm wrong in that intuition, if I fully trust Baba and let go of the fear, it will always work itself out somehow that I'm going to learn from it. So it almost doesn't even matter.

Laurent: That's great, Payam.

¶ Don: Incidentally, Payam, that refers back to one of the ... I think of the last meeting we had in this house. I remember ... saying and discussing let's say — the reality of the experience of Baba himself. And of course the whole question always comes up, again and again — "Well, gee, it's great for the people who were around [Baba] in physical form ... because you can experience Baba, so you can experience let's say the fearlessness that comes from really having known Baba. That's the real stuff." And then the thought was put in — but is that, nevertheless, an empty fear in the long run because even though one wasn't born, Baba has his ways, and if you go about life, and just let's say just keep an open mind, inevitably you build up an experience that can only be explained if Baba is continuing in an active form, right with you constantly. And you learn what he is. And then part of the inevitable consequence of that is that you lose more and more and more fear, as that inner knowledge — through your own experience that you can't argue with — becomes more and more real.

Now that seems to me to be one of the very, very most important fundamental aims of any sort of grouping of Baba devotees, to let's say, open oneself to that building experience which is inevitable if you just don't keep the barn door closed under lock and key all of the time — that Baba experiences get into your life. They're there. You experience them. By golly, he'd have to be around for that to work out that way. So, your own experience builds your own knowledge of Baba, and then suddenly, as a byproduct, you realize that your whole fear mechanism has changed — and changed radically — and you associate that with, let's say, really knowing inside of yourself through your own experience in life — that he is there, and that he does amazing things. That he is around in a terribly constructive and, eventually, totally reassuring manner.

Doug: One of the things which I experienced during my first few years with Baba was that I seemed to pay very close attention to only the seemingly important events of life. But gradually, without really being conscious of it, I began to pay attention to smaller and smaller events which occur during daily life and, finally, to everything. You bump your knee or stub your toe while thinking of something. He's there in every thought, reminding you of something. Like, I've had so many experiences like this. You know, I'm getting into a mental ...

¶ Don: You can go wacky if you're not careful. {Laughter.}

Doug: I'd be thinking really terrible thoughts about somebody, and then I'd smash my head against the door, or some other silly physical mishap would happen, which would get my attention. Stubbing my toe, or something like that, would happen. And then I go, "Okay, Baba, okay," like he's tapping me on the shoulder and reminding me of something. So I try to make a connection between my most recent thought and the mishap. This has happened so often, I mean every time — from the time I wake up until the time I go to bed — just the tiniest little things. If you can attribute all of this to God and try to learn something from each situation, then it transforms your entire life. And even if you're led into a really horrible situation, you're going to learn something from it. So that's not that bad either. So, that takes fear away.

¶ Don: Would you allow me to add some comment to what you just said? Yeah, I don't think what you said is quite wacky enough. {Group laughter.} That is another stage where you begin to suspect that his sense of humor in all these things that go on is just incredible. You know?

Sevn: ... There is this strong sense of feeling as if Baba initiated it.
¶ Don: He gave you the kick in the pants that got you to the right place at the right time for the right experience.

Sevn: Right. And there's a certain sense like — "Oh, there's the presence" or "this is His companionship." It's a sweet sense of knowing that He's the reason behind happenings.

Doug: And you're never alone.

Sevn: Yeah, that's it. And that's what really diminishes the fear.

Marnie: There's two things that Baba said that I found very helpful ... in the Supplement [of *God Speaks*]. One was obedience, the whole concept of obedience, and that, you know, initially I heard that as an onerous task. But now what I experience is that it's really a gift from Baba to be the vehicle for surrendering to him, and loving him and obeying him like that by doing all the — trying to do all the things. Not backbiting, being on time, and all those little things. It's a way of then reinforcing. The other thing that he gave that I find so helpful is conscious remembrance of him. So, between the effort to obey him — which I really have come to see as a gift rather than a task — because the remembrance does help with that journey, you know? And to me it's the way that I feel him, you know? Just — I remember that he is here. He is so close. He's right here ... It's so amazing what he's given us.

Sevn: I always get those confused. What was the gift between obedience and surrender? One was a gift from God to us, and one was our gift for God?

Laurent: Meher Baba said, "Love is a gift from God to man, obedience is a gift from Master to man, and surrender is a gift from man to Master."

Sevn: Right.

¶ Don: That's a beautiful confirmation, Laurent.

Marnie: Yeah, it's beautiful, and it's the way out. I mean that's what is so amazing in these words that Baba's given us, he's given us the way out. The way to be in the world, and the way to get back to him. And it's just — amazing! I don't know how else to put it.

> "Love is a gift of God to man, obedience is the gift of the Perfect Master to man and surrender is the gift of man to the Perfect Master." ~ Meher Baba, from Lord Meher, p. 4805

¶ Don: Well, Doug, have we continued on and perhaps finished off commenting on your particular intuition?

Danny: Doug, did that come out of *God Speaks* at all?

Doug: No — well, maybe it did. You never know. But ...

Danny: Because there is that discussion in *God Speaks* about the past, present and future being in the eternal Now, and ...

Doug: That may have planted [the idea] ... But I've never heard anyone discuss this thing of incarnating. And I did blur the lines ... and I think that was an error. ... Then we have to ...

¶ Don: Obey the rules.

Doug: ... that clarified that for me.

Glenn: Whether it's real or not, I have had the experience of accessing the past.

Doug: Well, I think that there can be past life flashes that we all might have sometimes. I don't think I've ever consciously been aware of one. But I do think ... with all the lives ... it's inevitable.

Glenn: Whether that — what that means and how it relates to ... I don't know.

¶ Don: I think we need to leave it there though, Glenn. I think Baba tells us about our mental body, what it has and what it does, to take that a bit further. Because he certainly makes it very, very clear that the mental body, in addition to all the other things that it does for a drop-soul, stores the experiences that that drop-soul has had from the very beginning. In the very early, primitive stages of course there ain't no mental body around, but I've noticed again and again when I became so conscious of the subject, in the editing work, that then Baba uses in the earlier stages of evolution the word "associated with."

Laurent wishes to add to this point, *God Speaks* has text which can be interpreted to say that the actual subtle and mental bodies are associated with the soul from the very beginning of evolution. To me, Baba states this clearly in *God Speaks*, Part 4: "Reincarnation and the Impressionless Equipoise of Consciousness," paragraphs one through five. In other words, Meher Baba makes it clear that the mental body exists (in the mental world) even in the first form in evolution, although not yet physically manifest as a brain. See also *Sexuality on the Spiritual Path* (London: Companion Books, 2007) p. 37-38.

And he simply says that when, let's say, the drop-soul has just been born a few seconds of imaginary time before, that the very, very first impression and the first iota of consciousness are associated with the drop-soul. And it doesn't mean that there is something that we can think of as a physical storage bin. Nothing even that evoluted, or concrete exists as yet. And so how under the sun it gets associated with — to me this is the scientific whodunit of all time. What under the sun is the thing that binds it? Golly, you know I must admit I sit around pondering these things inevitably, and sometimes can't control myself. And I just have to say — Enough, Don, go on, you have to get the dishes washed (or whatever). {Laughter.} But nevertheless, Baba certainly does point out to us that you as a human being ... have a definite body which has a great big storage chamber where all of these things are kept in a pristine condition. They're not going through radioactive decay, and naturally deteriorating over time. Now, you could be born for a thousand incarnations, and at the end of a thousand, inspect one of these mental bins and, by God, it was in exactly the same state as when the impression was originally stored there.

And this is a fact which has a certain, let's say, frightening quality to it. And I've been running into this so recently, I'm terribly aware of it, how you can have an individual who has become tremendously refined, sophisticated, honest, dealing with things coming along and developed just wonderful characteristics — and everybody thinks of them just sort of as being one of those saintly people, you know, who just knows so well, so deeply, so certainly so many things that they just always have — they end up doing the right thing and you feel good about it. And then, all of a sudden, and this happened to me not long ago, one of these people that you've just known for a whole lifetime, and venerated, and loved — and then all of a sudden they do something. You say, my God, where did that come from? Really, you're so shocked. And then you say to yourself in the next breath, how can he live with himself with that still in his nature? How can he reconcile that with all of these things that he must believe in? How did it happen? How can this go on in God's Creation? You know it can be that startling and that is disillusioning, if I can use the term.

And one of these things happened to me not terribly long ago. You know, I really had to suddenly sit down and go to work with this business. Well, where did it come from? How could Baba, and God, let such a thing happen in such a wonderful individual? And then you just go back to the fundamental nature of — what are the facts? What does the implication of a mental body — which acts as a storage point — and eventually you've got to clean out all of these cubby holes from all their energy content before you can go back to God. And it is so difficult that, lots of times, you've just got to have even a Perfect Master around, who knows and puts you through the right situations to get rid of some of these cubby holes. And when I had this terrible experience with this life-long friend of mine — he didn't attack me, but he attacked one of my closest friends in life — that's what I couldn't understand. So, at any rate, when you do understand that these cubby holes have to be cleaned out, and they sit there, and they don't compare notes, they don't have a telephone system with the next cubby hole and say, "what happened to you?" And the next cubby hole says, "Well, I got rid of my energy, and I'm enlightened in this part now." No.

{Group laughter.}

¶ Don: They don't mutually influence each other, they go on existing. This is true. And so, my friend said, "Don, this must be a blind spot in your friend." And I thought — my God, I think he's got to the essence of "blind spot," it is simply: you run across, or you've been in a situation which woke up that particular energy pattern. And once it is awakened by the possibility of exercising itself as it originally was formed — and that could well have been when he was sitting around in a cave, you know, and fighting for life (with a little bit of meat on top of the fire in the cave), you know, it can be that ancient. And just all of a sudden it wakes up and it wants to express itself. And it does. And probably this individual — this to me is what Christ said on the cross: "Forgive them, oh God, for they know not what they do."

> According to the Gospel of Luke (23:34) Jesus said, "Father forgive them, for they know not what they do."

When you're in a situation like that you don't think what you're doing or so on. The energy is expressing itself. And, at best, you sit around afterwards and you justify yourself like hell — I had to do it for these obvious reasons. But all it was, was a cave-ancestry-energy which was suddenly subjected to something that is a code system [which it] reacted to, and it woke up, and it expressed itself. You know these are realities, these are realities. And we have got to admit that there is just no chance under the sun that we are free and exempt from them. And then we've got to be capable to accept them, and then maybe even do something like apologize for it. Say, you know, "I don't know why I did that. It's something totally unreal, and I did it, and I'm just hellishly sorry. I hope you will forgive me." I think this is what real forgiveness is about. To let that cubby hole express itself and know that it's inevitable, that it had to, sooner or later. And all you can try to do is minimize the damage that is caused.

Mahmoud Ajang: You know, whatever we do we are creating sanskaras. So let's say, for any reason that you mentioned, I'm getting angry. And then I realize that this was a fact. But already I have created a sanskara. Even though I have lost most, or some, of the energy which was the cause to begin with for me to act as such. So how about that part, that I have already created sanskaras? Meaning that I have accumulated some energy again.

Laurent: But did you express it? Or did you hold it back?

Mahmoud: No, but I'm getting angry — I express my anger — what I'm saying, so this was the, you know, energy part of that sanskara that eventually forced me to behave as such. What I'm saying, even though I have this charge ... of this energy, but already I have created this sanskara. Meaning that I have accumulated some energy that eventually has to be disposed. So what are we [to do about] that?

¶ Don: Well, okay, if you ask me that as a deliberate question, I will try to reply because I certainly have reflected and experienced over quite a good many decades these things since I originally understood some of the mechanics from Baba. And so, I can tell you from the standpoint of a lifetime of trying to deal with these things and puzzle about them what the solution is.

At the time Don Stevens was 87 years old.

I think this is certainly the time to tell you about my summation — of what I simply call my life with Baba. And what have I observed? Because I had to think a great deal about this. I've often told you that some of the most important things that have ever happened to me came when our Spanish publisher (of *God Speaks* in Spanish) — my promise to him to try to write a biography — half biography, and half summary of philosophy, of Meher Baba. When I finally realized I was going to have to do what I had promised to get done, and I couldn't get anybody else, finally, to do it, then I said to myself, "Well, Don, if you do anything for this publisher that is of any value, it's got to be based on your experience of Meher Baba. And so what you're going to have to do is, first of all, relive really important parts of your experience with Meher Baba. Just go over it as if you were in the astral state looking at the movie that's going on there — so you're sort of doing it now, because you've been asked to do it, and this is the process you've gotta go through. Relive it."

And so I deliberately went just consistently over a tremendous amount of my experience with Baba, and in so doing I saw trends, and inevitably results, that were fairly conclusive turning up from that. And the thing that astonished me more than anything else — when I began following through several of D.E. Stevens' pet problems with D.E. Stevens — and saw, let's say, the memory pattern of what had been happening within, then I began to realize that without my knowing at all, Baba, by the frequent contacts that I had with him, kept checking very, very careful track of where I was with important things inside of myself.

So you might say I sort of went underground very early in this whole process back in the early 1950s. And Baba gave me so many things to do, one after another, end on end, it just seemed to me I would never finish off the editing projects that he kept dreaming up. And so, one way or another, Baba kept me terribly busy. And secondly, he kept in very, very close personal touch with me at the same time. And so, then, when I finally wake up — years after he has dropped the body — and the editor says, "Do this for me," I relive them. And then I see consciously, deliberately, what has happened to some of the most important energy contents of sanskaras. And it is certainly true that, let's say, I didn't suddenly become a perfect human being (or something of that sort). But I could see the manner in which Baba himself entered into the thing. And I simply take Baba as the example of what a great Master, who knows the things ... that exist in you, and the types of situations that can be brought up. I saw that Baba himself had consistently put me through experiences, where a gradual process of de-energizing — slow, controlled de-energizing — this is the expression and the reality I want to leave with you. It is not, let's say, well, so you get angry and so you just build up the same energy knot again. No, it isn't. When you, yourself, exercise some sort of a push on the thing — or when you're under the direction of let's say a Spiritual Master who is assisting you in the process, he sees that the thing is happening in a slow, controlled, stage that you can bear so it doesn't come to a great crisis.

But you can see — I saw when I would look inside myself, and say, "well what happened to that old business about being so terribly frightened of spending money? What's happened to that?" I had no fright of it anymore. It had just absolutely gone. And I saw how many situations Baba had put me through — deliberately exposed me to them one after another, in the course of my real, daily, practical life. And I saw the gradual manner in which my fear of spending money, and getting caught short, and suddenly and not being able to finance things that I had to do, and gradually it would disappear. But when a real Spiritual Master is there, or if you conscientiously are trying to live a decent life, and you know, more and more in a sane, balanced manner — when there is some sort of resource to keep the thing under control, each time that you go through you blow your top less the next time. And if, for some reason or another, if you're just so busy with things that are truly important, you don't sit around too much and waste too much time — Did I do that right? Did I do that wrong? — Or so on. You do it as best as you can when it comes up, and then you've got to go on to the [next] thing you know that's important that has got to be done. But Baba, of course, was keeping track all of the time. So, I realized when I wrote this book for the Spanish editor, that this was an invaluable experience, and that I should share with other people the results of having this happen to you.

That book was *Meher Baba, The Awakener of the Age* (Myrtle Beach: Sheriar Foundation, 1999).

That was Baba himself and the things that he asked. But the byproduct was that he handled the sanskaras in a fashion, keeping track of it, so that I didn't get upset when I did things in a lousy fashion. But he knew where they were and what the next stage had to be. So, gradually, over a lot of time just a whole market basket worth of Stevens' crammed-up sanskaric patterns just gradually ... I could tap around in these things — and you know I know myself well enough to know where the emotional, and energy stresses are, so I could tap into these memories of where Stevens' problematical nature was involved. And, one after another, when I tested them and sure, I live situations like that still, but I am not at all emotionally involved in any of them. I do what's got to get done. But I couldn't find a single one of the really major ones that had not gone through an absolutely incredible, decisive lowering of any emotional pressure involved. That's it in a nutshell.

And I would just have to tell you, and I'll be terribly personal with you, that of course the great big bug-a-boo of all, which is one's sexual drive, had gone through just a whole continental divide, a change in the general process. And then I realized that probably he, himself, had taken upon himself the defusing just by these — I'm sure I've told you this sometime or another in a group that I trust completely (as I do you people) — that I realized that the thousands of times actually — literally thousands of times — that I've been warmly, tenderly embraced by Baba, and sometimes a kiss on the side of the cheek and so on, holding hands here, holding hands there, completely publicly, no embarrassment involved at all, someway or another this just had gradually, gradually, gradually drained. I couldn't believe it.

In fact, when I realized that I probably better test this — and put myself into situations where if I had sexual arousal potentials within me, by God I would get sexually aroused — but when I didn't get sexually aroused, but just loved the person in the same manner that I have loved them for years, I couldn't believe what had gone on. And I realized that it was Baba himself who had done that with this procedure, that every time I came to visit him I got good embraces, and every time he sent me out to do something or another, when I was about to go out of the door he'd give me another good warm embrace, and affectionate words and attention, and so on. And so this is, let's say, a deliberate but very, very controlled fashion of allowing the energy to be awake, and then some of it drained off. Simply because it's not appropriate; the situation is not right to get in bed with somebody or another, and so you don't.

And you don't realize that something or another has taken some of the power out of the impulse itself. When that goes on, because I was around Baba for over twenty years, and a great deal of that time not in concentrated stretches, but coming to visit, going in and out constantly. So, I think I told you, that when I was making up my list of things that I thought needed to be discussed in the biography [of Baba], I realized that it was in this case that the Avatar himself had taken on the responsibility. And it had just, let's say, sapped, sapped, as far as I could say, the last little bit of energy. So I could really love without having any, any feeling at all that it is necessary to consummate this by any type of a physical act. And he simply laid down to me the guidelines through experience with him, where the limits are of not forming a new sanskaric pattern in this area. And that's the other part of the puzzle. What are those guidelines? I think they're just terribly good, and dependable, and satisfying — tremendously realistically, warmly, humanly satisfying.

Doug: And having Baba with you on a daily basis ...

¶ Don: Sure.

Doug: For all of us — you do your best and then occasionally at some point in time you blow your top, but then because Baba's there, you know, you process it with ...

¶ Don: Sure, you do it conscientiously.

Doug: Yeah, and then, you know — what would [Baba] want me to do here?

¶ Don: And that's real to you.

Doug: And then you do it. And it's like he's right — he is, not like he is, he is right there. And then you go through that process. And I think that's where the sanskaras can lose its energy —

¶ Don: Absolutely.

Doug: If you just blow your top, and then just don't think twice about it, and go on to the next thing, then you probably build it up. But if you consciously then work through it with Baba then it's ...

¶ Don: It's a real priority. It's not imaginary. It is for real. Your relationship with Baba, as you build it, is for real. And the things that you feel answerable to Baba, they're real for you, and you do something real about it. So it is a self-reinforcing thing that happens. It's not done in some sort of a mystic-ivory-tower (somewhere or another), and then it all goes ker-flooey when you come back into the first real situation of life, and blood and thunder and guts (forgive the expressions, my colorful language).

Sevn: "Self-reinforcing." I'm not clear on that term: "Self-reinforcing process"?

¶ Don: Simply, it is a natural process. The values are real. And the whole series of experiences are, let's say, the scenario as developed by the Master, or Baba himself, for you. And what it does, each time, some more of the energy is extracted. The next situation you go into, there's a bit more drainage, and the whole process, gradually, because you trust it — The master puts your nose so much to the grindstone, you don't have time to sit around and daydream, and wonder about it too much, and try to do too much controlling yourself. You don't have time to daydream, because daydreaming can do the reverse of being self-controlling, and self-reinforcing. It can be doing the reverse, rebuilding back.

Laurent: I was going to piggyback on something, because I really love what Doug is sharing. When Aspen was six, we were moving out of one house going to another one across town in Flagstaff. So, I was helping her pack up her room, and I looked and on the wall she had taken marker and started drawing something on the wall (and we were renting this house). So I looked at it, and I pointed at it, and I said, "Aspen, did you do this?" — you know, with lightning in my eyes. She looks at me, and she says, "You have to forgive me, Dad, I was out of my mind." {Group laughter.}

Laurent: So, my anger fell away. And, of course, I forgave her.

And I was just thinking about it, and listening to you — for some reason this came up, you know, and I'm thinking — she was out of her mind. And I think what that means is, when you're not present — like the Buddhists are into "mindfulness," about being present, and aware of what's going on and stepping through that — but if you're, "out of your mind," it's almost like you're letting your mind do what it wants. You're not in control. And, if your mind does what it wants, look out, because anything can happen! {More laughing.}

¶ Don: Can we go a little bit further on that, because I think this is a terribly important point about being out of your mind. I think it has, primarily, to do (to put a label on it and really concentrate on that) — is where your ego is, at the point of the event which is going on. If you are thinking — "I want this. I'm going to be horribly disappointed if he doesn't do that. If she does that I'm really going to blow my top." — and if you're thinking about what you need to get out of the thing, and what you have to get control of, or you're going to blow your top, it simply means that your ego is right there going through the experience, and that is when the dangerous phase of an experience is going — when the ego is right there dead center. Because, as you go through the thing, then all of this energy gets constellated back around the ego, and goes into the mental storage pot again. So instead of dissipating energy, going through honestly the event, you're building up a larger energy store to repeat it the next time. And it's going to be a more villainous event the next time, because there's more of the ego drive of emotions.

Elham Ebrahimzadeh (Elllie): Well, I don't know if it's maybe a question, or a point, but there comes a period of time where the ego is beginning to creep in — so all the justifications as to, "Why did this happen? And it should be this way. Or, why did this person do that?" — all seem to arouse the ego more and more and the ego keeps growing ...

¶ Don: It does.

Ellie: So how do you put the ego away before it just gets bigger and bigger? Because I mean sometimes I'm aware that it's happening, and I tell myself, on some good days, that "Oh look. Here it is again, my ego ... I'm beginning to get righteous, or I am getting too tunnel visioned." I don't know ... And on some bad days I don't have control over it and before I can recognize my ego's involvement, my reaction just comes out.

¶ Don: Well, one of the most powerful tools, that I know of, in this area was really brought back to light by Baba when he said, "Don't worry, be happy."

And if you stop to think of that — when you're trying to puzzle out all of these things and how to get things under control — and your ego is thinking how it has to be, and what it is, and so on. Really, what you are doing is simply worrying a situation around to the point where you think you're going to get the most emotional satisfaction out of the results, in a future situation. But, if you take Baba's advice seriously — "Don't worry, be happy" — the greatest chewer-upper of spiritual energy that exists is our own tendency to worry. This will do a tremendous amount to cut that way, way, way down.

> Beloved Baba shared about obedience and his will, "In the following lines a lover states how impossible it is to obey the Master: 'O Beloved! You have tied my hands and feet to a plank and have thrown me in the midst of a stormy ocean, and you command me that I should not get my clothes wet!' This simply means that unless the Master helps you and you trust him one hundred percent, it is not possible for you to obey him absolutely. I am God in human form. Be prepared to obey me with all willingness. I bestow the gift of love as and when I like. Better leave it to my will and pleasure. Don't worry, be happy." (from *Lord Meher* p. 5770) Also this: "Do not worry. Be happy in my love and continue to hold fast to my daaman to the very end. Rest assured that all will be divinely well. God does not abandon those who trust Him." *Lord Meher* (Vol.16, p. 5673) — LW

There's another thing that I would suggest (as another part of the process) that certainly, I think, has to be terribly important to all of humanity, and that is the Avataric gift of intuition. If it is true, let's say, as Baba says it is true, that when you've got a problem in front of you, you now have the resources intuitively to get the answer to that thing in nothing flat — instantaneously. And that means that if what the problem is, is an emotional problem, or a relationship, or an ego problem, just take an intuitive answer and say, "Baba says I can get it through my intuition." And so this simply means

> "To love the world and serve it in the ways of the Masters is no game for the weak and faint-hearted. Moral courage and self-confidence should be accompanied by freedom from worry. There are very few things in the mind which eat up as much energy as worry. It is one of the most difficult things not to worry about anything." - Meher Baba, *Discourses*, (6th Edition), "Qualifications of the Aspirant," Volume III, p.121

that your ego hasn't got any chance at all of building up this structure, and daydreaming about it, and trying to get into the center of it in the future. You say to yourself — well, I had an intuition to handle it so-and-so. And I'm going to do it. And you put it into action with almost no ego involvement, I can tell you that from personal experience. So, one of the greatest things in getting the ego out of the scene of activity is simply to trust your intuitive instincts in situations more and more, and simply feeling that if I don't get it intuitively right, I'll get it more right the next time this comes up. And, again, I'm going to let intuition take over, so your ego is necessarily much less present than it would have been. So, this to me, is something (quite frankly) I've just been really dabbling my finger into more and more in my own personal life, and realizing the extent to which intuitive answers (even for little things you're doing in housekeeping even) are strung around in front of you. First of all, it saves a tremendous amount of time. Secondly, the emotional content — the fear content principally — of so many living things is necessarily tremendously diminished. And the ability, let's say, to get through the action and not have the ego present — years ago I wrote a funny little chapter in a book, in which I compared it to my mother's hair-curler. And I said — the ego is sort of like a hot hair-curler. And if the hair-curler isn't around for the hair to wrap up on again, the hair's going to remain straight, and get out of the picture in nothing flat. So, just keep your ego hair-curler out of a situation, and this will do an awful lot. I think it's a beautiful simile. Just get the hot hair-curler out of the thing, and don't turn on the electricity. {Group laughter.}

Ellie: Well, I just wanted to clarify. If I have a situation where I'm beginning to sort it out in my mind — not intuitively, the mind will have a tendency to problem solve and sort things. This is when the

ego gets sucked into this and it becomes a vicious cycle, as the ego in its attempt to stay in control will attempt to solve the problem in a way that will preserve itself ... {To Don}: Is this what you are saying?
¶ Don: That's exactly it.

Ellie: So when I don't worry ...
¶ Don: Keep that under control. Baba said — don't worry. It's wasting my time. And he's dead right. And it is also, without your realizing it, getting the deadly hair-curler back into the scene of action, and making it worse the next time. So, if you can control that effectively, boy you're a long way ahead. A desperate situation is when you allow your mind to return again, and again, and again, and again — and this is the old fear pattern taking over.

Sevn: I've found it extremely difficult trying to get your hands around the ego let alone try to remove it. I have realized it isn't necessarily correct thinking that we should try to control the ego. But as Ellie was saying, I think the whole game is just the observing it when you are able see it. It's about noticing this and that as "Me, me, me" or, "I want this," and I think that's everything. Recognizing that the hair-curler is there is really the goal. And observing it's presence will facilitate its demise.

¶ Don: I will make one comment on that. It takes a real hero to be able to do this. It takes a hell of a lot of guts — and to mean it, and to effectively do it — *this is what I call a hero on the path*. And boy they get places, to recognize it and do something about it. Marnie?

Marnie: As we're talking, it seems, what resonates for me, also, is that usually these responses come up in reaction to other people and ...
¶ Don: Very often.

Marnie: ... and so, Baba has said (if I understand him correctly), that we should be thanking these other people because they are doing us a favor with these horrible things.
¶ Don: That takes a double-hero.

Marnie: But I think if one can — somehow I know, well, in my experience in that — so I had a question about this idea of not "replaying" — you know, going over and over again. And I've had some experience in the last few years where I have felt very betrayed, and have gone over, and over, and over. But what I've found — and I'm not saying that this is the correct thing to do — but that in the process of replaying that, and thinking about it, and then kind of reflecting, you know — what was my piece in this? How did I, what did I do here? — there has been, somehow, a way of finally the light bulb going on that this person really, really has done me a service. Because, this person put me into a position of so much hurt that I just couldn't let it go. I just couldn't go into the, "Don't worry, be happy." Because, in a way, that would be kind of pushing it under the rug. I just really had to struggle to come to terms with it. And, so, I guess I'm talking about two things. One is, is there a value in replaying? And two, Baba does give us, again, an out when we can reach — truly, truly reach that point of seeing the other person as his gift to us, and as them doing a service for us.

> Beloved Baba spoke about this: "On another occasion, when there was a quarrel between two women, Baba intervened and stated: Love and forget. This is the only thing that matters, and it pays. Almost all of you are weak. By weak, I mean taken up with desires. Anger is weakness, pride is weakness, and so on. If a mother found her child weak, she would love it all the more. So all love more. Don't you remember what I told you in Nasik? Learn to say 'Janay-doe' — 'Let it go!' Give up wanting the last word. Give up all wants and be happy. But you must try consciously. Now be happy. I forgive you all, but continue trying."
> (from *Lord Meher* p. 2289)

¶ Don: Yeah, I think you two-thirds solve the problem when you have that capability, seeing the person as a help.

Marnie: And what's the other third?

¶ Don: The other third? Grinning and bearing it, and not bitching about it.

Marnie: Letting it go. Really becoming that detached.

¶ Don: "I'm still alive, I'll go on living."

Marnie: Yeah, right. Right.

Jamshid: You know, what you said resonated with me a whole lot. The last year and a half, I went through a transition, work-wise, after twenty years of being an employee working in the electronics and computer field. I switched, and became self-employed, and relied on someone, who was my guide and so forth, into this adjacent field, brand-new for me, and I went in with total trust. And you know ... just dropped twenty years into it and switched careers, never done it in my life. And halfway through, I realized that he wasn't who I thought he was, and I was being completely taken advantage of, and I was being ... psychologically played with, and the relationship was dishonest, and so forth and so on.

And we had daily interactions where honest, open expectations were being thrown at me, the basis of those expectations, and so forth, being changed day to day, and games were being played daily. So I had denial, anger, I went through the whole process. And finally I came to where you were going with it. My experience was that — I realized that here is — okay, who am I? — what anchors me in life? And if I were to be a reaction to that which came from outside, that I would lose my own grounding — that I had to stop reacting. That it really wasn't so much about this person, and this experience, but the experience became an absolutely powerful — because it's in my face. It is hitting me at multiple levels, survival level — personal because he's family, and closely bonded to my family. And so, there's a daily interaction, all kinds of personal, emotional, financial engagement, right? So, I had to take it and say okay, so here it is. How do I deal with it, right, without letting it take me off of my base? Here's the path that I've been — as a human being — I've been going through, and this is hitting me on all levels, and basically if I react to it, I'll go a whole different path, multiple steps back. Right? I had to stop reacting.

So, at some point, I started valuing the engagement as an exercise in remaining focused on that which I wanted to remain focused on — not a reaction. So daily, I engaged with him. I come clearly from — what I'm there to do, don't give in, no matter what is said — I basically package it, acknowledge it in my own head and heart. Acknowledge it — here is something — here is some —whatever ... Put it aside, refocus, resume on what I want to get out of it, with specific intent for the outcome of the relationship, right? I want this relationship to end — not end, but this phase of this relationship to complete itself. Looking like this: meaning that he would feel respected, he would feel taken care of, no matter what he has said, or done, or whatever, right? And that I could look him in the eye, and feel good about him. In this particular case — because we're a family and it's a long term relationship — that he could feel comfortable, and even joyous. So, that's where I want to get it to. So, constantly pushing that aside, so it really has become that the only way I can do it, is if I see him as an opportunity for me. The challenge is an opportunity. Not being an effect of ...

Doug: Or a victim.

Jamshid: Yeah.

Laurent: Jamshid, can I ask two questions? Are you still in this relationship?

Jamshid: Yes.

Laurent: The second one is, do you believe that he is acting this way consciously or is it largely unconscious?

Jamshid: I think it's ...

Doug{to Jamshid}: You said it's a game. He's playing games, so ...

Jamshid: Yeah, but that's ...

¶ Don: {to Jamshid}: But he's doing what comes naturally.

Jamshid: Exactly. So I know that at some points he may even, deep down, question — I have seen him question some of his own ways of being. But, the bulk of the force naturally is the way it is, right? So, no trying to change, no trying to negate, no trying to fight. That's what it is. It's got nothing to do with me. I just deal with it.

Sevn: {to Jamshid}: Have you noticed any changes in him since you've made a shift in yourself?

Jamshid: Yes, in that we don't clash, it's happier. Right? I have even made it clear that I have no intent to continue after these couple of tasks that we're doing together finish. And, although he wants me to continue to work with him, but I've made it clear to him that I'm not going to. And that was another thing he was very upset about. But, by not reacting to who he is being, an opening has been created for me — freedom for me — and actually for him as well.

¶ Don {to Jamshid}: Do you think he is perhaps beginning to play fewer games with you? Or is it about the same tempo of ...

Jamshid: I think it is less, because rather than being right — someone talked about being right —rather than being right, I accept it, the expectations, whether right or wrong. Okay, so what, you know, I have to give in more, put in more ...

¶ Don: Sure.

Jamshid: ... than what was, to begin with, unfair and inappropriate? That's fine. At least I was able to end — stay grounded in (what I define as being grounded for me), who I am, where I am in life. And, I also can give the opportunity to him not to dig deeper in where he was going with it. So, it's been tremendous, the opposite way of the way I was initially being, which was righteous, resisting, and reacting and all of that — caused tremendous negative energy. The mind ...

Laurent: Oh, like a storm.

Jamshid: Oh yeah. Daily — and not even knowing — my voice, or maybe many of the things that I wouldn't even say, but he would pick up on the energy, on the hidden feelings that I had, and react further and further.

Sevn: Speaking of righteousness — I've dealt with that, especially in my professional life. There's something amazing about the ego wrapping itself around the thought of knowing it's in the right — "Obviously I'm in the right position. How can this person be violating what is right?" It's very difficult for it to reconcile with the other side.

Payam: Well, there's quite a bit in marriage, I'll tell you that!

{Much laughter in the room, and someone clapping a couple times.}

Laurent {to Glenn, Payam's husband}: That's a warning for you. {laughing.}

Payam: But you know, I have to say, a sense of humor has — it can take the edge off quite a bit. I mean, there are moments, and it's late at night, where like — dah dah dah dah dah — and we just look at each other, and we just burst out laughing, because — I mean it's like going nowhere and we've heard it like hundreds of times before. And then, you just get to a point where it's just funny that you get yourself there, and it's pointless, you know? And then you sleep, and forget all about it. I mean, that's the nice part about marriage, you know?

Sevn: Right.

Payam: It's not always possible in professional relationships, but I have to say, a sense of humor does take the edge off quite a bit.

¶ Don: Could I ask for a signal from the group? We've been talking, at least theoretically, about intuitions, and intuitions flowing from *God Speaks*. I think we've sort of danced quite a bit around both of those words actually, and in a realistic and fruitful manner. Has anybody done a homework piece, of something written down that, after lunch, they would like to take up still on — you do, Danny? Good. {Don looks at another participant} And you've got something. Okay, all right, so let's be sure that after lunch we continue on, and eventually finish off the intuitive part of the agenda that we had promised ourselves we would do.

Marnie: Are you going to talk about forgiveness tomorrow? Is that ...

¶ Don: Well, sometime or another, if we get to it this afternoon, because forgiveness comes up in a fairly large context. It, let's say, comes out of a series of events and reflections (and so on), and I'd like to talk about them also. So when we start moving towards the topic of forgiveness, I've got a preamble that might be fairly time consuming. So, even if we start with the preamble, we may not get to forgiveness today, but there's no reason it shouldn't hang over until tomorrow. And then, I have to confess to you — sort of a bolt out of the blue — and this has been an intuition that whacked me since I've come on this trip, a project I would dearly like to lay out in detail to the YPG, and say I have a deep intuition that this is the reason for being for this group.

{The group takes a two hour lunch break}

Saturday Afternoon: Shades of Grace.

Don: Shall we all be just simply silent for few moments with Baba, without a prayer, except internally.

{Silence.}

¶ Don: Thank you, Beloved Baba, for a wonderful morning feast. Now we had two hands that went up. I think it was Danny's and Sevn's, on intuition — personal. Danny, you being the elder at this point ... {Laughter.}

Danny: Well, when Don gave the assignment on intuition at the Myrtle Beach meeting for something from *God Speaks*, it didn't take me too long to figure out that what I wanted to focus on was the section on forgetfulness in the "Supplement," which I know is a favorite — I don't know if other people in this group, but a favorite in general I think of a lot of people ... So I took out *God Speaks* from time to time to look at it, and nothing was really coming to me. Perhaps I should have made a more direct invitation to intuition. But finally, a week or so ago, I just sat down at the computer and started typing, in much the same way I write a screenplay. Things just came to me at that time. So I don't know if I'd call it an intuition, but — although I try to write intuitively, I try to sort of let things come to me that way whenever I write. It did feel like I was — or like these words were sort of filling in that skeleton of *God Speaks*. Perhaps some — I don't know what part — veins or arteries or muscles or tissues or something. But it just sort of really seems like a natural extension of what's already there, and that I was just sort of elaborating what was already present. But this is what I wrote:

"Forgetfulness is surrender. It is not repression. In order to forget something, one must surrender it. The mind clings to that which it has yet to surrender. The state of forgetfulness is not-worrying; to remember is to worry." By the way, has everyone read this in *God Speaks* in the Supplement? Because this is a sense of forgetfulness, and remembrance, that a lot of people are probably not familiar with.

Sevn: Is it the act of forgetfulness chapter?

Danny: It's kind of early in the Supplement ...

Sevn: It's called active forgetfulness ...

Danny: ... where he talks about forgetfulness being the secret of happiness.

Sevn: Right.

Danny: So it's definitely not forgetfulness in the sense of — it states in there: not in the sense of forgetting to mail a letter or something. It's really a much more mystical state of forgetfulness. And it speaks of remembrance causing pain, and therefore forgetfulness being necessary. So, I just want to be clear that we're not using the conventional definition, that I'm really hyper-focused on what I thought was meant in *God Speaks* rather than using any conventional meanings for forgetfulness or remembrance when I wrote this. So, as I said: "The state of forgetfulness is not-worrying; to remember is to worry. The state of forgetfulness is faith; to remember is to lose faith and trust. The state of forgetfulness is joy; remembrance is a heavy weight on consciousness. To remember is to fear; to forget is fearlessness. To remember is to be attached; forgetfulness is detachment. Remembrance is anxiousness; forgetfulness is laughter." And then I felt the need to just quote Baba briefly, or not quote but just mention something that Baba says here, which is: "Baba says remembrance causes pain, and that happiness depends upon positive forgetfulness." And then I went on: "Remembrance is guilt; forgetfulness contains lightness and clarity. Remembrance is shame; forgetfulness is peace. Remembrance suffocates; forgetfulness breathes. Remembrance is sorrow; forgetfulness is joy. Remembrance is jealousy; forgetfulness is contentment within oneself. Remembrance is craving; forgetfulness is the spontaneous renunciation of desire. Remembrance is greed; forgetfulness is 'This is enough.' Remembrance is anger and hate; forgetfulness is forgiveness. Forgetfulness is one-pointedness; remembrance is many-pointedness. Remembrance is sin; forgetfulness is purity. Remembrance is lust; forgetfulness is love. Remembrance is separation; forgetfulness is Oneness. Remembrance is past and future; forgetfulness is the Now. Remembrance is compulsion; forgetfulness is freedom. Remembrance is looking at Maya; forgetfulness is looking toward God."

And then I asked Laurent to read this on the train. He wanted to add something to it, and I think it's worth mentioning here, because he wanted to bridge that gap back to the kind of remembrance of Baba, which is, you know, so essential with Baba, to always remember Baba. So Laurent added: "Remembrance of Baba is the beginning of Real Forgetfulness." {A moment of silence.}

> A major Sufi practice is 'Zikr', reciting the various names or attributes of God, or phrases in praise of God. In Arabic, Zikr directly translates as 'remembrance of God (Allah)'. - KM

༄

Sevn: I just read this article in a scientific magazine about the new research they're doing into memory. Scientists have found that when a person engages in the physical or mental activity of recalling a memory, it renders that memory in an unstable state. So when you recall certain pieces of your memory, there's a moment when the physical storage of the memory can become unstable. So they're finding that the memories people constantly bring to their attention, like pleasant things or wonderful moments in their life, were more often forgotten, or not as easily accessible when compared to other memories that they didn't recall as often. When I read this I was thinking about this chapter on Active Forgetfulness, and how memories are tied to sanskaras? Perhaps they're similar; perhaps memories can serve as a useful point of focus. The act of dealing with a memory or a mental process in your mind could be similar to the act of dealing with a sanskara. Perhaps the process of bringing something from the subconscious to the conscious is a very important part of forgetfulness from the standpoint that when it's subconscious, it's much more secure. Whereas conscious memories, things that are much more accessible, are more subject to becoming unstable. I think that the instability of memory could be related to active forgetfulness or the idea of de-energizing sanskaras. I feel that an important aspect of the Path is becoming more conscious of the different aspects of your own memories.

Danny: I have mixed feelings about what you're saying.

Sevn: Oh please.

Danny: On the positive side, or the part I relate to best I guess, is that we know on this path with Baba, that there's a way of all sorts of things coming up from the subconscious that have to be exposed to the light of day in order to be released. So that makes sense to me. But for us to consciously go out of our way to try to remember ...

Sevn: Right.

Danny: ... sounds like clinging to me. That's sort of like, essentially perpetuating something that I — for myself anyway — am striving to sort of let go of. Because there's like a fear sometimes in remembering that you're afraid of forgetting ... that bringing back even the unpleasant stuff, there's a part of you that's saying, "No, no, don't do that," it is overwhelming to the person, and perpetuates that. Yeah, I mean, but that's just what came to me while you were speaking.

Doug {to Sevn}: What you're saying about instability of memory, I take it that means that if it's brought back it can get changed.

Glenn: That's scientifically proven.

Sevn: It has to do with the chemical and electrical functioning of synapses.

Doug: I know a lot of people who — I know a lot of artists, you know, they spend a lot of time alone, and, you know, when you're working without a lot of people around you, you ... some memories can get amped up and changed. They can spiral into something that they weren't. But there's no objective sounding board, and so you can have a perceived wrong committed against you by someone, and then you spend six months pondering it, and it becomes more and more unstable to the point where you have invented an entirely new reality that simply didn't happen. But the result of that is that you can go "on the warpath" against some perceived thing. And they don't know where it's coming from, and so you've increased your sanskaric baggage by conjuring up the memory and allowing it to get polluted ...

Sevn: Right, right.

Doug: And a person's own mind, and his ego, can just run with it.

Sevn: That's interesting ... so you can actually change the memory and then it becomes a new story based on your sanskaric coloring of the actual experience

Doug: Right, and really the actual event, you're getting farther and farther away from the actual event.

Don: Laurent, would like to add something?

Laurent: Yeah, I want to piggyback on what Doug is saying because my father-in-law Randy is a therapist, and there's a relatively new field, it's about ten years old maybe, called EMDR. You may have heard about it. It's almost identical to what you're sharing about.

Doug: What does that stand for?

Laurent: I don't remember. But it's basically a trauma and stress therapy, and they're doing all sorts of work in this area which is very interesting. I had it done to me once because of something that happened. Somebody offered it when they heard what happened and I said sure. And it was, in my estimation, successful as a therapy. But what they're doing now, because they keep experimenting with this technique, is exactly what you're talking about. They'll have the patient who had a trauma, whether it was, you know, intentional or unintentional or whatever, bring up the memory, and obviously into this unstable place, and then have the family literally sitting with the person on both sides, or people who care, and just loving them, and focusing this loving care and attention on them. And somehow having the memory brought back, but now in

> EMDR stands for "Eye Movement Desensitization and Reprocessing," which therapy was founded by Francine Shapiro in 1991. - LW

this new context of being loved, has a healing effect on the trauma (which they don't quite understand either). But it's like it's been rebranded with new information somehow. It's kind of fascinating.

Doug: Well, because they are people that are supporting the person, as opposed to nobody.

Laurent: Right. But they're not changing the story. So they're not tweaking the information, they're saying, "Tell us what happened," and while that's all being brought up, there's this intense focus of loving care on the person. But it's fascinating. I think it's related to what Sevn's sharing.

Doug: I've also heard of an exercise where they have thirty people sitting around in a circle and the first person tells a little story. Just a little tiny anecdote of, you know, forty seconds worth of story. "So and so went down…." And only he had it written down. Then orally everybody's supposed to pass this on to the next person, the next person and the next person. By the time it gets back to the first person—totally different. Completely different. And everyone was supposed to recount it as accurately as possible. So you've got…change.

As practiced by EMDR-certified psychotherapists, EMDR is a standardized, closely defined set of protocols which do not include the experimental family support technique described by Laurent. A link to a clinical definition of EMDR may be found at emdria.org. - KM

Laurent: Makes you wonder about scripture.

{Laughter.}

Doug: I don't wonder about scripture.

{Laughter.}

Payam: Well, what you said rang very true for me because — well first I have to shift my mind from remembering Baba. And it's such a simple statement that I've just been so used to remembering Baba … so first I have to shift from that to remembering myself, the "I." So forgetting the "I" means exactly some of the things that you said, for me. You know if I forget myself, then I can be a medium. That's how I see it. If I forget myself and surrender and let go of what I want, or what makes sense to me, then all sorts of wonderful things can happen. And every time I've done that I'm so present to Baba — why don't I do that more often? But it's difficult {laughs}. So thank you.

Danny {To Sevn}: I might have sort of an inbuilt bias. There's an old, there's a yogic technique which I ... from my pre-Baba days that involved deliberately bringing up items from the past and then trying to release the energy out of them through breathing techniques and so forth. And there's part of me, now that I'm with Baba, that just really rebels against that way of doing things. And something you were saying just brought back ...

Sevn: Right. I wasn't suggesting it as a technique, but just presenting the possibility that the way we perceive memories could be a useful way to understand sanskaras and their functioning. It's not an identical match, but memories (like sanskaras) are often intangible concepts. For example, the way they come in and out of our short and long term memory, and also the way they then get stored in subconscious areas. I think there is a correlation here. It is known that our memories form our experience. For instance, you're walking down the street and you see a figure in the distance ..."Oh, there's Bob!" And then as he gets closer you realize this is not Bob. It is the store of past memories and experiences that trigger the mind to automatically fill in data that's not really there. I think sanskaras operate this way too. They form our experience — we are not always conscious of the way they do it.

Danny: Yeah, that can cause problems for me when that happens. It's almost like I might have a feeling of (like an intuition underneath it) that, "Oh, I knew this person in a past life." But then the feeling's so strong — like, "I know this person." But my mind starts filling in the details from this lifetime because that's all it has to work with in terms of actual memories, and then tries to associate the thing from this lifetime which really has nothing to do with the person in front of me. But it's just that overriding feeling underneath it which is true. And somehow the mind, to make sense of it, creates something false in order to acknowledge the feeling that is true.

Doug: It's like a drawing exercise. I took a course called "Drawing for those who don't think they can draw." And I can't draw.

{Laughter.} So I thought I'd take the course. So they put ... in front of you to draw that. So I started to try to draw it. I wasn't really drawing what I was seeing. I was drawing what my mind thought it was supposed to look like. And it looked like something a six year old would do. And then you do these exercises of actually drawing exactly what you see, and it started to come together. But the mind does fill in the blanks. That's what it does naturally until you can use some sort of principle ... and I think it's the same thing. These memories are like seeing Bob ... your mind was thinking of Bob, until you get closer ...

Sevn: I think it's because of habits that we have strong attractions towards experiences that are familiar. It's similar to some people's relationship to music. People like to listen to the same song over and over and over, because they recognize it, like pop music. It's popular because it's catchy, and you hear it, and you're like, "Oh, I remember that." It's like there's this natural habit to want to prefer that which is familiar.

¶ Don: Could I go back to — I think it was Sevn who talked about the psychological studies, and that in a memory an unstable condition of energy is produced. I don't remember exactly how they measured that unstable state of energy. But I'd like to go back and relate that to something that Baba makes pretty clear. And that is that in what is stored (in some fashion or another) in the mental body is in a state of complete quiescence. It's quiet, and it can stay that way indefinitely without doing anything at all. And then in some way when the individual who has experienced that and stored the memory, comes into an environmental

"The mental processes are partly dependent upon the immediately given objective situation, and partly dependent upon the functioning of accumulated sanskaras or impressions of previous experience. The human mind thus finds itself between a sea of past sanskaras on the one side and the whole extensive objective world on the other. From the psychogenetic point of view, human actions are based upon the operation of the impressions stored in the mind through previous experience. Every thought, emotion and act is grounded in groups of impressions which, when considered objectively, are seen to be modifications of the mind-stuff of man."
– Meher Baba (from *Discourses* (6th edition), "The Formation and Function of Sanskaras," (Volume I, p. 54).

situation, similar to in some key ways (and Baba didn't explain how the memory considers the key ways, and how similar it has to be) then the energy of the sanskara, the impression that has been stored, is as it were, awakened. And I regard Baba's usage of the term "awakened" as being similar to what you say the psychologist feels is an unstable state of the energy. I don't know how they measure what is an unstable state frankly, but I'm not enough of a physicist, nor an electronic miracle worker, to know. But nevertheless, I think we've got some important things here. I always myself simply think of it in terms of, let's say, a coded memory on a computer. You punch in the code, and then just a whole stored archive file comes up automatically and is active in the machine. And it seems to me there are parallels between what goes on in computer technology — and human beings, and particularly over into the field of sanskaras, which excites me frankly. So you remember that somewhere or another (and I can't remember whether Baba states this in exact words anywhere in his writings) then the awakened energy, which in some fashion or another has been put into an awakened, or active state, and ready to spring, as it were, then it wishes to, it has an ingrained necessity to express itself in the same manner in which it was originally formed. And if you reflect on that statement, that is dead dog-eye center in what we regard as being a habit pattern.

So this, as it were, coded energy needing to express itself in the same manner as it was originally formed is a terribly significant thing. It also gives rise to apparently — and I think this is a jump, but a terribly important jump — the need, as it were, to express itself in the same form in a habit pattern, gives rise to an emotional pattern which has energy to it. "I want this," and what it wants is to do it in the same manner. And so if it doesn't do it in the same manner it feels frustrated, and this starts getting into a pretty deep and important realm of psychology. {To Laurent.} Go ahead.

Laurent: It makes me think of kids who can speak, and they're pretty young, three or four or maybe even younger. When they do something they really like, they immediately say, {using his little kid's voice} "Let's do that again!"

¶ Don: Yeah. So that is a habit pattern with more energy that has been expressed and wants to do it again.

Laurent: Yeah, how much do we actually grow up from that state? {Laughter.}

¶ Don: Well, I'm not sure, but that's open to a lot of conjecture and study also. But then let's go on to how this happens. So far, I think the fact that we human beings have stored within us patterns which want to repeat themselves when they encounter something (and this happens automatically; it's not something that we've got control over apparently) — they want to repeat themselves in the same manner, so this leads apparently to one considering that as being, in some manner, *right*. "This is the right action. This is the right way to do it." So we, in some manner, also tack on to it, put a piece of scotch tape on it, consider that as being inherently right and desirable and necessary in some manner. And this sounds like the beginning of the roots of racial, or national, considerations of morality. And gradually I think it is subject to what happens when this sort of action is repeated enough times in the social whole, and people observe that it produces results that are beneficial to the social whole, or detrimental to it. And if it is [perceived] as detrimental, then you have other people who have not experienced this particular incidence (or experience pattern) who just say "No, that's wrong. People suffer when you do that." And they say this is a wrong action. And so you begin to find, I think, the roots of social morality and the mores of the tribe, or a civilization. It gets to be fascinating. And all of this flows from the basic things that Meher Baba tells us about.

You begin to realize how these very central descriptions of the nature of sanskaras, and the storage of them, and especially this business — the incredible fact of a stored energy, and this must have to do with the pattern which is stored with it — wanting to express the energy in the same fashion, the same pattern in which it was originally stored. You know I think this is an absolutely fundamental, earthshaking thing that Baba points out to us. There are so many things that spring from it.

Doug: Tribal rivalry ... and they go on for generations.

¶ Don: Well, it also means that ... [we] end up with a pattern of right and wrong, desirable and undesirable, which is very different from another. And you get warfare about a clash of ideas. "Yeah, we found this to be right. You Son-of-a-gun, you're off on the wrong track!" So, to see how environment itself, and differences in environment, can produce really terribly conflicting ideas, and people stick to them so very, very firmly. So their acceptance of a difference becomes almost a matter of — well, in a way it is a matter of life and death in some cases, because you can well have conditions in your part of the planet which are enough different from another part of the planet that accepting the other guy's idea can really mean a considerable detriment to the progress, or health, of the whole. I'm obviously being very quick and superficial, but all you have to do is to open that door that Baba gives us to the reality of the basic qualities of the storage mechanism, and that it is one part energy. Energy (and lot of energy), regardless of how it is stored, is an unstable condition in nature. It is sort of like a hill that wants to run down to flat sea level. It's a way of looking at it —

Laurent: Potential energy.

¶ Don: This is potential energy. And it's terribly important. And it's so important to human beings.

Doug: Relating that to what seems to be a human, the majority of people tend to say, "I'm right, you're wrong." They want to know they're right, and they have to make somebody else wrong in order for them to be right. And that ...

¶ Don: Well that can be due to a difference in ...

Doug: ... you know, grey areas.

¶ Don: Sure.

Doug: Then they want to have it out. That seems to be a comfort zone where you, and several other, lots of people like you, believe that they're wrong, and then vice-versa. For a person to break out of that and start looking, "Yeah, but ... " and then ... Most people don't want to do that. So it's sort of a, what it means really is that it's been perpetuated. Basically continual warfare. I think that is true — been going on for a long time.

¶ Don: Yeah. Well, I'd like to suggest, just off the top of my head, that a grey area, per se, itself is a discomfort zone, because one wants to have it all this way, where it is undoubtedly the way I've experienced, or all that way where it's obviously wrong, and I can just jump up and down and say it's wrong. But a grey area belongs to neither one nor the other, and puts the individual into an untenable position of acceptance and concrete action.

Doug: Do you think humanity as a whole eventually will be capable of that? Because you know some people are, but it seems like the majority aren't. They really don't want to go into that.

¶ Don: Well quite frankly I don't think there's any solution to a mass of humanity, because this is an energy which creates emotions. Energy and emotions get involved in the same person at different levels. And it relates to energy of sanskaras, and that is *unreality*. And the only way that energy ever has a final solution is in its annihilation. In other words, when you're getting on, well on towards being God yourself. So asking humanity to have the temperament and the sophistication to accept grey zones, and uncertainty zones, is asking for something that really can't be achieved — really achieved — until one has made an enormous amount of progress towards Godhood, which means the elimination of the energy of the sanskaras. And boy that's quite an advanced stage. {To Doug}: So how do you live with it meanwhile?

"The merging into the fifth plane is called 'Fana-e-Jabaruti' or the annihilation of all desires." – Meher Baba (from *Discourses* (6th edition), "The Stages of the Path" (Volume II, p. 24).

Doug: ... I mean really it's — I don't know ...

¶ Don: How do you do it? {To the entire group} You know, I just pose that to you as human beings who are wise (Baba wouldn't have had you sitting around here if you didn't have a certain amount of purchase on these subjects and insight), and so how would you

> "The intermediate steps of slimming down the ego and softening its nature are comparable to the trimming and pruning of the branches of a wild and mighty tree, while the final step of annihilation of the ego amounts to the complete uprooting of this tree. When the ego disappears entirely there arises knowledge of the true Self." – Meher Baba from *Discourses* (6th edition), "The Nature of the Ego and Its Termination: III," (Volume II, p. 83).

as people that the Avatar knows are pretty well along in the process, recommend, if one wants to put society in a condition where it can live more happily, and with less bloodshed, and more progress? This is the basic question for the Avatar: How to devise learning situations so there is minimum expenditure (or wastage) of the basic resources in getting there? So this is what Meher Baba's mostly been doing in this incarnation, as far as I see it, in setting up the principles for the new cycle of Avataric cycles. How to put the forms in place and get them into motion with a minimum wastage of the psychic energy that is basically the principle, the endowment, the formula, the energy pool from which God-realization is eventually to be achieved. How to use that? And that's where the whole thing of the "Beads on One String," and forgiveness comes in. So I'm anticipating what maybe we'll start to discuss this afternoon or tomorrow. And it is fascinating to see what I feel now excitedly Baba has made an enormous effort on, and I've been around some of it, and only realizing now what I'm sure he was up to. So excuse me, I'm getting too off field here.

Doug: No, I mean — when you posed that question, I mean ...

¶ Don: How do you help civilization along, really, practically, concretely?

Doug: ... the only thing I can think of is to try to live by the, you know, just by example. You live your life according to Baba. And maybe it'll spread.

¶ Don: Yeah, but how do you *awaken that desire to follow another example other than the dictates of your own habit patterns*? Boy, there is a great big, you know, empty valley in between there which is hard to fill in.

Doug: Well, some people can respond if they —

¶ Don: They can, but what makes them want to respond? What

makes them think maybe something's wrong and —

Doug: If they understand that by responding it will make them happier. But that assumes that they're ...

¶ Don: And how do you awaken them?

Laurent: And how can you ensure that by responding they'll be happier?

Doug: You can't. You know, I mean there was the idealism of the 60s. We all thought we were going to change the world. You know, humanity was going to evolve. We were going to have peace ... I don't believe that, after reading Meher Baba on war, and just, you know, that's never going to happen. Because of what Don just said, that the whole of what goes on with the energy and the sanskaras of people not wanting to look at grey areas, because it's so uncomfortable for them.

¶ Don: It is. It's inherently uncomfortable.

Doug: ... is going to ensure that we have a constant level of battles and constant levels of ... which is unfortunate, but I no longer think it's something that's going to change, unless Baba has something else planned, you know?

¶ Don: All right, so basically what we're saying to one another here, Doug, is that this is inbuilt into the process of nature, and the manner in which it is organized, which produces discomfort zones and tendencies to avoid things. And the avoiding of things creates problems and real battles. And how do you minimize this discomfort area and do something about it? Jamshid, here.

Jamshid: I have a question. Doesn't humanity — I mean, yes, grey zone, discomfort. But aren't there shades of grey in —

¶ Don: Shades of grace?

Jamshid: Shades of *grey*.

¶ Don: You see how my mind substituted the word I wanted? {Laughter.}

Payam: I like that.

¶ Don: I thought that was a cute substitution.

Jamshid: — that we are not as unconscious as maybe we were five thousand years ago, or two thousand years ago. Yes, our consciousness is evolving. And yes, there are shades of grey out there ... that we typically don't want to stand in until we reach a point where the cost of not accepting uncertainty, and being in the question, and not judgment, the cost of not being so ... that we choose to, consciously choose to not to be in a such position of judgment. And at least pushing that direction and trying to stay in the grey. But my point, I guess in the whole of it, is that what we called grey back then is different from what we call grey today. That our consciousness has evolved to a point where yes, from 1960 to 2007 we have not gone from, you know, 0 to 1,000. But maybe we've gone from 999 to 1,000. Maybe we've taken one step. Maybe context that in many different aspects of life, as well as abstractions and consciousness and so forth, we're not so — we're not even there, or the bulk of humanity today are. ... let's say, recycling. The concept of how we connect to nature — how we use nature, am I worthy of that which I am taking in? And how do I make sure that the next generation doesn't get affected by that which I consume today, or the way in which I consume what I consume?

Doug: Well, you know I think those practices are being embraced by educated people in an affluent country and it's totally wonderful. But, you know, as you go into parts of the interior of the United States, and a lot of the rural areas, places like Mississippi, Oklahoma and places like that: "Recycle?" ...

¶ Don: Can I try popping something in there? Well, what about thinking of the possibility that perhaps the critical thing — and I like very much Jamshid's suggestion. He hasn't put this in precise words — but the stage, the state of civilization of the people can effect certain changes in the living habits so that what was not acceptable or possible becomes acceptable in a later generation as that civilization so-called matures. And I would tell you, if that sounds interesting to you then I would go back and say then let's consider even a more fundamental initial property, and that is the amount of leisure time within which an individual is not *fighting to live* and has the opportunity to reflect. Is this perhaps a critical element and that the basis of civilizing depends upon that? And then the retention and passing on to the next generation the fruits of what the reflection has produced.

Doug: Well I agree. I really, and I ...

Laurent: And that's what we're doing here.

Doug: Sometimes I ... and I look at other things and I get kind of shot down again. But you know if we talk about the evolution of the human, and we look at recorded history, I'm really in awe. Yes, I mean ... slavery used to be accepted. Now it isn't. And that's definitely a step in the right direction. Some of the brutality of the Dark Ages, the Middle Ages on such a huge scale —

Laurent: — is only done by the CIA. So we're making progress. {Laughter.}

Doug: But then just sixty years ago we had the Third Reich. We had Pol Pot, and all of that. If survival is not the issue anymore then other things are possible. I hope that we are slowly evolving.

Payam: Well, I get into that kind of dark abyss with it. And at the same time I hear Baba's made us a promise. He said there's a New Humanity. And I just accept that, that it is coming. I don't know when, and—

¶ Don: It's here.

Laurent {to Payam}: Maybe you're it. {Laughter.}

¶ Don: It's it. It's here.

Payam: I mean that living the brotherhood, sisterhood. But for all of humanity, not just the few or the people I know immediately.

¶ Don: People are much more conscious of brotherhood and sisterhood than they were when I was a kid even. Even I can feel the difference. Enormous. How about you, Ellie?

Ellie: The question that you posed was, How do we in our day-to-day interaction *Don was born in 1919.*
you know with the sanskaric, the conundrum of the sanskaric energy — how do we affect the world or our surroundings? And Doug was saying, yes, by being an example to others. But for somebody

> "Love is essentially self-communicative; those who do not have it catch it from those who have it. Those who receive love from others cannot be its recipients without giving a response which, in itself, is the nature of love. True love is unconquerable and irresistible. It goes on gathering power and spreading itself until eventually it transforms everyone it touches. Humanity will attain to a new mode of being and life through the free and unhampered interplay of pure love from heart to heart." – Meher Baba, *Discourses*, (6th Edition), "The New Humanity", Volume I, p.24

else to want to change they have to be touched in their heart. Love comes ... In their mind if they're touched by love then they're going to want to make something shift. I don't know how to explain it or what it is, but when people are touched by love they're compelled to do something different than they used to, or act differently. And if there's enough of that that keeps happening then, you know, this brotherhood isn't so farfetched.

Doug: Well you know it actually, when people are touched by love, they like it. They want more of it.

Ellie: Right, they want more of it.

Doug: And so maybe that's what we ...

Sevn: I think that's a key point, but if you look at some of the people in the middle of America, they're not happy. The look in their eyes is that of suffering. People don't want to suffer, so I think as the consciousness of the New Humanity is unveiled, it will be contagious. There are theories of a magic threshold number. I think it comes from Judeo-Christian mysticism, and says something like, when 144,000 individuals become either enlightened, or reach the threshold of the subtle plane, then *bam*, the rest of the planet will become enlightened. Perhaps this is a kind of fantasy but I think there's a truth to the idea that when we reach a certain threshold of people sincerely seeking truth, that it'll be contagious and the world will change out of necessity. Baba says the real job of spiritual workers is to destroy spiritual ignorance.

Marnie: So this thing of falling is sanskarically connected ... there are going to be some people who are at a certain consciousness who are loved, which has touched them in their heart. There will be other people who are at the more material sanskaric level that practical suffering that comes from not recycling or polluting their atmosphere or whatever is being ... that incite them to make changes ... Baba will use all those different means to ... Make change and then it's probably pretty small but ...

¶ Don: You're pointing out their practical considerations that have to be present and fulfilled for something to happen fundamentally, basically, naturally enough for it to have an important effect on humanity. And, could I give you an example that Baba gives very clearly? And it's the basis of his "Don't worry, be happy" recommendation which he pushed so hard. He says very simply in one chapter of the *Discourses* that the ability of the involuting drop-soul to overcome barriers on the spiritual path depends on the availability in him of psychic energy, spiritual energy, which can be used to eliminate the barriers along the route. But he said, so often unfortunately the individual has no availability. They have so exhausted it and frittered it away in various different things they do not have the psychic energy available to apply to these barriers when they come to them. As a consequence, they're slowed down or stopped almost indefinitely. And he said of all of the things which exhaust needlessly this supply of psychic energy, worry is the one that fritters away the most.

Payam: Wow.

¶ Don: And so then he starts saying to everybody, "Don't worry, be happy." And I have only in recent years suddenly said, "My God, that makes so much sense!" {Laughter.} And the Avatar, who is planning for the next cycle of cycles, who identifies this and said — This is something I can do about it. So I'm going to sit down my spiritual devotees with cards and with radio programs and university lectures, "Worry is a terribly important thing and you've got to get rid of it."

Doug: Well this brings us back to Danny's point, because if you remember, you worry. But if you forget, you forget yourself. I mean, you can't be tied up in yourself and self-absorbed. That would be worry. You would be worrying.

¶ Don: Yeah, and principally because of the fact that the self is the thing that winds it back on the hot iron curler and makes it at least as available as it was before. If your mind is focused on non-Truth, and the ego is the furthest thing away from the Truth, then a maximum amount of the energy is going to be tied back into a further, maybe even more strong sanskaric energy pattern. That's it in a nutshell.

Mahmoud: What you just mentioned makes sense because, "religion" — a strong relationship with what's happening in today's "religion" ... connected on the basis of false religion.

¶ Don: Based on false religion?

Mahmoud: Yeah, I mean, the religion, the sense is correct, but what they have created around this religion has totally changed it. The whole concept of the religion.

¶ Don: Well yes, and unfortunately also this whole energy balance tremendously. Even the sense of competition between religions destroys an enormous amount of this really valid psychic energy devotional aspect of the true religion. But then, if you go ahead and spend what you have saved up in your own store, and a great big battle on concepts of who is God and who's got the best Avatar — {Laughter.} You know, well it's all frittered away, or a big portion of it is. But apparently the Avatar has seen that the general level of civilization worldwide has gone on far enough so that he can do something like pointing out that all of this inter-religion warfare and competition is destroying a huge percentage, much more than is necessary, of devotional energy from promotion of individual progress through the barriers on the spiritual path. So that he can now say to them, "Look, you have got to stop all of this silly argument about who's got the principles, and who's got the best messiah, and save that energy and cooperate, and carry all of civilization along. It's a monumental — everybody has always known that truth is truth, but why hasn't anybody done anything about it? I think it has just been because of what we've been saying, that people are so blessedly preoccupied with *satisfying their own idea of what has got to be*, that they're always fighting each other, and they have no energy. And fighting *themselves*, and what they expect to get out of it, worrying about this, worrying about that. But the Avatar has seen that the stage of civilization has grown to the point where people are beginning to reflect, finally, and be dissatisfied with the situation. And if you come along and say, if you stop quarreling with that Muslim over there and that Jewish person over there about whether Christ is the best of all, or whether he had indoctrinated people with the best formula for civilization, and [instead] cooperate with them on the basic fundamentals: there's one God, and there's such a thing as love, and so on. Then you will have an enormous supply of energy to get through the real barriers, and the spiritual path can then be done more efficiently. Well, that should be the Avatar's job: how to choose the potential for present benefit most efficiently. More and more of it is available.

Doug: ... give humanity a push. And so during his manifestation, and afterwards for a time, perhaps some of these things will be mitigated. There will be more cooperation. There have been times of cooperation between Christians and Jews and Muslims who were living in harmony at one time ...

¶ Don: Quite a few of them were, and quite a few of them weren't. At the same time they were doing wonderful things in Spain for awhile.

Doug: Yeah.

¶ Don: Going up into the Balkans and the center of Europe it was the reverse.

Doug: It was in Spain that they really had it together for awhile.

¶ Don: Yeah, they sure did.

Doug: But then things will deteriorate again and He has to come again. But you know —

¶ Don: They will deteriorate, but they will never deteriorate to the same level they were at before. And meanwhile his more efficient principles that he has gotten enough people excited about to spread some sane, decent, healthy principles, will help the whole thing again with another leap forward.

Doug: Well what you're saying then is extremely optimistic.

¶ Don: I am an optimist. {Laughter.}
Doug: I believe you. {Laughter persists.}
¶ Don: Doug, sometimes I say I'm a "hopeless optimist."
Doug: Some of the things I say are devil's advocate stuff. But if each Avataric advent is just a little bit better —
¶ Don: Mm-hmm. But look what has happened in the world. To me, archeological studies show that the world has constantly been advancing little by little. But now I think the age of the planet, and the age of civilization, and the age of our remembering processes are good enough that it is gradually even accelerating. Now that's where I get to be a hopeless optimist. {Laughter.}
Doug: No, that's good, that's good.
¶ Don: Yeah.
Laurent: Well the last advent, if we look historically—because I've been studying a lot about this—the last advent was during the 7th century with Mohammed (Peace be upon Him and His family). So all over the world it was tribal. All over the world. And suddenly with this present advent we're global. So we have a global humanity aware of things that, we don't know if it's ever been like this before. We can assume maybe not.
¶ Don: Certainly not.
Laurent: It's hard to know what was in the ancient, ancient past. How did they build the pyramids? Who knows? But —
¶ Don: I'm sure I've been sitting on my memory lately.
Laurent: Don knows how they built the pyramids. But we've got a global New Humanity coming that's obviously radically different from what was going on at the last advent —
¶ Don: Radically new potentials.
Laurent: — which was tribal, you know, tribal up the wazoo, right? It was tribal in Europe. It was tribal in Arabia. It was tribal in Persia. So this is radical already.
Doug: There's still a lot of tribal, because you —
Laurent: I know, but we're making that shift from tribal to global.
Doug: Oh yeah, we are.

Laurent: And I just wanted to tack on this, because you [Doug] were saying about introducing Baba as, "You'll be happier." That was an interesting idea.

Doug: I didn't mean — I meant ...

Laurent: I know.

Doug: Ellie and I were talking about, you know love is contagious ... if someone touches them with love ...

Laurent: Sure. Yeah, sure. But I think it's really interesting that Baba said, "Don't worry, be happy." He didn't say — Don't worry, I will make you happy! And when I hear that, "Don't worry, be happy," it's one of the simplest and most difficult things in the universe because he's putting the onus on each one of us.

Sevn: Right.

Don: A "do-it-yourself" process.

Laurent: Yes! And what he's saying in my estimation is, "Change your attitude. Don't expect me to make you happy. Change your attitude and be happy!"

Doug: But don't you think that an unhappy person after being touched by love, in whatever it is, can take that, and make it grow within them —

Laurent: They can with the right attitude.

Doug: — like a seed.

Laurent: With the right attitude they can nurture the seed. With the wrong attitude they can kill the seed.

Doug: — and then they can decide whether to be happy. But at least they'll have some raw material with which to be happy if they want to continue to experience more love. Or forget about it. I mean it's not like Baba's making them happy ...

Sam: For many of my generation the word "God" holds strong negative connotations. The word, when used in most contexts, evokes thoughts of hypocritical institutions, political agendas and mandatory duties to be performed against one's will. This is not due to a lack of fascination with the Divine, the Spiritual, the Sacred on the part of today's youth, on the contrary; it's because of an innate, intuitive understanding of the ineffable within young people that so many of them conscientiously avoid using the word "God" to describe the awesome power of the unity they see in the world around them and feel deep within their own hearts.

Not too long ago I was speaking with a friend of mine. He was about twenty-four years old at the time of the conversation, and struggling to find his path in life. Although he had been raised a Christian, he had no real interest in organized religion or spiritual communities, and looked towards music and creativity to provide meaning and purpose in his life.

The topic of conversation had started with music, but soon moved on to philosophy, and in turn spirituality. And then, without warning, this unassuming twenty-four year old came out with, what I felt to be, a profound piece of wisdom. "It just seems obvious", he said matter of factly, "if God is anything, then he has to be everything; he is everywhere and everything, and he is all of these things all of the time. God can't be just the things that we humans deem sacred, if God is indeed God then he is all the things that we deem sacred-less. God is hate, God is love, God is death and God is life. If God is infinite then he must be everything that is finite as well. And by extension, it's basic logic that we are all a part of this... thing ... called God."

And I think, in one brief statement, my friend summed up the feeling prevalent among a vast amount of today's youth. It's obvious, it's intuitive, it really couldn't be any other way. *We, and everything else in all of existence, are just a piece of one multi-versal God.*

And while this feeling within my friend, which reflects a greater feeling within today's youth, is unfocused, almost unconscious of itself, and can easily be mistaken as skepticism or ambivalence, it does indeed exist. And its power is yet to be realized.

Danny: I know what you mean. I've seen that in so many young people. You know, that potential that's just not being focused somehow —

Sam: Right.

Danny: —not being quite grasped onto because there are so many distractions.

Sam: Yeah.

Doug: Well the media will, they measure spirituality in a country by the number of churches. If there's more churches built in '07 than '06 that means spirituality is growing.

Sam: Right, yeah.

Doug: And you know, I don't know how else you'd measure it. It's subjective. But that's the only way for ...

Sam: Like Laurent said earlier about how personal experience is the only real gauge you could ever have about something like that. For me it's like a personal experience, like you were saying ... at a vast rate. It's just not recognized on the global scale.

Payam: So Don, you left us with a cliffhanger.

¶ Don: Oh? {Laughter.} We're now getting terribly close to that cliff top, by the way. That's why I was just looking at my watch. I was going to suggest maybe we'd better quickly now get to the second remaining intuition that Sevn had to offer.

Sevn: Okay, mine was inspired by a quote from *God Speaks*: "If the soul is conscious of impressions, then the soul must necessarily experience these impressions through proper or suitable media."

So if the soul is conscious of impressions or sanskaras, then it must necessarily experience these impressions through the most proper and suitable media. I'm going to summarize the different ways this has unfolded for me. It has been comforting for me to know that whatever I'm experiencing at any moment in time is the most ideal situation possible. I'm being provided with the perfect media and the perfect vehicle to experience this according to exactly what I need.

> The term 'sama' means 'hearing' or 'audition'. Two of the Sufi orders, the Mevlevi of Turkey, and the Chishtis in Pakistan and India, utilize a combination of Zikr, music, and dance to create the possibility of creating a 'Hal' state for the participants, which may include visions and loss of normal consciousness. However, knowing how easily the human organism can become addicted to the unusual, the exotic, some teachers discourage repeat experiences: "If a novice is attracted to sama, you can know there is still in him a remainder of falseness." – Junayd (KM)

This has evoked an intuition related to meditation and yoga and the desire for people to take on yogic practices as a means to seek occult experiences and direct visions of the subtle realms. From personal practice, I have come to know that state in meditation that you come to know that is very blissful and wonderful. I think this is samadhi in a lower sense, not Nirvalkpa Samadhi, but nevertheless one of the most blissful states that a person can experience. I think that this is what most people that are really into meditation and yogic practices are looking for. They're looking for this state of bliss. I have this deep intuition that they're just looking to experience something that is inherently there when they drop their body and that temporarily liberating the body from the limitations of the gross realm may get bliss, but it's not really doing anything spiritual. By seeking bliss you're not really discovering any greater truth. Being that we have a body that exists for a hundred years or so, it is strange that people seek an experience that will inevitably occur after death? For me, the fact that I have a body that suffers pain and emotions is evidence of a proper and suitable vehicle. This is so important, because a lot of times in my life I've tried to find ways to transcend my body, because it feels a lot more comfortable. But I have a strong feeling that transcending the body isn't necessarily transcendence at all. It isn't God-realization. There's nothing special about it because this body is the most wonderful and perfect tool for experiencing the world. It is a relative waste of time to think that the mere absence of the gross world, gross sanskaric influence, and the gross body, is any closer to the spiritual realm. The gross is just as much God as anything else. Seeing Baba in a picture with your eyes is just as perfect as having a dream where he comes to you in white glowing light.

Doug: So you think that the seeking of those experiences is like an escape through some kind of intoxicant?

Sevn: Yeah, the gross world has a lot of limitations and pains and it's nice to escape them.

Marnie: And then what you're saying is that that's spiritually not moving forward. It's through experiencing the gross but with the consciousness of Baba as being a source of ... that is the means for spiritual...

Sevn: Right, right. I don't know all the means for spiritual advancement ...

Marnie: No. no.

Sevn: I just know that from my experience — I don't know why it took me so long but — that this state that I was looking to experience in life wasn't any closer to truth than what was right in front of me.

Danny: Isn't it pretty much like the "masts", you know? They might be blissed out, but they're stuck.

{Laughter.}

Sevn: That's the extreme, yeah.

Danny: And Baba had to unstick them, which they didn't like, because they were being pulled out of bliss.

'Mast' is the term Meher Baba used for those souls that are 'God-intoxicated,' and it is an abbreviation of 'Mast-Allah.' – LW. For more see: The Wayfarers: Meher Baba with the God-Intoxicated, by W. Donkin (Myrtle Beach: Sheriar Foundation, 2001)

Sevn: Yeah, exactly.

Danny: But it was necessary if they were ever going to get God-realization.

{Silence}

☙

Danny: ... I did have that sense just from everything I've read about Baba that taking that temporary samadhi — as blissful as it might be — and it might be a million times more blissful than my daily cup of chai — {Laughter.} Nevertheless —

Laurent: We'll call you "Chai Mast."

Payam: "Chai mast." That's a good name! "Chai Mast."

Danny: There's probably already some mast with that name. {Laughter.}

¶ Don: Well, I wonder, Sevn, whether Baba's statement in writing that at the end of the subtle plane review between lives of the drop-soul, it is the sanskaras [which] demand rebirth in the world. And it is absolutely necessary, for the sanskaras to be eliminated, that they be carried back into the environment of the physical world. And that is where the real work is done. So what you are suggesting is that your just deep basic feeling, that as wonderful as it is inducing a state of bliss somewhat outside of those worldly experiences — in fact, deliberately putting them into a state of unimportance, at least for the time being, is actually counter-productive for the drop-soul, to put it rather bluntly. And I think what Baba says implies that. And certainly it foreshadows his statement, which he makes very clearly, that all God-realized masters, inclusive of the Avatar, *far prefer that their devotees be carried under the veil*, and never knowing spiritually where they are, and not having esoteric visions and experiences. And that is a pretty blunt statement, and it upsets quite a few people of course.

> "The Master usually helps the aspirant through ordinary means and prefers to take him under the veil, but when there is a special indication he may also use an occult medium to help him. Special types of dreams are among the common media which are used for touching the deeper life of the aspirant." - Meher Baba, *Discourses*, (6th Edition), "The Place of Occultism in Spiritual Life: The Value of Occult Experiences," Volume II, p. 85.

Danny {to Don}: That might be a little extreme, just because I've known too many Baba people who I think do have [visions] — I mean it's more the exception than the rule, I think — but I've known those who do have [experiences], it's just a part of their normal daily lives, they just sort of — maybe they've always seen ghosts, or they had visions or whatever. And it's almost like part of their challenge that they go through in this lifetime. Maybe they don't even want that.

¶ Don: Mm-hmm.

Danny: They struggle to stay centered through that and keep it in the proper perspective.

¶ Don: Well, I don't know what the proper perspective is; I just have to say that really a fairly appreciable percentage of my closest, and most admired and loved, friends are people who just commonly sprinkle [in] their conversation — Baba told me this, and Baba advised me to do that, and he warned me about so-and-so. In other words it's just daily experience as far as they're concerned. And I think I've told you here my general — these are people you know I've known for years and love dearly and respect highly. At some point or another I have told them (or do tell them) that I simply prefer to be what I am. I'm not psychic at all. *And I think that there is a very, very real possibility that their experiences have a considerable amount from their own unconscious of personal coloring. And if these are terribly important, then as a first measure of hygiene they should admit to themselves there is a very, very strong probability that there is important subconscious coloring of their experience, of what they call Baba, of their own subconscious mind. In other words, mental body storehouse influences.*

Danny: Those aren't the cases I'm referring to though. I agree with you, I have the same kind of suspicious reaction when ...

¶ Don: Sure.

Danny: I mean, Baba told me that I should be suspicious ... {Brief pause.} I'm kidding. {Laughter.}

¶ Don: That's the first principle of what ...

Danny: You guys looked so serious when I said, "Baba told me." I didn't think I was going to have to actually explain that I was kidding. {More laughter.}

Danny: Anyway ...

¶ Don: You better be pessimistic. {Laughter.}

Danny: But, yeah, I mean, I think everybody's story is different. But I'm sure people in this room know people who — or at least some people in this room — who do have experiences. And that's why I just wanted to mention, even though I generally agree with most of what you're saying — I'm not one of these people, I don't really have those experiences. But I have to allow that sometimes that just might be their experience or their path in this lifetime or their sanskaras or whatever, that they're going to have experiences outside the gross, and somehow have to integrate that into their life with Baba. And it doesn't mean Baba appearing to them and telling them things. It may just be seeing, you know, things from the subtle world, or whatever, or the astral. Or just having visions. And that can be really hard on them I think, because then they still have to get up and go to work. And it can be hard to go back and forth between the two states of existence. So I just wanted to allow for the fact that I don't think it's always like a 100% veil with us Baba devotees. It's the fact that it's not the same for everybody.

¶ Don: No, it isn't. It certainly is not. But Baba lays it down very clearly on the line.

Doug: But Don, what you're saying is that there's a danger in wanting the ego to masquerade as ...

¶ Don: Well, it's a great temptation.

Doug: A person wants to do something, then they can somehow juggle things around and make it sound like Baba's wanting them to do that. But in actuality they want to do it, and justify it.

¶ Don: Well this is where subconscious coloring ...

Doug: You get tricked —

Danny: Yeah.

Doug: It's a tough, I think it'd be tough to, you'd have to be brutally honest with yourself in order to make the distinction.

Laurent: That's where the role of companionship comes in I think.

Doug: Yeah. The truing.

Laurent: Yeah.

¶ Don: Sharing with companions. Opening your mind to their feelings.

Danny: And I agree and that happens and I don't want to take away from that point at all. I just felt like I had to allow for the, you know — I didn't want to let some sort of bias get created against these occasional exceptions to the rule.

Sevn: I don't think those are exceptions though. I don't think the experience of the astral realm is anything near subtle consciousness or the subtle world. I think psychic phenomenon and experiences in the astral world is actually very gross. The astral is the threshold, but for all intents and purposes it's gross. This is a common mistake.

Glenn: And I don't think that's occult.

❡ Don: *It's the interplay between the two worlds.*

Sevn: Even the lower occult powers are fabulous, like levitation, but Baba said these have nothing to do with the subtle world.

❡ Don: And they have nothing to do with spirituality.

Sevn: Right.

Danny: I wasn't really thinking about levitation. {Laughter.} But it's interesting that distinction between the subtle and the astral, so thank you.

Glenn: Forgive me, I'm going to mention something not from Baba, it doesn't have Baba's authority. But I remember reading something — I hope I don't offend anybody — that Edgar Cayce wrote in a reading he did on someone's past life. And it came up around some, a particular kind of psychic experience. And the gist of it was that pretty much everybody on the earth has been, in the past, in a place where these kind of, what we consider psychic experiences, came most naturally. Because that was just the way people did things. And it probably was less evolved spiritually. I believe it's in the supplement in *God Speaks* and other places. When these souls immediately attain 100% mind before they — later on we evolve a closer balance of head and heart — they're able to manipulate matter and energy in tremendous ways just with the thought itself. And these are not natural things nor are they really occult things, it's just they're more like baggage of the past. And we all come with different baggage from our lower forms. You know some people skip lives and might still have an instinct to bury bones, because you were a dog in a previous life or something. I think some people just come with ...

❡ Don: {Laughing.} So that's why I like to do that.

Sevn: In *God Speaks* Baba says that minor occult powers are a result from sanskaras from a previous lifetime[1] — and then the major are usually — or is it the other way around?

Danny: Yeah, I know the part you're talking about. I can't remember exactly — but it can be a natural result of even like if you

See Part II of this volume wherein Don shares a large number of his personal intuitions on the subject of forgiveness.

get — maybe some good karma or something.

Sevn: Right. Exactly. I think that's what...

¶ Don: You know this is the place where I think we have to introduce a terribly important topic and that is that certainly intuition itself involves subconscious processes and subconscious contact with deeper layers of the individual human being. And therefore it has certain elements which are psychic. There's no question about it. So it's impossible to do anything really important with intuition without going right to the brink-edge of the unconscious, and dealing with some of the things which are occult in the long run. So if we do what Baba says, utilize and experiment with it, and use it in your daily lives, but always remember you must check it with logic and reason. Don't forget that ... But when we go into the whole subject of getting the beads on one string, and the great problem of hate and how it might be relieved, I'm certainly going to say that I am convinced that we must absolutely as a group, and this group in particular — go much further into intuition, intuitional processes. And we're just going to come bump right up against the usage — right next door to deliberate usage of the occult powers. If we do any work together over a period of time, I'm certainly going to read to you on occasions various of my own intuitions.

I'm going to bring up at least one either late today or early tomorrow dealing with the subject of forgiveness. And you will notice that the intuition talks about things that Baba gave out, and the intuition came through as, "I have done so and so." Now I just want to skirt a little bit of historical background on this, because it's important that I do so now. I have had quite a great deal, since Baba talked about the Avataric gift of intuition, realized that I have used intuition in a lot of creative things, even in scientific reports when I was a laboratory worker.

> Don worked at Standard Oil of California, which later became known as Chevron.

And I recognize now how much intuition I have used importantly in my life. It has been a fact. It has been a very important contribution to my professional career, for instance. And I have deliberately — in the last four or five years since I had prostate trouble and woke up every morning about three o'clock to go pee, and then I wanted to get back in bed, and I get warm and go to sleep again — had in that sort of completely dead intellectual time really terribly important intuitions. And I have deliberately fostered those in the last four or five years. But in all of that time there have only been three or four of those intuitions in which I suddenly said to myself, *well those words are exactly in the same style of using words that I got familiar with, with Baba.* This is Baba's style. And those I accept as having come from Baba. But I don't attribute them, nor do I attribute infallibility to them. So I want you to understand that I deliberately skirt a very, very dangerous ground. We're all going to be. We're running risks with the occult, and our own unconscious mind, and our own subconscious powers, which are pretty powerful as a matter of fact. But I think what I have to steer clear of, and have, has been to become dependent upon those as messages from Baba. I don't feel they are. I think he would, someway or another, find a means of knocking me over the head if I started trying to attribute them [to him]. So there have been only four or five times when I had such a definite feeling — this is Baba — getting a terribly important message through to me. I said that almost has to be a special, special one, and Baba wants me to know that it's important. Stevens, wake up and take it for serious. Is that a clear statement? I'd like you to understand it. {Pause.} You know I wonder, Sevn, if maybe I should read that intuition, which is so central to what we'll be discussing much of tomorrow?

Danny: Is this the forgiveness intuition?

¶ Don: Yeah, it's a forgiveness intuition. {At this point Don reads aloud from "Forgiveness 3" (dated September 14, 2007), an intuition he received):

"Forgiveness is the ultimate test of the ego. To condemn is the ultimate declaration of separateness." In other words, when you condemn, this is saying — I'm me, and by God you're something else.

Laurent: "And you're going to be punished."

¶ Don: Very likely, yeah. {Don continues to read}: "In this incarnation I have reserved for my true devotees the expression of complete forgiveness. First in their own lives, and then in the teaching to others of the example that they are qualified to make for others."

¶ Don: Notice this. This is certainly, on the straightforward use of the words, Baba talking. Talking to his real devotees. Take it as seriously as you want to. But I took this terribly seriously as a major statement of principle, and it made such great sense to me. I'll read that part again: "In this incarnation"— that means now, although Baba's dropped the body, "I have reserved for my true devotees"— that means you and me. And to me especially it means this particular group who are very select and a quite young selection from his devotees. "I have reserved for my true devotees the expression of complete forgiveness first in their own lives"— in other words, look at your own bag of tricks. And who do you feel really head-up and mad about whenever you think of them? And gee, I could never forgive them for that one. That was too terrible. But first of all, go over that list, and say — by golly, if what Don was reading out there is a statement from Baba, this is terribly important. And make just a mental inventory of people who have really wronged you, and every time you even think about them you just have to close the door, and try not to get upset again, or figure out if there's some way you can get back at them.

So, "first in their own lives, and then in the teaching to others of the example that they are qualified to make for others." Having really tried to do something first of all about it in their own lives. You can't talk theory or hypothesis on something this serious. "Do not confuse my function in this lifetime with the activity I have included importantly in other lifetimes when my lovers have built religions around my words."

In other words, remember his statement in 1932, in London to the press — I have not come to establish a new religion.

In other words, take that for serious now. God, just about everybody I know expects the same thing to happen as Christ and

Mohammed, and so on, and so on. Unconsciously. And that's what they're preparing for. Isn't it amazing? {Don continues to read the intuition aloud}:

"As I told the press in London on my first visit in the thirties, I have not come to establish a new religion in this lifetime, but to revivify the world's existing great religions and gather them together like beads on one string. With my repeated visits with Eruch, as he has recounted to you, and the lengthy work I have done repeatedly at those spots and through other means as well, I have cleansed these and other focal spots of great and sincere veneration, from much of the residue of hate and competitiveness which has so encrusted them, and readied them to be placed side by side in the great fact of Oneness of all truth. This basic chore of the scouring of the filth of hate and condemnation, which has been such a constant heritage of the relationships so often rampant between religions, must be completed by my devotees."

> "My object in coming to the West is not with the intention of establishing new creeds or spiritual societies, and organizations. I see the structure of all the great religions of the world tottering. The West is more inclined towards the material side of things. I intend to bring together all religions and cults like beads on one string, and revitalize them for individual and collective needs. This is my mission to the West." – Meher Baba, in *Celebrating Divine Presence*, by L. Weichberger, et al (London: Companion Books, 2008), p. 350.

¶ Don: In other words, he says — I've already started the cleansing process of this hate and condemnation. But the true, final, really putting it in place and living, has got to be done by my devotees. Everything that I have seen Baba do bears out completely this statement of fact and responsibility. It's important. {Don continues reading}:

"It must be completed by my devotees and those others they bring to this central task which I have confided to them in this final period of the last cycle of Avataric cycles." So this is the part of the completion of the old, and the form for the new, and it's an important part of the structure of the new. {Don continues reading}:

"Let there be no mistake, the assignment I give my true devotees is not that of building more churches and receptacles for the bodies of new believers in Meher Baba, nor Jesus Christ, nor of the Avatars and still other incarnations, but their task is in preparing through forgiveness of the base for true and complete harmony at the deepest levels of feeling and being." Boy, that's a powerful statement.

Laurent: It sure is.

¶ Don: And how distant we are from that now, even after Baba's done a lot of the basic cleaning.

{Don continues reading}:

"This has never been done before and will take great insight and patience to accomplish. The problem, of course, is the old one that has existed since the beginning of time: that of the 'I' and 'me' and 'mine' of the ego. Just as the great receptacle of the ego becomes that of feeling one has become religious, so the next great refuge so dangerous to the functioning of Truth in the new cycle of Avataric cycles is that the ego will find its haven in the act of condemning those who have deviated in their opinion from the Path of Unity. Instead, they are to be forgiven to allow them their real opportunity to join the surge of true unity that I have made possible in my deep efforts in this direction during my lifetime as Meher Baba. Do not be confused. True forgiveness is now absolutely necessary to clean out the last dregs of resistance to real Oneness between the great religions themselves, and the reality of this true forgiveness is now to be lived and practiced in the world by my devotees as their act of love and devotion to me. There is no other task as central and important as this, which I am entrusting to them and embodying in these words to you."

¶ Don: Well, that's sure laying it on the line, isn't it?

{A moment of silence.}

☙

Laurent: It blew my socks off.

¶ Don: It did? Oh, so that's why you haven't worn any since?

Glenn: Don't give any importance to occult experiences. {Don chuckles.}

Jamshid: I heard, "progression of consciousness."

¶ Don: Progression of consciousness?

Jamshid: I did hear that, because clearly in this Avataric incarnation, this is a goal set forth for [humanity]. Right?

¶ Don: Yeah. Mm-hmm.

Jamshid: [This has never been done] before. It is not easy, but it is possible. It wasn't before, but it is now. Isn't that progression of consciousness?

Doug: Yes.

Jamshid: The possibility is there? Now? Not before?

Doug: Well, the question remains: how?

¶ Don: Yeah.

Laurent: I think the answer's in the title.

Participant: Yes.

Doug: What's the title?

Laurent: "Forgiveness."

Glenn: Well, you know, forgiveness is kind of like ... forgetfulness. It discharges a lot of the strength. The force of something comes up. You use the positive plateau. You access forgiveness. Or is that ... What is the plateau?

Laurent: Neutral.

¶ Don: The neutral plateau.

Danny: It seems to me that forgetfulness and forgiveness are intimately related. Because when Baba describes forgetfulness in *God Speaks*, he talks about "awareness without reaction." Without mental reactions, which are ... so I think that's what forgiveness is.

Marnie: I think that, forgiveness feels to me like it's even more than that. That conscious forgiveness is working with the self to — the detachment is from all the churning of feeling and emotions and stuff that — we talk about righteousness. All these things. It's the work of facing the ego in itself, and taking responsibility for that, and then transforming that into acceptance, and forgiveness, and really love for the other who is the subject of forgiveness. And then from that comes forgetfulness.

¶ Don: Forgetfulness is an aspect of it, but it's not the heart-core of it.

Marnie: Yeah, but forgiveness is this other thing of facing the self …

¶ Don: You come to basic grips with your own ego to be able to forgive important wrongs.

Marnie: And that's why it's so hard.

¶ Don: It is terribly hard.

Payam: Well, there have been a few instances, for example at the L.A. Meher Baba Center, where there have been disputes between people who had very long friendships. But when we sat down together in a group meeting to bring more harmony, there was a real experience of love. We each had to get more in touch with the love than the act of injustice. And there was a lot of working through. Sometimes a person can't do it on their own.

Laurent: Mmm. They need help.

Payam: Yeah. Yeah, right.

Laurent: Can I piggyback on what you're saying or are you still going?

Payam: No, but it just brought that memory up, and it's beautiful because when Baba is at the center of it, then I think it's so much easier than if I were, say, in my work setting where I might be trying to facilitate that for people who don't have the commonality of Baba (or God) or anything else.

¶ Don: But I would certainly make a suggestion that when you become deeply involved in the clean-up process, as I think of it, you in your own facing in your own life of forgiveness, you can't leave your work out of it. You're going to have to take that in as part of it.

Laurent: Mm-hmm.

¶ Don: There's no way to escape it.

Laurent: I thought forgiveness was part of the homework assignment, so I wrote a little something about it.

¶ Don: Yes, well, I thought we were going to include it in words but I'm not sure that we had a chance, did we, Sevn?

Sevn: Yeah.

¶ Don: We did? Oh, that's great. Because I wanted if possible some work to have begun before the group met, and maybe some people have found, gee there are problems here, and this needs discussion and a lot of it.

Laurent: So when Payam was sharing just now, I felt inspired to share what I wrote on the train as my homework assignment about forgiveness. {Laurent and Danny arrived on the AmTrak train from Flagstaff.}

¶ Don: Great.

Laurent: It says, "Forgiveness frees the guilty from the bindings of justice. Forgiveness is a gift of love from the more wise to those less kind. Forgiveness is a sacrifice on the altar of consciousness whereby the ego can leave behind a piece of itself, surrendered to the Highest. Forgiveness is expansive, and touches the wronged, the guilty, and those who bear witness. Individual forgiveness takes one stone off the old wall of separation, while group forgiveness ... "

¶ Don: That's a nice term.

Payam: Yeah, I like that.

Laurent: Thank you. " ... While group forgiveness works to remove the entire wall. Forgiveness speaks the language of Oneness, while justice speaks the language of separation. Forgiveness is unexpected, while justice is Divine Law. Forgiveness is above the law, and is a divine attribute."

¶ Don: Very nice.

Sevn: You know I like that all except for one line.

Laurent: Which one?

Sevn: "Forgiveness is a gift from the wise to the less kind." I don't know — I feel that forgiveness can't be one-sided. We can't just say, "Well, I forgave them, I'm clean, it's up to them now." Forgiveness, like love, has to be given and received.

Laurent: Oh, that's interesting.

Glenn: You know Baba used the same gesture for love and forgiveness. This is in more than one Baba video. Mani explains that the gesture for love and forgiveness are the same.

Sevn: I strongly feel in everything that I've been taught and I believe, that — love, for instance, love in order to be complete, needs to be given and received.

Laurent: No, I want to focus on forgiveness.

Sevn: I have a feeling that forgiveness should fall along the same line.

Laurent: But say the whole thing about forgiveness because I need to respond to it.

Sevn: In order for forgiveness to be complete, it needs to be given and received.

Glenn: Not one sided.

Laurent: I know, but here's my problem with that —

Sevn: And the reason I say that is because there's a certain righteousness out of, "Oh, I forgave them. You know, I did my part. It's done."

Laurent: Here's my struggle and problem with that: Because this assignment has led me to the point where I'm just about to be ready to forgive my father for committing suicide. So now how do I deal with that under your framework?

{Silence.}

&

Sevn: Hmmm. {Laughter.} Well —

¶ Don: "Well."

Sevn: — It's going to involve occult experiences. But I totally believe that's possible.

Laurent: What's possible?

Glenn: That your forgiveness could be received and he could even be aware of that.

Laurent: But I feel —

Sevn: ... simultaneously received.

Laurent: As a Meher Baba follower, I want to forgive him. I haven't done that. And I don't want him to have to be able to receive it for me to be able to give it.

Marnie: Well I think it's setting up expectations, which I think are a big mistake. And —

Laurent: Which one is?

Marnie: That if we predicate true forgiveness is only possible if the other person receives it. One can give something that another isn't able or willing or wanting to receive. But it doesn't mean that the act of forgiveness, which I think we internalize in the self, it's not dependent on the external. It's strictly an internal process, which if one then does the internal part —

Sevn: No.

Marnie: — to forgive the other, then it doesn't matter what you're —

Sevn: No, then that's just all about you! Then you're feeling good for yourself.

Marnie: No, no, that's from an ego place.

¶ Don: I knew this would stir things up!

Marnie: Because you're doing it out of one's desire to love Baba. You're not doing it because you'll think I'm great, or I think I'm great, or "I am great." I'm doing it because I want to be closer to Baba, and as long as I hold onto anger, hurt, resentment ... I'm not forgiving them. Separate ...

Sevn: I think this is the same as generating good karma, and good karma is no more desirable than bad karma.

Danny: Well, I think what Marnie might be saying, is that you'd want to be able to [forgive] without any sense of expectation or need from the other person involved. And I think what [Sevn] might be saying is that there's no separation, so that person can't help but receive —

Sevn: Right, I'm saying the reception process doesn't have to be them writing a letter back to you saying "Oh, yay!" I think it has to be heard. But you have to tell them physically. You can't just keep it:

"I resolved the forgiveness in my mind. They're forgiven." You have to communicate with them. They have to hear it. They have to take it in somehow.

Female Participant: Yeah. Yeah.

Sevn: ... Receiving it and accepting are probably —

Doug: ... talking about the situation I had this morning ... [with] this person. But then you know he majorly retaliated. And so I apologized to him. And then I, you know, I tried ... I think he was, you know he was out of line too, and so I really tried to forgive him. I didn't say that to him because he didn't think he'd done anything wrong. But I wanted to apologize, which I did, and he accepted that. I did try to figure out in my mind, what would Baba want me to do here? Because I want to do what he wants me to do. And then I need to try to put this behind me. And so I tried to mentally go through the process of forgiving him. There was no acknowledgement from him. But as far as I was concerned, I apologized and I'd forgiven. And there's nothing more I could do. Now, you can turn that into a self-righteous ego trip. But you don't have to. It doesn't have to be that. And so I think it can be one-sided as long as it's honest.

Laurent: I think Don has something he'd like to share.

¶ Don: Yeah, I would like to — Oh my golly, it's three minutes to four. {This session was scheduled to end at 4pm on Saturday.} This came up particularly in my mind when I was having a series [of intuitions] in relation to three words that came to me intuitively one morning when I woke up: "When, where, and how — forgiveness." At what point do you take the person — do you invite them home? Or do you call on them? And how? Well, do you say it to their face? Suppose they're dead by that time for instance. And this was really a stickler and as I began to go into it, and I really, really tried to think up, really what is involved in real, real, what should I say, terribly, carefully thought out and planned insult or damage or wounding? And what are the mechanics of it? And then if you do forgive, how do you measure the results of it somewhere? If it has any reality, it ought to be measurable, at least psychologically some way. What do you do? Do you get out sort of a mass questionnaire and have a consulting opinion society go around and measure so many thousand people and their answers, to what it's done to them? How do you measure these things? And then I thought of the one that just really buffaloed me. What about this Balkan situation? And I can't tell the story on that one totally today, but I will tomorrow. Here we have a situation that is a result of actually an invasion of Christian territory by Muslims going way back in the Middle Ages. And it is one of the greatest, greatest social sources of "unforgivableness" and just blunt, racial hatred coming from original misdeeds, or invasions. And how do you go about such a thing? How under the sun? Because all the people who were involved in it, even the people who commanded armies, kings and princes or whatever not, or emperors who commanded legions to go out and do this and that and the other thing. How under the sun is the thing, how does it work out? How do you reach back that far in time? Are you trying to reach astral people or reincarnated souls by that time? How do you go about it? What's the mechanism for the whole thing? And so this really is where I got really buffaloed on it.

And I want to foreshadow my own position here. I am totally convinced that I personally know enough of the background of what Baba did on this, and really having Eruch's confirmation of the principle parts of what I did, and what he did for Baba, which I'll tell you about tomorrow. And this thing is too well established in my mind to be a figment of Stevens' [imagination]. And the manner in which the results are at least really beginning to be startling and striking are the manner in which Baba has revivified these certain religious spots of devotion, especially in India, which I've been to repeatedly. Here I've got my own memory of repeated visits to these places and seeing what's happening. So the revivification process is something that is established beyond any doubts in my mind. *But how the hell do you go about a consistent process of forgiveness?* And how do you reach some of the most intractable — you can't touch them — sort of situations, because they happened centuries ago and resulted in racial hatred so deeply indoctrinated? How do you go about it?

And I just absolutely confess that I know intuitively that this very key word forgiveness is somewhere right around the center. But how when, and how where, and how under the sun do you establish any measurement of results and try to improve those results, or block things that are beginning to react against it? This is just so enormous, enormous and important. You know it's a great idea — I think so, a wonderful idea. But nevertheless one has got to come down to practical realities in the here and now, in the universe with people involved. And why, let's say, trying to cover a situation of the difficulty of being realistic about it I think would be an unforgiveable sin. So I just have to say to you, usually when I get excited about something, I know not only the outlines of the history of why I am excited about it, but the general outlines of what I am convinced is a practical route to follow. I don't in this case.

All I can do is to sit here and say you're some of the best people I know in the world, you're close to Baba, you have some of the best potentialities that I know of anywhere to make a real, real central push on this thing in this coming generation. So the credentials are there, but I certainly cannot be any sort of a realistic guide. All I can say is, we're friends, we're companions. I'll certainly work hard as I possibly can with you. But boy, don't look to me for solutions.

The fact that I was around Baba maybe more (statistically) than you were doesn't get us any closer to a solution. I don't got it. I just have this keen, keen feeling the word forgiveness is a central tent pole. But I don't know that it is all of the tent poles. I just don't know. I think it's just as perfectly possible that tomorrow morning, at five o'clock, Marnie is going to wake up with a second central tent pole. And cheers and cheers and wonderful. This is where we are. This is huge, and I am convinced that it is one of the most important things Baba invested, and I've got reasons for that. And, by God, I don't like to leave Baba even a tiny bit in a lurch. So, I'm in the dark where we go from there. But boy I know it's —

Laurent: Well, it's pretty bright darkness.
Participant: Yeah.
Marnie: Do you have a copy of that [intuition you read], or would you rather —
¶ Don: Oh sure, it's on a disk. You can get copies anytime.
Marnie: I'd love to read it again and reflect on it.
¶ Don: Yeah. Well, there are nine already on forgiveness.
Marnie: Really?
¶ Don: Nine intuitions. And there's a lot of good stuff in it.
Marnie: Yeah, when you feel ready to share, I'd love to read ...
¶ Don: Well, look, anything I've got on any sort of a Stevens' intuition is available to you. The worst that can happen is we just make, let's say, a copy onto a floppy disk for you.
Sevn: Or we'll just put it on [Don's] blog.
Marnie: Does he have a blog? {to Don}: Do you have a blog?
¶ Don: This is part of the story. Yes! Hey look, I've got the blog addresses.
Laurent: The posts are amazing.
Marnie: Yeah, you'll have to give us that blog address.

As of October 2010, the site is still up at: http://sharingbeauty.blogspot.com with nine posts from Don.

Sevn: Sharingbeauty.blogspot.com
Marnie: Okay. {Background chatter.}
Laurent: Here Danny, pass it out. {Laurent hands Danny some photocopies.}
¶ Don: Look, you've got your night-time work. Identify the closest computer and go and spend until four o'clock ... Tomorrow morning. {Laughter and mock shock.} We try to prepare ourselves, even when we don't know the answer.
Laurent: It's good. It's good. {Various chatter as the group passes out and begins to read papers.}
¶ Don: In fact I think I brought the — ah, I brought the first three blogs with me ... I think those are the ones. Mm-hmm. Yes, these are the ones, those are the blogs. You know if you want I'll just leave these copies of the first three blogs that have gone on, if any of you

would like to skim it. It's a first attack from a different avenue on the subject of forgiveness. It's a beginning from a different direction. And I'll tell you tomorrow why. {To participant eating snacks}: Hey, you're stealing things there. Don't look so guilty. {Laughter. Various chatter.}

Danny: I can only read one of these at a time, if somebody else wants to read one?

¶ Don: There are three there.

Danny: Yeah. Do they have to be read in consecutive order?

¶ Don: No. My intuition might excite somebody. Get them started thinking. But these are blogs on beauty.

☙

Marnie: Don, I would just like to say one thing ... {to Jamshid}: I feel like, in sharing your experience this morning with your family member and all that — I think that was a beautiful description of a model. For me, what touched me so deeply, was it's the practical — because it practically feels better and is more true to ourselves, who we are, to forgive. And also then the spiritual in terms of that desire that we have to love Baba, to feel Baba with us all the time. And so it's like those two pieces together, if we can address the practical, and then the spiritual comes.

¶ Don: Yeah.

Marnie: I just felt that was such ...

¶ Don: It was gorgeous. Absolutely gorgeous.

Marnie: — really such an inspiration.

¶ Don: Yeah. And then, how can one apply such principles into something so complex as ancient heritage of hatred which is still very prevalent and important today?

Marnie: Yeah. And I do believe that although you know there's all this ego stuff within us, there is that beautiful, true higher self, if you want to call it — whatever the terminology is — that knows the right way, that wants to do the right thing. And then if we can

access that then ...
¶ Don: And I think it's by intuition—
Marnie: — just that — by intuition.
¶ Don: Yeah. Inevitably.
Jamshid: Now you did not necessarily mean at all to limit the scope of the question with that specific example of the Balkan situation?
¶ Don: It was just one of many, many — there have been horrible religious wars, but it's not been only that type of hatred or warfare between let's say one religion and another, but let's say between one concept of good and truth and others. It's been — it's gone all up and down the scale.
Jamshid: There is hatred and suffering all over. And there's more that is being brewed and justified — or pushed over —
¶ Don: Yeah. We're in a very active stage of brewing things now. That's the unfortunate part. I'm appalled by it.
Payam: It so happens that the last few days I've been listening to some inspirational words. And one has to do with the Rwandan atrocity —
¶ Don: Oh, that was a horrible situation.
Payam: — and a beautiful example of forgiveness was a survivor of that. And there was a book she wrote a book called, *Left to Tell*. I don't know if you've heard of it.
¶ Don: No.
Payam: By [Immaculée Ilibagiza] ... she lived through, and it's an incredible story of trusting God, and being open to hearing that intuition.

Left To Tell: Discovering God Amidst the Rwandan Holocaust, by Immaculée Ilibagiza (Hay House, 2006).

¶ Don: Mm-hmm.
Payam: And everything she did is actually miraculous, what she endured and what came out of it. And then maybe tomorrow I can just share a paragraph from that book that deeply touched me —
¶ Don: Please do.
Payam: And then there was Nelson Mandela, who — miracu-

lously again — in his act of forgiveness, brought about, in an unbelievable way, the end to Apartheid, without the —

Jamshid: Typical bloodshed.

Payam: — bloodshed that could have —

¶ Don: Well, Mohandas Gandhi was another example of somebody who did amazing things through peaceful means and affected the whole world in the process.

Jamshid: And another perfect example is from India, who loves ... {Laughter.}

¶ Don: Right. Yes. I should say so. {Laughter.}

Marnie: ... means of societal process of forgiveness.

¶ Don: Well the important thing here is the problem is enormous and composed of so many parts which have been generated in so many different ways that the manner of attacking things has a challenge to an infinite variety of mechanisms. That's why I think that it's going to have to be a fairly important group process, with a smaller group giving the main part of the push on the thing. And then, depending upon a tremendous inflow of inventiveness and ideas, and an awful lot of experimentation with those ideas. It's not going to be something that's going to be done in five or ten or fifty years. We're talking about something that's likely to take several hundred years to make a real dent, with enormous inventiveness. But this I know already from my own experience, that Baba has left resources that are incredibly powerful and specific in relation to it. And when a person touches one of those resources, some of these I can identify quite frankly. When you touch a Baba resource, then things happen in a fashion you would have said — impossible — just incredible. So remember we've got Avataric investment on a major scale in back of this. So expect to see the incredible and the impossible happen. But boy it's going to have to be based on a very, very powerful conviction within oneself, started off by seeing what happens when you try forgiving one or two or three of your pet peeves or hatreds. Somebody who has really wronged you or wronged your family or wronged one of your closest friends or something.

Jamshid: Inventiveness …

¶ Don: Absolute key: Inventiveness.

Jamshid: When I was in India, the first and last time, last November, the only time I've been in India, we met a father and son. A teenage son. I cannot remember the last name. They live in Hawaii right now. And they have a very good business of horticulturists. And there's been all kinds of experimentation with growing plants that are — that naturally are not — they don't lend themselves to growing in the region. Right? It's so hard to grow plants in different regions. And we were having a conversation about unity of all life forms. And what he said was that he is going to go back to Hawaii with his son, sell their business, and go to one of the desert locations between Israel and I believe Egypt —

¶ Don: The Sinai Peninsula?

Jamshid: In between … location, harsh, typical of that environment, not some place that's very uniquely vegetation friendly ecosystems. So someplace semi-harsh. And set up an institution to teach Arabs and Jews, Muslims and Jews, to come there and learn how to grow, and feed their people that which they love to have, and that which is difficult to grow in their climate. And send them back to where they came from to produce food. But most importantly the message, the experimentation, the exercise of working together, being together, and understanding the commonality versus the differences. Inventiveness.

¶ Don: Sure.

Jamshid: Not political per se, but …

Laurent: Everybody needs to eat.

Jamshid: Yeah.

¶ Don: Well, could I suggest that the witching hour of our second part of today is finished. And it doesn't mean nobody can talk anymore, but shall we just have a quiet period with Baba again, and you do the various things you must do. {Silence.} Dearly Beloved Baba, guide us to see the intent of Your Wish. Amen.

End of Saturday

Endnotes for Saturday Afternoon:

1. Regarding Sevn's comment about how Meher Baba explained the existence of "occult powers" in *God Speaks*, we felt this was important enough to quote the passage directly:

"Other occult powers have nothing to do with spirituality or with the mystic powers of the planes. These occult powers are of two types:

   a. Superior occult powers.

   b. Inferior occult powers.

"The one who has these occult powers can make good or bad use of the same. Good use of occult powers helps one to put himself on the planes of the Path and may even make one a mahayogi. Bad use of these occult powers makes one suffer intensely in the next human form. Good use of superior occult powers puts one on the fifth plane of consciousness after four lives (reincarnations).

a. Superior types of occult powers are derived from tantrik exercises such as chilla-nashini or repetition of certain mantras, etc. The one who holds these powers can perform the so-called miracles such as levitation, flying and floating in the air, dematerialization and materialization, etc.

b. Inferior types of occult powers need no tantrik or any special exercises. They are had through sanskaras of past lives. For example: if someone has done certain good deeds many times in the past, his next incarnation may give him the faculty of inferior occult powers without undergoing any strenuous exercises. His sanskaras give him the faculty of inferior occult powers such as clairvoyance, clairaudience, healing, producing sweets or money seemingly out of nothing, etc.

"All such capabilities form part of the lower or inferior type of occult powers. If one makes good use of the inferior type of occult powers, he derives superior type of occult powers in his next life without undergoing any tantrik exercises. Likewise, the one who puts to good use his faculty of hypnotism gains the superior type of occult powers in his next life."

From *God Speaks*, by Meher Baba, Supplement, p.p. 217-218, (2nd edition, copyright (c) 2011 Sufism Reoriented).

Two Spontaneous Short YPG Interviews
(for the fun of it)

Laurent: What's your name?
Sam: Sam.
Laurent: Where are you from?
Sam: London.
Laurent: Where are we?
Sam: L.A.
Laurent: What did we do today?
Sam: Had a YPG meeting.
Laurent: What's YPG?
Sam: Young Person's Group. Baba. {Laughing.}
Laurent: Ah. And who were you meeting with?
Sam: Don Stevens and companions.
Laurent: How did you like it?
Sam: It's amazing.
Laurent: Thank you, Sam.

ℰ↷

Laurent: What's your name?
Payam: Payam.
Laurent: Where are we?
Payam: Well right now we're in our house. {Payam & Glenn's house.}
Laurent: What are we doing here?
Payam: Oh, we're having the most wonderful get together, celebrating just — love! I just feel so inspired.
Laurent: Me too. Where are we going?
Payam: To my parents' home where we're going to see Don.
Laurent: Oh, Don who?
Payam: Don Stevens! Don the Don!
Laurent: {Laughing} Thank you, Payam.

Don Stevens at the Avatar Meher Baba Center of Southern California, October 2007.
Photo by Douglas Frank.

Don Stevens at the Meher Spiritual Center YPG gathering, December 12, 2005, with (L to R): Cynthia Griffin, Danny Sanders, Kira Olson, Doug Frank, Marlena Applebaum, Marnie Frank, Nicola & Heather Masciandaro, Laurent Weichberger, Ben Wolbach, and Glenn Russ.

Don at the YPG gathering April 19 – 20, 2008, near Atlanta, Georgia. Photo by Douglas Frank.

Don Stevens with Sam Clayton at the April 2007 YPG Gathering in Myrtle Beach, South Carolina. Photo by Heather Masciandaro.

Don at the YPG gathering April 19 – 20, 2008, near Atlanta, Georgia with (L to R): Danny, Marnie, Sevn, Heather, Nicola, Doug, Cynthia and Richard. Photo by Ed Legum.

Sunday Morning

{The session starts off with Laurent asking Don a few questions about whether he slept well, and if Don's "plumbing department" was in good working order, to which Don gave the group a laugh with some short stories about how Baba would give him a laxative at Meherazad if needed.}

Don: Life has its interesting things. But one has to have an experimental attitude. I was just finishing off suggesting, because I touched on it briefly yesterday but I wanted to repeat it, and that is: *try the experiment of using intuition in some parts of your life on things that are just totally unimportant, but they've got to get out of the way.* And I found immediately whenever I was going to make a decision how to handle just a simple little household situation, that before I launched into it, when I reflected, there was an instant pattern that suggested itself to my own mind, but my immediate reaction always was — well I've got to reflect on this and think it through. So I'd go through my usual laborious examining and making a decision. And one day I said to myself — my God, I wonder if this is another aspect of intuitive information—intuition, which is just there. And maybe I'd better experiment with it and find out how dependable and trustworthy these things are that just immediately chart out a course of action to take in a situation. So I began doing it. And really, you know I got a little nervous — am I getting too cocky about these sort of things, and maybe getting into dangerous ground here? Better watch myself.

But at any rate, especially recently as I began to gather a little bit more assuredness, and recognize with a certain background of, let's say, success and failure, if I just immediately adopted and go ahead, I haven't turned up one yet that landed me in a pickle. That is really amazing — but then, and this is the really important point here. I find A: it saves time. It really does. It's instant. And you don't sit around even to make a fast decision. You don't. You just go ahead and act. And then the second thing is, I had not realized how much nervous energy unconsciously I was spending…

Laurent: In imaginations.

¶ Don: — in imaginations, well what if it goes that way or this way, and so on and so on, and what does that do, and do I stub my toe? I've gotten over a lot of that since being around Baba, but there's still a pretty good hefty portion. Just the net saving on nerves at the end of the day is appreciable and very impressive I must say. So try it out and see what happens.

Laurent: I never appreciated that "saving of nerves" until I had my second child, Cyprus.

¶ Don: Really? Now you needed to save your nerves.

Laurent: Now it's like a very important factor. {Laughing. Group laughter.}

¶ Don: Keeps you alive and sane.

Laurent: Absolutely.

Payam: Well I, have a simple situation that's come up since yesterday. And I actually told this to the group in terms of intuition. So I have this little Rumi couplet in English that we recently bought, Glenn and I. And I have posted it on the wall in the bathroom so I can see it every day. So I've had this urge to share it with the group. It was just a connection I made. An affirmation of what you felt in your Urge? You should pay attention and go with it. But it happens in other situations too, and I sometimes think — am I looking for signs to validate what I was feeling, or is that really something I should pay attention to? And that's the question I had, and then I'll share this poem … there are things that come up in day-to-day things, and my tendency is, unless there's an absolute knowing that this is an intuition and I need to act on it, most of the time my tendency is to say — oh well, I don't know. I'll think about that. I just put it aside and, sometimes, I mull over it for a long time, and sometimes I just disregard it. That's kind of my working out what rings true as an intuition versus my own stuff.

¶ Don: Yeah.

Payam: So I wanted to ask if people do that, you know, kind of see some connection between what they're feeling inwardly and ...

¶ Don: Well, who in the group has had enough of these situations and at least tried a tentative name-tag of intuition with it, and any experience after doing that?

Marnie: Well, I find that my intuition works in some areas but not others.

¶ Don: Really?

Marnie: Where I'm intuitive is in terms of understanding others, I've had a lot of intuitive understanding of other people that I totally trust. So for me it's very selective. And I'd like to know how to expand it.

¶ Don: Maybe by a simple decision to act instantly in some of these other fields that you have, let's say, tended to shoo it away [from] or not follow up. And see what happens.

Marnie: Okay.

¶ Don: Because that's pretty much my case. I just felt that when I'd suddenly have an intuitive idea on something that I was shirking my responsibility not instantly to sit and do the boning up and putting a bit of logic together in relation to it. But it wasn't until I decided — God, that almost has to be an intuitive product, and I should test it out. And then testing it out was just incredible. It has really picked up speed.

Sevn: One thing I've been experimenting with is the idea of intuition as an inner process, and the effects, or fruits of intuition, being an observation or happening in the external world. The intuitive mind is more easily recognized as a quiet and centered state of being, but what about when you're in a crowded area or have to make quick decisions in the presence of others? How can you act from an intuitive place in the midst of chaos? When you understand the challenge of this, the synchronicity between the inner and outer becomes clear. It's almost like a specific awareness of the subtle forces affecting the gross world. For me it's always there, but most of the time I don't recognize it. I feel that intuitive process in my life empowered by intention; the active process that initiates the expressions of my heart. I've been practicing to become more aware of the threshold where action and intuition meet, but for the most part I'm still dependent on quiet time and meditation as vehicles for inspiring inner recognition.

¶ Don {Chuckling}: That helps. It sure does.

Sevn: ... it's still more difficult to get it in the active situation.

¶ Don: Glenn?

Glenn: First of all, I'd like to follow that thought by ... the type of life I've led, I've found that certainly being quiet is optimal, I've felt that, but I have found that I can shift into that quiet space even in the midst of a chaotic and active environment.

¶ Don: Bless your heart. That's a big discovery.

Glenn: That's kind of my experience.

¶ Don: You can protect it.

Glenn: It would appear to others maybe like I checked out for a second.

Sevn: Right {Laughing.}

Glenn: But I think if it's something important ... actually ... other noisy situations or whatever. But I think that's possible. At least from my experience it appears to be possible ...

Doug: I believe it to be very important to trust one's own gifts and intuition. I happen to know someone who is very perceptive, but she doesn't trust her own perceptions. This has to do with the fact that her family discounted her perceptions from a very early age and so became a script for her ... don't believe in your perceptions because they are false. I've been in situations where I felt very strong intuitions. For example, I was with a friend of mine photographing in New Mexico and we were heading for this huge butte rising out of the desert ... And the closer that I came to this thing, the more and more uneasy that I felt.

¶ Don: More and more what?

Doug: Uneasy.

¶ Don: Uneasy, yes.

Doug: ...When we had come within a couple of miles of the butte I said to my friend, "hey, you probably won't understand this but I cannot go any further. We must turn around now and get out of here because there is something about this place which is extremely dark and is projecting very negative energy to me." So we turned around. I've been in other situations like this, many times in very remote forests. Sometimes I will have an idea about what the negative energy is about and sometimes I don't, but when a place is giving off very negative energy to me ... I leave. I believe that listening to my perceptions and trusting them has served me well in my life.

¶ Don: Yeah. An intuitive process.

Doug: Yeah. But they come real fast.

¶ Don: Sure. You just know.

Doug: Yeah, I feel that I do. I'm more impulsive than Marnie, but sometimes I'll be in my studio, and I'll be working on a project and a new thought will come into my head, or I'll see something on the shelf and I will impulsively and completely change my activity. Sometimes, by reacting in this way, these course changes have led me to places which became very, very positive, but it all starts with some little window of thought.

¶ Don: Yeah.

Doug: So I usually act on them.

Laurent: I wanted to piggyback on something Sevn was saying. I like Sevn's approach, also in the sense — not so much in the setting aside quiet time, although I think that is really vital to the process, but when you're in the act of daily life and trying to tune into your intuition, that's obviously more difficult. I think there is a built-in feedback loop in the intuition process where if you're very clear about: okay, I had an intuition. Just believing that. And then clear about your decision about whether to ignore it, or act on it. And then tune into that feedback loop of — all right, what is the response around me to this decision? And trying to listen for that. That that's really a pretty vital part of the process where you can be pretty clear sometimes. Wow, that was fantastic, or, if I had obeyed it — you know, let's say you ignored it. If I had obeyed it, this would have been a different experience. And just enjoying that whole process all the way through, with the feedback of the result, if you can tune into that.

Doug: Sometimes you can't see them all.

Laurent: Right. But I mean, sometimes you really can. So, just being attuned into your inner process, your decision about — to go or not to go, and just keeping your finger on that pulse is a really profound process unto itself.

Sevn: I think intention goes hand in hand with intuition. Perhaps intention is a means of programming intuition. It's not a just a matter of consciously entering a state where intuition is available, but rather a natural process of intuition arising by itself, because an intention was set. This allows our use of intuition throughout the day to be more spontaneous.

¶ Don: I think Glenn had something you wanted to add a few moments ago.

Glenn: I went through much of my life, I feel, having intuition, often very clear intuitions and not acting upon them.

Laurent: And NOT acting on them?

Glenn: Not. And because, you know, I had a practical mind. Typically I had reason ... what made the most sense and research and so forth. It wasn't until just observing, well that would have made sense, and research and so forth. But there was no evidence I could have relied upon to, other than I had this ... so anyways I guess, the one thing, and because I think it's ... is a very individual ... one thing I've learned in life is that you learn an enormous amount more about any problem space from making mistakes than getting it correct, or accurate, whatever, because you don't know what you did right ... but when you make mistakes you start learning the boundaries of what it is that you're experiencing and how it works.

¶ Don: You do a little bit of practical analysis and identify, let's say, which part of the event went wrong and you're going to have to steer clear of.

Glenn: You can't be afraid to just jump in and see what happens.

Doug: Somebody told me a long time ago that if you're gnashing your brain about whether to do this thing or that thing, just ask yourself this: what's the worst thing which could happen? You know? And then just do what you feel is right and learn from it. This process can hone one's trust in one's own intuitive process.

Ellie: A lot of times, if I'm trying to make a decision, and I'm not sure about what I'm supposed to do, the question is there and I just let it go and I go about my day, and something invariably happens — I get something that I should do. It doesn't come to me instantly {snaps her fingers}. I mean, in some very simple situations, you know, that are very mundane, I get a feeling to do something and I do it. But when I'm trying to make a decision, I'm not actually sorting it out. It's a question in my mind, and as the hours go by in the day ... do it this way instead of that way. That seems to give me peace. And I don't think my mind was in it. But it's one of those things that doesn't happen just like that {snaps fingers again} all the time.

¶ Don: So it's a progressive thing that is going on.

Ellie: Right. And I'm sitting with it. *And I try to keep my mind out of it.* Because you can go anywhere with that and you never know, I never know whether it's accurate after that or not because then my mind ...

¶ Don: Yeah, the mind tends to turn up the process of listing the various different ways you can turn instead of identifying a direction.

Ellie: Well the question I was asking is, when you get these signs, is it dangerous to do that?

¶ Don: Inevitably you're going to be experimenting with that.

Doug: ... test them out, yeah. You gotta test them out.

Laurent: But I guess what I'm wondering is, are you talking about these signs as confirmations that your intuition was valid?

Ellie: Yes.

Laurent: See, for me that's different than trying to make signs into intuitive messages.

¶ Don: I misunderstood then. A good point.

Laurent: I mean, I believe that Baba does confirm for us whatever he's trying to get across to us. I feel that that's part of the natural process with Baba. So if you feel that confirmation, I think that's healthy. If you're following an intuition, I don't think you need to be fearless. I think you should allow yourself to be in whatever state you're in and follow it. So if you're following your intuition and fearful, that's okay. I don't think following your intuition means you can't have fear. Because then you'd be limiting your own ability to move forward in your spiritual process. But I don't think you have to wait until you're fearless to follow your intuition, personally.

Sevn: There's a difference between looking for signs to confirm an intuition and recognizing how it actually unfolds. For me, sometimes I have looked back years in the past to actually be able to identify the intricate pattern that was the manifestation of intuition. Along the way it's not always apparent.

Glenn: I woke up from an earthquake ... {Laughter. Much chatter, people talking over each other.}

Payam: I have to say, the mind is powerful. It is so powerful. And it can be dangerous. I really see the danger in it, too. You know, I've gone down the street and said, you know, I really want that car. And it's there on my mind. I like the car. And then three weeks later it's for sale. I mean it's ... that's eerie, you know? I mean it's ... call it whatever you want to call it. Or you know, sitting at the table, having this conflict, should I move to Los Angeles or not? If God would only give me a sign — like an earthquake. And at three o'clock in the morning there was an earthquake!

¶ Don: But why not take a positive attitude that maybe this is an inbuilt gift which you are endowed by grace to help you on the Path and make life a bit more easily accessible in accomplishing things? Why not look at it as something positive in your life and see what happens? I think you'd probably end up finding it's very natural and very helpful and very valuable. Don't tie it up with a lot of knots. You'll never get it solved and worked out if you do. Go ahead and experiment, and be optimistic about it. You're under Baba's thumb, you've got every right to be optimistic.

Payam: Yes.

¶ Don: If anybody has got a right to be optimistic, it's somebody who knows they're under the Avatar's thumb. He's not going to sit around indefinitely and let you go puttering off on a wrong track. He'll find some way or another to suggest to you that things have gotta change there. So you can afford to be optimistic in your experiments in things like this that come up in your life. Take a positive approach. It's faster. It's a hell of a lot more comfortable. And it progresses a hell of a lot faster then. Exciting, too.

Can I try out something on you that is, again, so recent in the Stevens department of using intuition? I'll give you the blunt fact summary. I am almost certain that every object gives out signals which your own physical body senses and reacts to.

And that, for instance, I know ... the physicists have been astonished that if you have something sitting here, and you have deliberately identified something, let's say, a few billion light years into space, and you do something to this object here, and some way or another there is an association with that other thing way over there, when you dabble with this part of the dual here, the part over there knows instantly and responds to it. So this has been really puzzling physics. I wonder, what's the communication system? And it fascinates me, and inadvertently I started experimenting with it, and just particularly when I was looking for something that I had misplaced, or when I wanted to find something that would help me do something in the household, do I have such and such a thing hidden around somewhere or another that I can use in this situation? And I would someway or another, increasingly recently, have some sort of an impulse to it. Yeah, it's over there in the closet. You left it over there. And so this could be, let's say, this sort of a retarded memory that you've unearthed, but that doesn't seem to fill the bill when I really try to explain the situations.

But when I began assuming — this also rolled out of the fact when I began talking, I think I've told you all sometime back in my life I just tried the experiment of talking to my body, and a certain problematical part of it, let's say, as if it were my friend. Because I suddenly realized that that part of my body and I were desperate enemies. I was always swearing at it, why under the sun can't it be more cooperative, and so on. And just suddenly bolt! out of the blue I had sort of an intuition such as at that time I would never dream of having. If I got it I would cast it away immediately because I thought it was so silly. But something said, Don, why don't you try the experiment of making friends with that part of your body? I couldn't believe it. You know, it was just like the kid I'm going to tell you about later today who obviously made the experiment of thinking — maybe I could forgive my father. And it was so incredible that it produced results. So is it then possible that every part of our body is also living and sentient? Maybe even has some sort of a communication system? Just as if it had a telephone system and could link up with your brain. Give it a message. You give it through the telephone system through your own — you don't even have to link it up through a phone. You just tell it what you're thinking about. And, God damn it, incredibly as it may seem, it seems almost instantly to respond. Particularly if it's a friendly message — "I've got confidence in you, or at least I'm trying to have confidence in you." So then I began to think — well gee there are some things, and particularly this business where I located several things in a row that usually I've spent hours or days searching for, and I just sort of open myself up to getting some sort of an intuitive signal. And, by God, as soon as I would do it, I had an impulse to look so-and-so. And I said, for heaven's sake, how did that happen? And then it occurred to me, one of the logical things is, as improbable as it sounds, that is a living, sentient — anything is living.

Anything in Creation is living, regardless of how simple its form is. And if it's living, there must be some sort of, way of, communication that goes on. Or else how does it meld in and stay around other objects without the whole thing falling apart? At least that's the way my mind looked at it. And so I just began to think — well by golly, is it possible that each thing is someway or another like a broadcasting radio station? And it is sending out messages, "Here I am." And you know where it is, and you also even, desperate as it may sound, know somewhat of its state of mind. Could I say that? Suppose a rock is over there. Does it have a state of mind? Well, I'm afraid I believe pretty thoroughly that it has even a pretty sophisticated state of mind.

Laurent: Doug has something, and I need to share something too.

Doug: ...There exists a subtle energy which science cannot address.

¶ Don: Exactly.

Doug: I was reading about honey bees the other day. They send out a group of worker bees from the hive to go and scout out an area, which might be 20 miles away! Then these workers come back and somehow they communicate to the rest of the bees the number of workers which will be needed to cover this particular area. The hive then sends out just the right number...

¶ Don: That's a pretty good planning committee, isn't it?

Doug: Well, these bees are communicating with some sort of energy which we can neither understand nor measure. There is presently a crisis going on with honey bees disappearing. Various people have come up with theories about this. One of the things which has changed during the past five to ten years is that cell phone towers have sprung up everywhere. These towers emit microwave radio energy ... we're just being flooded with microwave energy 24 hours a day! One scientist has suggested that such energy may be interfering with the abilities of honey bees to find their way back to the hive. The point is that with most scientists, in the absence of instruments which can measure something, then that something could not really exist. And what you're saying about a pair of pliers or a rock having some kind of broadcasting ability is completely plausible ... although un-provable.

¶ Don: Can I stop you just a moment and say — because the point you're raising is fascinating to me — I simply at one point said now maybe these things exist within the knowledge of oneness. They don't think of themselves as separate. The more important fact is that they are really a part of the infinitude of oneness of God. And so there is instant communication that goes on within oneness, where there is no separation.

Laurent: Mm-hmm. Well, oneness is the medium.

¶ Don: Oneness is the medium, really. And they exist in it. And they don't have "I"s all obsessed by the fact "I'm separate from that screwdriver over there."

Doug: Well, in that sense then you could say that one could travel a million light years in an instant.

¶ Don: Of course. Within oneness there's no space or time. It's instantaneous. It's the only thing that makes total sense.

Laurent: I have to share something because this is kind of spooky what you're talking about this morning. Payam knows this story because we talked about it. I got an email yesterday. I snuck into Mahmoud's office to check my email. There was a message from my God-daughter, Emma.

¶ Don: She's already on the keyboard?

Laurent: No, her dad typed it for her. But she dictated it, "Daddy, tell Laurent I want him to send me a rock. It can be any rock. It doesn't have to be from India," she says. "So that when I'm lonely, I can speak to the rock, and the rock can speak to Laurent for me."

¶ Don: Well, that's an incredible statement, isn't it?

Laurent: It just fits with what you're talking about this morning. So I got her a rock last night on the beach.

¶ Don: Is it talking to her?

Laurent: I gotta talk to it first. I'm going to tell it — listen now, you need to help me. {Laughing.} But look at the timing of it. That it came yesterday, and what you're talking about today. It's just perfect.

¶ Don: Well, let's go back to intuition, because we need to have some sort of — these are lovely stories, but I think that their implications in relation to intuition, and the importance of what Baba has said, his Avataric gift to make intuition available to all human beings. So what we're saying is, well, rocks communicated in the past, but through Baba's gift of intuition, we can pick up the signals much better than before, so that a vast amount more of people can pick up the rock messages. And this is an important thing. In other words, there is a whole maneuverability of knowledge and practical use of this sort of thing that has opened up which hasn't existed before, and where this becomes terribly challenging and important. So intuition in such case, and if what we're talking about — each object in some way or another has got a radio transmitter within oneness, unity.

This is pretty important because this is information that is accessible to everybody if they just begin to understand that new resources of information have been opened up, and start opening up the plugs from their ears.

Doug: How would they do that? I mean, how does a person do that though?

¶ Don: Doing such things as we're doing right here. Sharing experiences and saying to one another this is worth an experiment. See what results you get. And I'm pretty damn certain we'll get results without going off the rocker doing it. (This is said for Payam's benefit.)

Sevn: I've learned that this is a big part of Zen training. Its not so much communicating with objects, but rather the authentic understanding and realization of the unity of all things. Its about completely and fully experiencing an object, whatever it is, not just looking, feeling, or hearing it, but really being one with it. Seeing a cup exactly how it is different than conjuring a picture of a cup in your mind.

Doug: ... Take any person. Who knows what is the best exercise to use in order to train one's mind or to experiment? Perhaps the

---

It is said that Solomon spoke with plants and Moses with animals. For Solomon see, The Old Testament, 1 Kings 4:33. For Moses see, The Masnavi, by Rumi, (translated by E. H. Whinfield, 1898), and an on-line story by Rumi here: http://www.mythfolklore.net/3043mythfolklore/reading/rumi/pages/09.htm - LW group can share experiences about this.

Laurent: But maybe even the receiving of the exercises could be an intuitive process. Because everybody's at a different stage of development, maybe just tuning in intuitively to what exercise is best for you right now.

¶ Don: Baba was very clear on this point. It is not that some people are more prone to be able to intuit. Baba said, very flatly and definitely, in the two times that he talked about it, he was equally definite on this point, *that the Avataric gift of intuition is a gift to all of humanity*, not to a certain minority who have special adaptation or gifts. And this is an important part of what he conveyed.

Doug: So basically he set this in motion for all of humanity.

¶ Don: For all of humanity. He just unstoppered the intuition plug in everybody.

Laurent: I think some people misinterpret it as Baba's gift to Baba lovers.

Doug: Okay, he's un-stoppered this thing ... but there's a certain amount of guidance then which would be required. I mean ...

¶ Don: But there's one thing that I can think of which keeps coming into my mind ... intuition is something like a weak sound or a weak radio signal. And it's not a part of our habit pattern yet, amongst other things. So one can actually foster the process by deliberately trying to do some quiet time in one's life so that they can register. Life to me is sort of something like static. And there's so much static coming into our ears that it's pretty easy to lose a quiet whispering sound. And this is the responsibility of the individual to recognize that this could be a pretty serious problem. And that maybe I can do something to assist that part of it. The signal's there, but have I got so much static blaring in my ear all of the time, and I listen to the static, out of force of habit.

Marnie: As we're talking, one of the things that keeps coming into my mind, having lived my adult life (since the 70s), is the whole New Age movement, having really witnessed people experimenting with psychic powers.

¶ Don: Don't forget, I said the whole area of intuition is right on the edge of just plain psychic phenomena.

Marnie: Mmm-hmm. So I think, for me, one of the reasons I've kind of dampened, and not paid attention to, some of my intuitive abilities, is because we've seen so much in this New Age stuff which the ego has grasped onto, and people have used it in really manipulative ways with other people ... And how dangerous that is. As you've been talking, it seems that if one does this and uses intuition as a way to remember Him and to gain a sense of oneness through inanimate objects: it's a way to remember Him and to experience him ever more deeply, to become more and more sensitive to His presence ... This can be ... a way to keep ego from grasping ...

¶ Don: Marnie, I have to tell you, that the instant Baba said that in Mandali Hall, something inside of me just leaped up with a bellow and cheered — thank God, now when Baba drops the body we will still have the intuitive means to be in touch with our Beloved. And then, after I cheered that, and I said to myself — my God now what's the difference between this, and a psychic experience? And where does one begin, where does the other end off? And then I just had to come to the conclusion that after all, if I follow through even the logic that Baba puts out so clearly:

Here Don is paraphrasing Baba so we don't put this statement in quotes. — LW

> A drop-soul is God. And the only difference between you and me is — I know I am God — and you don't know it yet. But your drop-soul is God. It's got all of the components, all of the aspects of God.

And so, all right, because the Avatar is one with God, my drop-soul knows Him in its own drop-soul. *So, I can have a conversation right in my own soul with Meher Baba, and that certainly is not psychic.* The only thing that is dangerous, I think here, and which one has the responsibility to discipline themselves and think it through, and feel it through, and intend it through, is am I somewhere or another opening myself so that my cognitive and decisional process is being put aside, and Doug over there is putting his on top of my system and using me? That is a psychic, thing. But, if Doug and I some way or another are talking inside, and he is part of me, to me there is no danger there. Now this may sound just absolutely batty, but this is an important question one has to deal with, and really dealing realistically with Baba's gift of intuition. Where does this begin, and end off, and then often where does that begin, and turn into a danger? You know there are no easy answers to this terribly important and powerful tool and there are terribly important possibilities of — I use the word invasion — that are involved here.

Sevn: Can I add something here? Actually pose a question. Now, Baba said use of superior occult powers for positive means can actually propel —

¶ Don: Assist you, yeah.

Sevn: He also said on the fourth plane, the use of superior powers can propel you to the sixth plane. So I guess the question is, do we play it safe, or trust that since Baba is our master, the use of these tools and can actually be an accelerator on the path?

¶ Don: Anybody like to jump in?

Marnie: ... That's what I was just about to write down ... if in this time, if we learn correct use of our intuition, it begins the training for our souls for the time when we are advanced — and we are all destined for that time (whether we're veiled or not). I think it does develop, it begins ... training for correct use of powers, as opposed to avoidance of powers. I think for myself, the way I've chosen to do it is an avoidance of powers. But this is very helpful in terms of ... power, and knowing correct use, and not letting the ego take it over, but through surrender and love for Baba.

Sevn: Is it possible without the guidance of living Master or a guide?

Marnie: Well, unfortunately, no, but I'm thinking on a level now — infant level of one who loves Baba.

Sevn: Right.

¶ Don: We've got to go back to that or Laurent's going to go crazy if he doesn't get his comment in.

Laurent: Yeah, I mean, I shudder to think that there could be an answer to Sevn's question that would apply to everybody. It's such an individual circumstance. Everybody's got their own temperament, their own development. *I believe that Meher Baba is here now and is our living Master even though he's not a physical being,* so I rely on him for guidance, and I rely on spiritual companions to be part of Meher Baba's guidance. I don't think it's one or the other, you know? And I would imagine that there could be no one answer that could satisfy everybody.

Sevn: Right. I see.

Doug: Thank you.

Payam {to Don}: I want to make sure I understood what is the distinction you're making, because it seems very important, especially in my work too. Not that they're psychic, but you know, being in the position of advising, even. That ... so unclear about that. I do that by remembering Baba or ... that.

You know that so then Baba does whatever. So the distinction you're making if I can understand it is that the intuition that you have and that you use together — meaning that, I don't know, it's too abstract, maybe you could say it again ...

¶ Don: Well, then I'll have to remember what I said. {Laughter.}

Payam: That misuse — you know that fine line of intuitively —

¶ Don: Mm-hmm. Yeah.

Payam: — feeling something and yet where there's the misuse of that being imposed on someone else.

Laurent: Yeah. That displacement. That kind of displacement that you were talking about with Doug.

Payam: Can you say more about that because I'm not sure if I really understand it.

¶ Don: Well, it's a huge subject and so much of it depends upon this word that we haven't brought to the surface here, "intent." What is the intent of action? And certainly I know this gets into the realm of "control," that is the never-never land. I remember that Baba said to me personally, "Don, that I never give instructions through another person."

Laurent: But you should tell the Sam Lewis story, maybe, because that's a perfect example, isn't it?

<small>Don knew Samuel Lewis personally, as they were both Sufi mureeds under Murshida Rabia Martin — LW</small>

¶ Don: Well, unfortunately it is. This is the thing that completely soured me on any kind of occultism. When Inayat Khan left America in 1927, to go back to India, and amongst other things make contact with the Chishti school of Sufism, and pray at the tomb of his Chishti master, Murshida Martin said to him, "But Inayat Khan, what do I do when something important comes up, and I need your guidance, and you're way over in India? What do I do?" And so Inayat Khan said, "Well Samuel Lewis here has psychic capabilities, and can communicate instantly actually, and so if in a difficult situation you tell Samuel what your problem is, and Samuel uses his psychic capabilities to get in touch with me, I'll get an answer to you quickly."

And then of course Inayat Khan, in a fairly short period of months, takes desperately ill, and finally dies of an infection. And Murshida Martin is left knowing that Inayat Khan has not disappeared, in fact he's probably no further away than when he was in India. And so, when she gets into a difficult situation where she needs Inayat Khan's guidance, now without a body, she still relies on Samuel Lewis. And Samuel Lewis just happens to be a person who is a very *human* human being, with very strong likes and dislikes.

༄

And so Murshida Martin, for the rest of her life, is left with an instruction from Inayat Khan that she knows was given to her by him, and should operate perfectly trustworthily even when Inayat Khan doesn't have his body around talking to her. And so, she spends the rest of her life practically crucified because her deep instincts tell her, every once in a while, this is something Samuel Lewis' own personal likes and dislikes are so deeply involved in that it is probably Samuel Lewis talking now, and not Inayat Khan talking.

And she just said to me — forgive me for being so personal about this — but to me, it is a classic ... story, and so deeply touching. She said, "Don, you cannot imagine what a cross this has been to bear, ever since Inayat Khan died." And those were some of the last words she said, and I saw the poignancy of the suffering when she said that to me. It was sort of a deathbed confession. I don't think she said it to anybody else. And it meant so much to me. But this, to me, epitomizes the sort of problem that can arise through psychic powers, and the misuse of them, or the possibility in the strong personality of their being misused to further the ends of the ego of that individual. Huge.

Danny: {Danny mentions having met a Baba-lover years before who told him a story of meeting Sam Lewis during the 1960s.} If anyone wonders what happened to Sam Lewis in the years to come, it maybe puts the exclamation point on that story.

¶ Don: Well, after he disappeared I made no effort to stay in touch. Actually, I liked Sam during Murshida Martin's lifetime.

Danny: And I should tell you later, I actually worked with a guy at my company in Flagstaff whose parents were followers of Samuel Lewis.

¶ Don: He had quite a few followers around ... Doug, you started to say something?

Doug {To Payam}: Well, you're a psychologist. Would it be helpful to you to be able to literally look inside of a person's mind? Would this allow you to be more helpful as a therapist? If so, you would be using psychic powers to help someone. Would this represent the misuse of one's powers because you would be invading one's most intimate and personal thoughts, even while helping them?

Laurent: What about interpreting what you're reading?

Doug: You mean you're saying that it would be false or tainted because it would be going through your own filters?

Laurent: Well, absolutely. Let's say you hear, or read, something. What does it mean? It has meaning in the context of their being. What does it mean? It's a contextual situation. Then you take it and put it in your own context. What does it mean? Suddenly it's devoid of its context.

Payam {to Don}: Well, I know what you bring up as an example. But for me in a very simple way, you know, going back to something you said many — well not many but several years ago, about "dressing yourself in Baba." And, I try, I don't always remember to do that, but I try to do that in every interaction that I have, and sometimes I don't even, I'm not even present to it being intuitive. But it's a connection, that maybe I'm connecting with [people] at a different level than I would have been without doing that. And so, then, I don't even know how to describe it. I mean, I do all the practical things that I have to do whether I'm ... or doing them. But eventually I can't even describe in words what happens when I...Something that happened. And I think that remembering Baba, bringing that into that exchange makes all the difference. So the result might be that I....whatever else happens. But there's something intangible that happens. That I think that's probably more significant than anything else that I do, you know?

Doug: Well, especially in psychology...

Payam: Mm-hmm.

¶ Don: Can we sort of use a mechanical model of a human being, for a few minutes, and see where it might lead us? I would say that there are, almost certainly, and I think we know enough from Meher Baba's description of what human beings are and, psychic forces are, to say, "Okay, all right, we have Payam. Now Payam actually has two major communication system possibilities. One is, she is really first of all a drop-soul. The drop-soul is God. And God is infinite and everything is contained within God. So, she has one means of communication even with somebody sitting over there on the sofa, because that person sitting on the sofa also, in another way, in another reality, is right inside herself and part of her own drop-soul. There is nothing that says that one part of her drop-soul cannot know something about another part of her drop-soul. So there is every possibility of Payam communicating with Doug within the drop-soul communication system. I think this is not just hocus pocus, or anything, but a very, very important reality.

In addition to that, there is Doug over there, and it is perfectly possible, let's say, that you Payam as a physical human being have available to you various different types of waves that you can send out and receive back if you're sensitive to them, and which bring you back information about Doug. And it's what we were talking about the stone somewhere on the system of a few millions light years away is true, that stone is also let's say a part of infinite unity, and can communicate — God, a rock, it's a primitive form of consciousness associated with a rock's drop-soul, but still, that drop-soul of a rock also is God. And so you can have communication. There are two ways that this rock can know what's going on with this other rock on planet Earth. One is by communication in its own drop-soul, which is instantaneous. Or it can do it with some sort of intangible waves that we can't see.

Now to me, the people who are psychic are depending upon their external type of communication through intangible forces and waves. And there a great problem for some reason or another, that is I think from everything I know the external type is much more susceptible to ego and ego-influence than the within-God communication. Does this make any sense?

Participants: Yes. Yes.

¶ Don: And here's where the great danger is, because you as a psychologist, if you're intuitively talking from your knowledge of that individual, your ego doesn't exist within that communication. Your ego gets involved when it gets down to the mental body or something like that. But if you are let's say using a psychic knowledge which is using let's say something like broadcast waves and two different entities, then you get into something that boy, mother Ahlstrand explained to me quite clearly. She said, "Don, I often think that this business of the danger of mediumship, for instance — mediumship actually involves two separate physical entities — and if one is trying to influence another person deliberately, it means that somewhere or another you are trying to displace their sentient decision-making system and substitute yours."

She says the first danger is that you will try to control the individual. In other words, your ego can get into that situation quite easily. And she brought up another point which we've never discussed and I think is hellishly important. She said, she always looks at it as something that the communication system in an individual, from their highly refined decisional process and so on, down through the mental and subtle body, and down into the body, is something like let's say a piece of furniture — it's an oversimplification, but in a piece of furniture, of course, if you handle a chair roughly, you can maybe break a leg of the chair. And so you get out your glue-pot, and you put the chair back together again. And then maybe you're rough again and you break it a second time. And if you're careless maybe you'll break it several times. And the repair that you can do on that leg finally is so bad that the chair is never going to be worthwhile and strong enough to hold human beings. So you may, [cause a problem] by too much involving of this breaking of the tie between the refined part of decision processes. The high part of the consciousness and the physical body. If it has been broken deliberately by medium types of contact it gets into something irreparable. And this is the second huge danger in let's say any type of psychic communication. I think this is what Norina did to herself —

Laurent: Hmm.

¶ Don: — and she didn't recover from it. She broke the leg too often. And I think it is a desperate tragedy. And not even the Avatar could do it under his rules of creation. So Baba could come around

> "Mother Ahlstrand," is a reference to Ms. Katherine Ahlstrand who was Don's psychologist before he became a Sufi. She was a preeminent student of Carl G. Jung, and it was through her that Don was introduced to Rabia Martin. — LW

> Norina Matchabelli gave a series of 'thought transmission' presentations in the 1940's in which she channeled Meher Baba. Baba himself stated that Norina was capable of this connection with him. Don apparently is referring to the eventual cost of this psychic activity on Norina's health. — KM

and sympathize, but not correct it. Doug?

Doug: I've always believed that all people fall within a bell curve with regard to sensitivity. Each one's ability to receive these energy transmissions varies tremendously.

¶ Don: Sure. It is a gift.

Doug: Yeah, I mean that some people are over here on the left end of the curve and you know, they're kind of dense. They don't even pick up on everyday cues.

¶ Don: Mm-hmm. The only thing they can pick up is a kick in the seat of the pants. {Laughter.}

Doug: Correct. In the middle of the curve is the way most people are. On the extreme right end we have psychic. This end of the curve represents all of the varying degrees of ability to receive the most incredibly subtle energy transmissions from another soul. If one recognizes oneself as truly being on this end of the curve, then one might think of oneself as being gifted, but it is almost impossible not to get one's ego involved with this. I mean, if one were to be regularly picking up these subtle signals, it would either drive one completely insane and you'd want to kill yourself, or you would know that you desperately need a master. Even then, we all have egos, so it becomes like a no win situation.

¶ Don: But even for the gifted psychic, they are breaking the integral communication system in the individual that they are giving a psychic experience to. The individual may feel that it's great, but they are breaking it. And if that is repeated too many times, that leg, that particular piece of furniture is permanently weakened. And I've seen this happen to psychic people. There has been a leg broken too many times. And the piece of furniture is just finally weak. I mean, they get sort of huffy and puffy and pale, sort of absent.

Doug: Completely depleted.

¶ Don: They are. Yeah. And it's sad to see. I've seen this happen to highly sensitive people. What do you think?

Sevn: You talked about, two fundamentals, psychic and intuitive. You described the intuitive as going to that oneness, that place of unity in God.

¶ Don: Yeah ... drop-soul where all of creation is.

Laurent: I see it as an internal process.

¶ Don: It is an internal process, there's no breaking of legs, ego is not involved, there is no separateness.

Sevn: As opposed to the separateness of one.

¶ Don: That's right. Totally different kind of communication.

Sevn: Do you remember that [Baba] quote, "Don't love the many in one."

¶ Don: I've heard it but I can't remember it.

Sevn: "Love me as the one in many ... don't love the many in the One?"

Laurent: It's in *Discourses*?

Sevn: In the "Love" part, yeah.

Payam: Should I go get it?

Laurent: We also need to hear the Rumi quote.

Payam: Yes.

Ellie: To clarify though, our own intuitive process, we're drawing from within ourselves.

¶ Don: Within ourselves. There's no time or space. There's only infinite unity.

Ellie: Right. And so whatever one ... based on that intuition that compels us to act or say something —

¶ Don: It doesn't compel you. It's a signal from within oneself.

Ellie: Right. That's safe. And our job is to ...

¶ Don: So Payam is perfectly safe if that is the source of the knowledge of her patients.

Ellie: ...

¶ Don {to Payam}: Your own drop-soul knowledge of everything. And it's almost certainly, I would say, that for somebody who loves Baba, you are so closely under Baba's thumb that there's virtual certainty that any sort of intuition about your patient that you have comes from your own drop-soul. And there you are in intimate contact with Baba also.

Payam: So, I will share the Rumi couplet. And I think it's very much related to forgiveness.

Sevn: "Divine love is qualitatively different from human love. Human love is for the many, and Divine Love is for the one in the many." ...

Laurent: Yeah.

Payam: Here is the quote from Rumi: "Be like the sun, for grace and mercy. Be like the night, to cover others' faults. Be like running water for generosity. Be like death for rage and anger. Be like the earth for modesty. Appear as you are. Be as you appear."

Laurent: That is wonderful.

¶ Don: That is super.

Laurent: Oh wow.

¶ Don: That's lovely. I'm glad you shared that.

Marnie: Yeah. Beautiful.

Payam: And you know we were interviewing this wonderful lady — who founded and is the director of Kian's preschool — she gave it to us.

¶ Don: That's going to appear in the next *OmPoint* journal. I predict it.

Laurent: {laughing} How do you say grace in Farsi?

Payam: Ohhh ... I have a dictionary; I can look it up.

Don is referring to the OmPoint International Circular available at www.ompoint.com.

Glenn: ... I think some of the words that we use in English are very generally applied — we often use the same words to mean several different things ... whereas in Farsi you have a plethora of words that grace is ...

Marnie: It reminds me of the *Hundred and One Names of God* prayer, all the different names of all the different forms of God. And in English we have "God," basically. Maybe a few like the Holy Ghost, and a few other things. But ...

¶ Don: Is Payam looking for something?
Payam: Yeah.
Glenn: The [Farsi] translation dictionary to translate the word "grace."
¶ Don: Oh, I see. Mm-hmm. ... Oh boy, he's found the tome. {Various small chatter, and laughter.}
Jamshid: [Grace in Farsi] is almost half a page.
Participant: Oh really?
¶ Don: Oh boy.
Laurent: Well, we could save it for lunch time. It's not important.
¶ Don: Well, is that what the group would like to do? Save that for lunch time?
Glenn: I think what might be useful in this particular instance is discovering the actual Rumi poem in Farsi then we can know what was intended by the word grace in the translation, rather than trying to infer ...
¶ Don: Well, I would like to suggest one thing at this point. This is not intended to cut off prematurely a fascinating exchange of ideas. I'm just awfully glad that we have taken some further time this morning to flesh out another part of intuition which is desperately important and that each one of you are gonna have to deal with at length, and practically, in your own personal lives. Because I can't imagine a single person sitting here who is not going to be deeply involved, for the rest of their lives, in intuition and its use. So there we are, and you know — I said that I hoped that this group, as long as it exists, will use the subject of intuition as an important agenda point in permanence, and suggest also my own conviction that the greatest challenge that I know to a Baba lover is to use intuition in their working with *God Speaks*.

In my own personal life I can see that the interaction between the deliberate effort to use intuition, become aware of it more and more, and the long term projects that Baba has put me into on *God Speaks* itself; this combination of active awareness of intuition and working on *God Speaks,* has been probably the most fruitful thing that I've ever done. I simply feel that the import, the real flesh and blood and guts of *God Speaks* is filled in by your use of your own intuition. And it's a long-term process. It's incredibly valuable, I've found.

So can we leave that particular one, and I also said to you, and this is what now I'd like to spend the rest of the day on, but I had a very strong intuition just a few days ago that really the fundamental purpose in bringing together this particular group is to train them in the whole ... project that Baba carried so far during his life, the one that I always call, and many people now call the "Beads on One String" project that Baba set underway. And in particular, carrying it on into the stage where my own contact with it has led in the direction of the pivotal key word: forgiveness.

The muck, the real memory patterns that are so desperately important in human conduct of lives and politics now is so tied into this business of what religious wars and misunderstandings and enmity have produced, that it is, I am sure, a huge proportion of devotional power is frittered away, as an individual, as Baba pointed out, fritters away a large part of his own personal stock in worries. And so, the Avatar is dealing with I think two unnecessary and desperately important fritterings away of, spiritual power, I would label it, desperately needed in the individual's ongoing on the spiritual path. I think that Avatar Meher Baba decided, all right, this has gone far enough and the next phase, the next cycle, of Avatar cycles, we have just got to get that fixed. His first very simple push about of how much we do lose in worry. And I think that his, "Don't worry, be happy" just as simple and almost ridiculous as it sounds, has already made a huge dent in that particular thing. And I have the feeling that Baba is pretty satisfied with what he set en route there. But then when we get into the other part of the bloody wars and the competitions, desperately cruel, that go on and have gone on for centuries. There, I feel that he got to the point of putting a great big Avataric charge into it for the people who are going to be carrying the thing out into daily life and in racial contacts.

So, that is going to call for some tremendously creative discipline and persistent effort. And I can't think of anything more challenging or exciting than that particular project. To try to carry on, and put one's real creativity and persistency to work invested in that field. And that is why, I guess, I had the intuition that this group is perhaps, let's say, in Baba's relation to it, brought into being to be a real help. I don't mean to tell you that I think Baba's just trying to use you for one of his pet projects, but I think there is a synchronicity of "Ike and Mike" here, that they belong together. And I seriously propose to you that as we go into, principally after lunch, the forgiveness part that we promised we would go into during these two days, that you think of it every once in a while: is this something that I have a deep internal link with already, and that now it is going to start coming out, where I can see it and understand it and consciously, deliberately invest in it? So think of it occasionally, as we talk along in that direction, of your own personal relation to it.

Now if I have intuited up a wrong alley, also be frank about that, or if you feel that for some reason or another you just don't have any sort of internal linkage with it, be honest about that too. It's certainly possible that I have misread my own intuitions, or Baba's intent in this thing. And you know, you listen to it and say — well, I think that's fascinating and terribly important, but for some reason or another, I don't think that we're especially linked into it, or I'm not especially linked into it. But it's almost as if we're coming to a point of decision in the group's existence and its focus of attention. And I don't want to side-step it. But I don't want to try to force it. All I want to do is present to you, historically, my association with it and the evidence that I have put together over the period of the last years, from my experience with Baba, of Baba's relationship to it and the potential for you personally.

So I will start by, I think I've just about got time to do a quick summary of historical things that I believe most of you are familiar with, at least the essential outlines of them historically — the principle things that enter into this business of the "Beads on One String," and the possible position of the word "forgiveness," as a critical element in its moving ahead now in the next phase. Does this make any sense?

Female participant: Mm-hmm.

¶ Don: ... I am sure that I told you about, but I quickly remind you, because this is key to that important part of Baba's gift to humanity: of going down across the end of the lower Meherabad Mandali Hall, Baba said, "You know who lives there?" And I said, "Yes, Mohammed the Mast." And he said, "Have you gotten to know him?" And I said, "Well, Baba, yes, I have gotten to know him but quite frankly he is still very strange." And I implied by that, that I didn't particularly make friends with strange people so I had no incentive to get to know him better. And then I thought — Oh my God, he's the only one of the masts who's been around Baba months, and years, so I am just as much as saying — you're a lousy psychologist Baba; he's still a weirdo. {Laughter from the group.}

Mohammed Mast was one of the God-intoxicated 'masts' or 'majzoobs' contacted by Meher Baba over a period of many years, mostly in the 1930s and 1940s. Mohammed was such a favorite that he lived in Meherabad, Maharastra State, until his passing in 2003. — KM

Then when I realized that, I practically wanted to fall through Mandali Hall floor — make a permanent dent in the Earth. So, anyway, when he said, "That's interesting, Don, you know there are two problems with the masts, the first is the bewitchment[1] (and the bewitchment is the psychological focus of attention problem) and can be cured by psychological means, and so I use psychological means to un-bewitch them, but there is the other problem that is not well known at all, that I want to discuss, and that is that their emotional experience that they have is so powerful that actual physical brain damage occurs, and because of course I simply say creation should not be herniated by miraculous things or efforts, I don't do any sort of miracles, and so they are left in that condition to their death with a damaged brain, so that's why Mohammed still has some of these very weird traits and characteristics." But he said, "However, the point is that when they are reincarnated in a new body, they not only have [a new] body but also a properly functioning brain. And then, with a properly functioning brain, all of these tremendous, real, spiritual achievements that they have undergone in this great experience ... that caused all of this, then those gifts, knowledge, abilities, will be completely available to humanity." And when I heard that, I said — My God, what a treasure trove, this is incredible. Now, do you realize that that was apparently, as far as I can gather, the first time Baba had ever said that? Even Dr. Donkin in his Introduction to his book on masts...

Laurent: Wayfarers.

Don: *The Wayfarers*, points out that he pestered Baba again, and again, and again and again, "why Baba are you doing this to these masts?" And Baba would never tell them.

Doug: What year was that, that he said that to you?

Don: Well that was not terribly long before he dropped the body.

Doug: So it was in the 60s some time?

Don: Yeah, it was in the 60s, yeah, well into the 60s.

Doug: We had never heard that, and when you told us that in Paris, it was such a bombshell.

Don: It was.

Doug: He was preparing these souls for the New Humanity by repairing them and preparing them, to be let loose in the world at some future time with all faculties functioning normally. Who knows where these souls are today?

Don: Yeah. It's an incredible resource when you stop to focus on it.

Laurent: You want to hear something really bizarre though? When I first came to Baba, in New York, I spent a lot of time in that closed circle I told you about where we would meet after work, and one of the people was extraordinarily intuitive, and he said this.

Don: He did, really?

Marnie: Oh, is that right? That the masts were going to be coming back, or...

Laurent: That Baba had worked with them so that he could fix them, like you are talking about, and then when they reincarnated they would be this giant spiritual force in the New Humanity.

Marnie: Wow.

¶ Don: Well, nobody particularly spread his theory though.

Laurent: No, no, but ...

¶ Don: But this was Baba, Himself, who said it.

Laurent: Yeah, we were in a closed circle, it wasn't about spreading anything...

¶ Don: Yeah.

Laurent: ... but I had heard it and I took it in then, so when you told me that Baba had said it, for me it was just like — intuition can be that clear — that he obviously was tuning into something with Baba.

¶ Don: Yeah, sure, obviously.

Payam: Well, I always saw it as Baba was doing his Universal Work ...

¶ Don: It obviously is coming to fruition as the new cycle of Avataric Cycles is starting. So, this is another one of these tremendous investments of Avataric time and energy to get it off to a good start. And his atomic bombs on his special words is another one, because Baba spent a hellish amount of time on his writings, and especially two or three things that he gave out in this very-very special way. And he impressed upon me, and — repeatedly, that this was, a great treasure to the devotee who had contact with those words — even if he didn't understand two words — that he would still soak up that spiritual energy.

So, investment one: the words with the special atom bombs. Investment two: the rebirthing of the masts in Creation. And then, third, it was not until, not terribly long, again I've told you this but I want to repeat what are, to me, the high points of the logic of what the Avatar spent his time on, for this new Cycle of Cycles, to set the stage. And the third is, go back to his statement in London[2], in 1932, in Kitty Davy's family garden with the press, and Baba said — I have not come to establish a new religion, I haven't come to do this, I haven't come to do that, but I have come to revivify the world's great religions so that the truth will be available to the devotee who is searching, and I will collect them together like beads on one string. Now, that's what Baba said. And such an earthshaking thing as that, and he put it (to emphasize it), can you imagine — maybe you don't even realize — but facing Chapter One of *God Speaks*, is this exact quote. Baba had it put there.

<small>Since we give the actual quotes from Meher Baba in the notes, we didn't put Don's paraphrase of Baba in quotation marks — LW</small>

I didn't really tumble to the fact that that is a terribly important statement of Reality and God, wake up, because just about everybody who loves Baba {Don starts reading to those gathered from *God Speaks*}: "I am not come to establish any cult, society or organization; nor even to establish a new religion. The religion that I shall give teaches the Knowledge of the One behind the many. The book that I shall make people read is the book of the heart that holds the key to the mystery of life. I shall bring about a happy blending of the head and the heart." Nobody ever quotes that! {Don continues reading from *God Speaks*}: "I shall revitalize all religions and cults, and bring them together like beads on one string."³ So, this particular one does not say — "so that it shall be available to the devotee."

Laurent: This is concise.

¶ Don: Um, hmm. Yes, this is slightly abbreviated I think.

Laurent {in response to one of the YPG members, regarding what Don read}: Facing the start of the *God Speaks* itself, facing "Part One." It doesn't have a page number.

{Some talking among the YPG members}

¶ Don: It's just before the first page.

Laurent: After all the introductions and prefaces. Facing page...

¶ Don: Page one, Chapter One. You got it, isn't that amazing?

Marnie: Yeah.

¶ Don: There it is. Nobody takes it for serious. God, when I think, you know, to me, this is simply saying — Okay, in my past Avataric incarnations you got busy and you collected my works and published them, and you built churches, and you built cathedrals and so on, and not this time, there is something else to be done. So, this is what I was talking about just a little while ago.

Sevn: What struck me about this, is that Baba is different, because it wasn't his intention to destroy the previous religion, like many of the previous Avatars did.

That any Avataric advent "destroyed" a previous religion intentionally seems to be a misunderstanding of divine intent. — LW

¶ Don: Baba reinforced them, that I experienced, yeah. So, at any rate, that was the next building block that Baba sent me around, this is number three in that, and had me take motion pictures of places, and I thought that it was a grand and glorious, uh...

Laurent: Sightseeing tour?

¶ Don: ... sightseeing tour that he was making up especially for Stevens. Until he sent me on the second one, and I said — No, he's got something else. I always wondered — now what the hell is going on? And, in this, there was a high point that became a key in many ways for me, and for my understanding things eventually collected around... he sent me two times under his instructions to the Ellora Caves, and especially to Kailash Temple. And the first time it was purely a sightseeing expedition. The principal thing that happened on that one was this old man, beggar man, when we stopped for tea, going to Ellora, who came up and I thought he was going to ask me for alms, and then he reaches down in his dirty tattered garments and draws up three beautiful oranges, and I think — ah, he's got a new wrinkle on this, he wants to give them to me, or sell them to me, and that way he'll get a lot of money out of me.

So, I just waved my hand and shook my head, and the driver said, "Oh, no Saheeb, he want give oranges, give oranges to you." And I said, "That's terribly kind but how can I get them? I should probably give him some sort of money for them, because he obviously doesn't have anything." And he said, "No, no, no, Saheeb, he make gift, spiritual gift." And then Adi Sr. (Adi K. Irani) and Francis Brabazon, who were with me, came out and I told them this story and I said,

"I just have to do something for this poor guy," and Adi said, "If you do, you will spoil his perfect spiritual gift to you. Don't, please don't." And that set the stage, that was my first trip to India.

Laurent: And you accepted the oranges?

¶ Don: I accepted the oranges, and he was so happy after we left. And that formed my knowledge of India. It was my impression. I knew India through that gesture. And it has been absolutely invaluable ever since. And on the second trip, that Baba sent me on, he said, "Don, you've already been to Kailash a couple of times, but this time I want you to go when it is just dusk. I've been several times with Eruch and I stay up at the palace, guest home, of the Nizam of Hyderabad, and I've made the same arrangements for you. And when it's dusk, the chief guard has allowed us to substitute Eruch as the guard for Kailash Temple, so you will be alone. I want you to go up to the chief temple room and sit there. And then when you're done..." He didn't tell me what he wanted me to do {laughs to himself}. I knew for some reason I should not ask him what he wanted me to do. I'm supposed to have been enough of a spiritual student to know that intuitively, of course. {laughs to himself}

I wasn't that intuitive, I was in a horrible quandary. So, I go up and when I get settled down there and I felt — Oh my God, there's somebody in this room — and I screw up my eyes, and I don't see anybody moving or anything, and the sense of the presence of somebody gets stronger and stronger and stronger, then I feel this strange pressure, that I've never felt in my lung-cavity, starting to form, and I thought — Oh my God, I've picked up a virus infection in my bronchial tubes and boy is it galloping. I'm going to be sicker than a dog! And then it got worse and worse and worse, and I said — My God, I've got to get out of here, something's going to bust inside and I'll have to go to the hospital. I was so worried.

So, I got the hell out of there. And Eruch said, "Well, Don, what happened?" And I told him. Eruch just looked absolutely as if this happened every Sunday at 2 o'clock. {Laughter}

He said nothing, no comment, no queries for it, changed the

subject. Drove back and the next day Baba was there in Mandali Hall, and he said, "Well, Don, what happened?" And I explained exactly what I had told Eruch. Baba looked at me, nodded his head, changed the subject. *Never, until he dropped his body, referred to it again.* So, all of this was just, you know, Sunday at 2 o'clock, apparently, for Baba.

So, this was stowed away in my mind with a great sense of failure, but Baba didn't toss me out, so apparently I hadn't *failed* the examination! But I knew that I had failed to get to the import of it, even intuitively. And so, it wasn't until years later, when this group in London, who had been egging me all this time, said, "Now, Don, we know that Baba didn't tell you why he sent you to photograph these places, but if they were important enough for Baba to want you to film them for him, they must be important to him. And if he has gone to Kailash Temple, himself, with Eruch at night, there is something going on there, and we want to see these places." So, finally, I did it. And when we got to Kailash Temple, you remember I told this story to you, but I want to repeat it once more. When we got to Kailash Temple, I told the group, "Now, here we are, and there are of course thirty some-odd more caves around here, which are beautiful, and after you are done getting your fill of the beauty of Kailash Temple, you just go ahead, but I've got unfinished business here.[5] I'm just going to stay here, if you will forgive me."

Two, or three of the people in the group stayed with me, and they kept at a discrete distance because I was not in meditation or anything, but they just felt that I was not in a talkative mood (which I was not). And then I was leaning against my favorite pillar, and as I was leaning there I suddenly began to feel a strange sensation in my body and particularly in my chest, and all of a sudden I said — My golly, this is the same thing happening to me now that happened thirty to forty years ago, when Baba sent me here the second time.

Laurent: Over forty years.

¶ Don: Yeah, it was thirty to forty years. This was 2004. Can you imagine? And the same thing happened to me. And then, *all of a sudden*, I knew — there was no question — absolutely this was Baba's Avataric stamp of power that he had left in this place.

Participant: How did you know?

¶ Don: How did I know it? Because I'd had a similar feeling, not as strong or as acute, several times with Baba when he took me on public occasions. Usually to visit a group he hadn't seen in some time. And something very strong and powerful would happen, and being close to Baba I would feel, suddenly, this surge of power and I would have to say — this was Baba's Avataric Power, because I'm feeling it, in this particular occasion, for me it is palpable.

And, when I was sitting there in Kailash, I said — that was what I felt. And I knew it was not antagonistic; *he hadn't wiped out the devotional power of the other people, but he had added to it, and confirmed it.* And so, well, that to me was a terribly important identification. And when they got me back to London, after collapsing on the plane, I spent three to four days there [in the hospital] and got back out. As I was getting out, all of a sudden I said to myself — My God, now why didn't I remember that? This is the *Beads on One String*, and Kailash is a powerful example of it. And this is also, obviously, what this business of revivification of the existing religions means, and I've experienced it, and strongly, in Kailash.

And when I told Baba that the pain in my chest was so great I couldn't stay any longer, he knew I had felt his presence and he didn't have to tell me. He knew one day I would identify it, as what it really was ... yes, Doug?

Doug: Well it's important, and I thought that Kailash was a Hindu temple?

Laurent: Yes, it's a Shiva temple.

Doug: So, why would that key into "Beads on One String" for you, because it was just one of the beads?

¶ Don: Oh, one of the beads! I can't say that I had the same sensation in the other places, but when I got out of the hospital [in London, in 2004], and remembered the Beads on One String, then I said to myself — My God, so the places he had sent me to, maybe they're not all of the beads on one string, but there are some important ones that he has sent me to.

Doug: What area? What traditions? Jain, Buddhist, Hindu ...
Laurent: But, you know, it's interesting, because we were together on that trip. When we went to Mount Abu, and the Dilwara Temples, you were visibly moved to tears by being at the Dilwara Temples.
¶ Don: Especially, yeah.

Laurent: And it's almost as if each bead may not have the same quality of power, or wisdom, but they're each charged for sure.
¶ Don: Very special.

Doug {to Don}: But you were being given a message about the Beads on One String... because he was so powerful ... his presence there ... eventually that's the reason he sent you in the first place?
¶ Don: Oh, absolutely! No question at all, he was building up a series of experiences, that were then powerful for me. I didn't know what it was all about, but he knew at some point or another, he had put enough dots that I would connect up the dots and get a picture out of it, and by God, that's exactly what happened.

Doug: Thirty-five years later.
¶ Don: Yeah, right. But, you know, by that time, I'd had enough of these experiences where an unexplained thing would all of sudden fit into a reality, and I would understand it. So, that was part of the joy and the excitement, it was part of an adventure story with Baba. So, at any rate, that then became quite clear in my mind, that this had to do with the "Beads On One String." And the next powerful event was towards the end of Eruch's life. Again, I've told you this story, but I repeat the key elements.

Close to the end of Eruch's life, he got in touch with me, and actually on that occasion, it was some way by telephone. And he said, "Don, you know, I finally after all of these years, finally got to see the film that Baba had you take of those various different places." And he said, "Now that I see the film, I have to tell you that the places Baba sent you to photograph[6] are exactly the same places that he got me to take him to, each one of these just the two of us by ourselves. And when he got to the place, then he would go into meditation,[7] deep meditation for hours on end." And he said, "Now he did not do this just once, but he did that repeatedly for each one of these places. And he never told me either, why he was doing it, I just knew it was an important part of his Avataric work. But I wanted you to know that they are identical to the ones he sent you to, to film."

Laurent: And in some cases, Baba slept there too.

¶ Don: Well, that was on the Dilwara steps, Dilwara Temple steps. Eruch had told me that, the first time that I visited Dilwara. He did it just sort of to confirm that Baba himself was so fond of Dilwara he had been there a number of times. Eruch said, "He would deviate, our return home from a mast tour, so we could go by the Dilwara Temples, and at night time then he would roll up in a blanket and sleep on the bottom step[8] going into the principal temple at Dilwara."

Doug: Were these places receiving the Avataric stamp? Were they all from different traditions?

¶ Don: More or less, yes, generally. But there are some things that were not actually religions, for instance, the fortress of Shivaji[9]. And he sent me also, had Meherjee stop once, at a stop point, not a stop point even, on the freeway going up the ghats towards Pune, and then when I got back he said, "Don, I had Meherjee stop there because that was where one of the most important battles of Shivaji against the Moghal[10] invasion was fought." And he said, "I haven't told you this, but one of three minor incarnations that I took, *veiled*, before coming as Merwan, was as Shivaji. Another one was as a sweetmeat seller in the Himalayas..." And the third one I could never remember and that's a whole story in itself.[11] But at any rate, that was the first time I'd ever heard about three minor incarnations, and I think ...

Female Participant: ... Three minor?

¶ Don: Three minor and Shivaji was one that he particularly wanted me to know about. He wanted me to go up, with Dr. Donkin, and film Shivaji's fortress above Satara.

So, at any rate, I don't pretend that Baba sent me to all of the beads, and I don't pretend that he hasn't revivified others, in what he has done in visiting Saint Theresa in Spain, and Saint Francis of Assisi in Italy, and also the cathedral in ...

Laurent: St. Mark's.

¶ Don: ... St. Mark's, in Venice. Certainly would lead one, me to believe, that's he's collected some other beads, or done some terribly important work. Anyway, I don't want to pretend, or limit it to just the ones that he filmed and that he went to with Eruch.

But, nevertheless, the point is that I know, for myself, the impact of Baba's energy because I have been around him on these public occasions, when smaller versions of it I have felt, and that is Baba, no question at all about it. And I know that what he left, for instance in Kailash, is a monumental supply, and he had to be leaving similar investments in these other places.

Laurent: And, the Muslim bead is the Qutub-e-Irshad Moinuddin Chishti's tomb in Ajmer.

¶ Don: Yeah.

Laurent: That was phenomenal. Oh! {Don and participants talking} Oh man, oh my God.

¶ Don: Now, the next thing that I wanted to explain to you, and I am not sure that I have to the group here before, is what I call the population chart stored in my memory of these places, because, the places that he had me film are so beautiful, almost without exception, that always when I had a friend coming to India for a first time, I would say, "Be sure to see ... " so and so, and, "be sure to see," so and so ... And in several instances I went with them, sometimes I went to these places, and sometimes I went back for different reasons. But I want simply to repeat to you, that for various reasons I have been back to most of these places he sent me to film. And because of my generally photographic memory, I remember what it looked like. And I suddenly said to myself — My golly, I remember, roughly, about how many people there were around there, and what sort of people they were. And I just started rapidly, when this memory pattern started taking place, did a "population chart. "Every single one of these places, from when I first saw it, none of them had anyone around, quite frankly, almost nobody around. And then the next time that I would go, there'd be a few groups around, the usually gawking school kids and a few tourists and so on, but more people, *and a few people who were obviously devotees.*And so, and then the next time, more. And, my God, you remember when we went to Moinuddin Chishti's Tomb, you practically ...

Laurent: It's like Grand Central Station [in New York].

¶ Don: ... the first time I went there, there was almost nobody in that whole God ... excuse me, courtyard. {Participants laughing.}

¶ Don: {chuckling to himself}: Things do slip out.

Doug: A lot more people being drawn to these places ...

¶ Don: Yes. And so I said to myself, my God — revivification — *I have experienced the revivification that Baba talks about in that address to the press.* Revivification, there it is. And also, the sense of devotion of many of these people, was totally different as time went along. So it was for real. But then, I also said — well, now, what is my sense about the purpose of all of this? And, certainly, what Baba was doing, he cut off ... any public aspects of his visits to these tombs. Nobody, there are almost no Baba devotees who know anything about those visits, to them.

So for some reason or another he did not advertise, or leave almost any trace, of the Avatar's presence there. Except for Eruch, and then Eruch telling me that where I had been filming for Baba, he had been there meditating with Baba. So, that was terribly important to me. But then I began to think — but what is the purpose aside from revivification? Why did he cut off, for instance, any public knowledge of his participation? And then I began to think — is it perhaps possible that so much of the devotional deposit of the people who come there for their own religious purposes, being someway or another spilled away, just as Baba warned us *worry* was doing about our own spiritual energy?[12]

Are these places really intended as Power Houses for civilization? Broadcasting points for it? And, did Baba add power to it, and confirm it? And now it is time, somewhere or another, to do something about what obviously has been a tremendous drain on the resource of devotion, deposited in these places. The religious wars that have been fought, in their name, constantly, constantly, constantly. And, what's going on right now? I hear, in our civilization, it's a terrible situation that we're in. It would be a crazy Avatar who would allow a powerful drain of that sort to go on, when Baba warns us about worrying, which we can do something about individually. And if he didn't do something about that tremendous drain on the whole deposit of devotion, that has gradually accumulated, much of it around particular places of devotion such as the things that he sent me to witness, to film for him — and so no, he certainly has not left that there to be frittered away. And, how under the sun, {Ajang home doorbell rings} can one do something about these enmities and hate, that goes on so much in the world? {Someone answers the front door.}

¶ Don: Now, this is the last ... {Don looks at his watch}: Oh my God!

Laurent: It's time for lunch.

¶ Don: It is. I'll just quickly tell it to you. I got to be very, very, friendly with the President of Johns Hopkins University. And so he did a lot of personally inviting me to various different things that I would never have known about even. And one of them was a special meeting held at the university's foreign campus at Bologna, in Italy.

Johns Hopkins is Don's alma mater.

And addressing them was one of the editors of the *International Herald Tribune*, a very highly respected "gent." And he gave a discussion of major things going on in civilization at that present time, which were tragic in view of the height that civilization has reached in our time. He was talking about the things that are residual hate, from original religious wars, and he pointed out for instance, the classic situation in the Balkans[13] where the invasions are several hundred years back, and they still go to war with each other, and lethally let each other's blood.

And, so, he said — "And I've been reflecting on this." and he said, "You know it's time that something was done on this tremendous drain on civilization and its forces." And he said, "I've thought a lot about it, and I just have to share with you my thought. *The only thing that I can think of, that can possibly act as an antidote to all this horrible hatred, is just irrational, unconditional forgiveness.*"

Laurent: He said that?

¶ Don: He said that. Um-hmm, yeah, that man said that. And I loved him for saying it, so I got a special introduction from the President of Johns Hopkins University, and went and visited him and took him out to lunch.

He was a wonderful guy. I really had great admiration for him. But, at any rate, that word stuck in my brain, and then, rather recently, I would say in the last year, easily, suddenly as I was thinking — what next in relation to Baba's tremendous "inpouring" of energy, into these Beads on One String? Is it simply to revivify the religious philosophy, or is it also to do something fundamental about all of this tremendous hate pattern which wastes so much beautiful devotional energy? So, then, just suddenly, I said — what good can one do?

And then I remembered what he said about the religious wars and the Balkans. And he said, "The only thing I can think of is — forgiveness — unconditional forgiveness. And people are capable of it." He was an optimist, and it stuck in my mind, and it just suddenly banged down. And I said — so that's why I went to that Bologna meeting, to hear that guy say that. Because, I think it's the only thing too. And then I began, just quite frankly, to say — well, Stevens, let's put your intuition to work and make deliberate intuitive progress. What are the mechanics of forgiveness? How does it happen? How does real forgiveness happen? And then gradually enough built up and I saw the huge complexity of it. And as I saw the complexity, I said to myself — my God, this is a whole new field for civilization to tackle: to do something about forgiveness itself, and the mechanics of it, and the results of it. And how to improve the efficiency of forgiveness. And I was getting nowhere in trying to dream up any — how do you go about measuring, or what's the methodology of forgiveness?

How can you, someway or another, sort of formulate it? And, tell other people about it and how to go about it and measure its efficiency and how can you improve it? And I was all tangled up in these sort of things and finally I came back, from our month in India together in August 2004, and was getting nowhere with my intuitions. And I just said — I've got to start talking to groups that I'm close to, because this is too important. And I know Baba means that this is the thing, that his real devotees are gonna have to do. So this is the thing, instead of building cathedrals this time, and so on, no new religions to build cathedrals to, but put the energy and the resources into this project of forgiveness.

And I don't know a stinking-Hades-business about how to go about it, but nevertheless I've got to talk to — I've just got to start talking to groups who love Baba, about it because it's their responsibility. So, I tried it out with the four groups in France, and each time that I brought up forgiveness, and said, *"Now look, this is terribly important. But I've got to be blunt with you, I cannot imagine that you can do anything meaningful in forgiveness unless you clean up shop in your own corner first. So, go over your own pet list of peeves and hates, and so on, and just say — can I forgive that guy? Can I forgive that situation? Can I forgive that gal who tripped me? And so on. Right at home, go through it, point by point. Then I think you will, when you find out a bit by bit how to do it in your own backyard."*

And I said, *"Let me tell you one thing: I just feel this is Baba's project, and you're gonna have a powerful assist from Baba, but it's gonna be tough. And do it. And then when you know a bit about it, and the forces involved, then you'll be in a position to affect and influence other people, but not before."*[14]

And boy, it was just as if an earthquake hit each time that I said that to a group. And the instant that I said that in one of the groups in France, there was one guy that we all love to pieces because he is so good hearted, and so peaceful, and so non-critical, he just pitches in and quietly does things.

And we all love him for it. The instant that I said that, he burst out, "Well, I can't do that... no, he did that to me ... grumble grumble ..." and he was muttering I thought — My God, I tapped into a psychic wrinkle in this guy, and he's going to a nut house, what have I done?

And so, I tried to do it all more sweetly, and so on, and then once I said, *"And incidentally, the way you react, you're a perfect living example of how necessary it is to forgive..."* and he didn't take kindly to that, and started muttering...

Laurent: {Laughs heartily.}

¶ Don: ... about fifteen minutes later, we all had to break up and be quiet with Baba, but all during the few seconds we were quiet he was muttering {Don mimics this muttering ... grumble grumble ... "he did that" ... grumble grumble}.

Participants: {Laughter.}

¶ Don: Oh my God! And so, when we were going home in our cars, his car was taking him home to his part of southern France, and just in front of ours, and he is muttering...

Participants and Don: {Laughing}

¶ Don: ... and he's going on and on {grumbling} out the driveway, and out the front gate, and into the distance. So, I said — Oh boy, I just cannot imagine what is going to happen next to this poor guy. I hope he doesn't go to a lunatic asylum! So then a couple of days later I realize that I'm going that weekend up to Brittany, and then I go over to London and from London I go to Mexico City — my God, it will be a couple of months before I see this crazy guy. I can't leave him in a state like this. And so, I telephoned a friend of his (who knows him pretty well), and said, "By any chance, do you have his telephone — I never managed to get his telephone number." The friend says, "You know, he's very cozy about his telephone number, he doesn't give it to me either." And he says, "But now, wait a minute Don, if it's really very important, I do know the guy who lives next door to him. And maybe he'll know where ..." And I say, "I've just got to get a hold of him, and make an appointment to get together, and save him a trip to the nut house ..." And so, ten minutes later, my phone rings.

The guy himself is on the phone. And says, "What can I do for you, Don?" And I said, "Well, you know, I was just so sorry that this business about forgiveness was so upsetting to you, and I just wanted to talk with you a little bit, we've just got to work out — to be able to sit down quietly together, before I go off for several weeks. And I just can't leave a close friend as I am leaving you now."

And so he said, {Don says it in French first and translates it as}: "That's not worthwhile. "So I thought — Oh my God, he's been thinking for several days now and just seen that: there's not any chance, and he's come to the conclusion, it's not even worthwhile. And: "I'm mad, and there is no way that I can participate in the forgiveness project, or anything of the sort" — and I thought that was his conclusion.

So, I try a sweeter voice and sweeter emphasis, and so on, and I'm only two sentences into my highly attractive spiel and then he breaks in again and says, {Don says it in French and translates the end of the sentence as}, "Already done!"

"Already done, what are you talking about?"

He said, "Well, Don, you know when I was driving down the driveway... {Don laughing to himself} ... He said, "All of a sudden, I suddenly saw the situation. And I saw, the basic real facts, the important facts between me, and this person," who happened to be his father.

And he said, "The force of the real, real facts, and the blood relationship and responsibility compared to these picayune things, they were really small, yeah they were disturbing, but in comparison to the real value of the relationship, I thought — how could I be so stupid?"

And he said, "You know, as soon as I got back I called him up." And [the father] said, "I feel exactly as you do, and let's do something." So they made a date to go to the most expensive restaurant on the Cote d'Azur[15], two weekends later, and live it up — and, relive their friendship.

Female Participant: Wow.

¶ Don: And so, this to me, was my confirmation that the intuition that Baba had that the energy and the way, so that if you've got the courage to touch the Doorbell of Forgiveness, by God you link into a circuit where things happen that are incredible. End of story.

This is why I think forgiveness has Baba's touch, and I can predict that anybody that's got the courage to try it is gonna have something to experience and really be amazed about — working with the Avatar on something that the Avatar has put his heart and soul into. And Baba has done it, I know it.

Laurent: And by the way, Don's next book is going to be called, *The Doorbell of Forgiveness*.

Participants: Oh ... Wow ... {Laurent and others laughing.}

¶ Don: Listen here Little Bear ... Little Bear! Please be little and don't laugh so big. {Don and participants all laughing.}

¶ Don: Shall we be quiet with Baba for a moment? {The whole group becomes silent.}

¶ Don: Dearly Beloved Baba, please keep that doorbell polished. Amen.

Sunday Morning Notes:

1. In fact the terms that Meher Baba himself used when discussing the masts with Dr. William Donkin for his book, *The Wayfarers*, were, "divine intoxication," "divine stupor," "divine madness" and "God-intoxicated." Donkin wrote about the mast Chatti Baba: "Meher Baba, who is all too rarely communicative about his masts, told the mandali one day in Ranchi that there was no equal to Chatti Baba in the whole world, and that he was inestimable for the help he gave him in his work. The moods of this great man were extraordinary, and would fluctuate from a sunny expansiveness to a truculent attitude, without apparently much provocation. He was like a child, quick to change for a very little thing, but he had a bewitching enchantment about him that made him loved by all." See: *The Wayfarers: Meher Baba with the God-Intoxicated*, by William Donkin (Myrtle Beach: Sheriar Foundation, 2001), Part One, The Difference Between Ordinary Madness And Mast States by Meher Baba, available on-line at: http://ambppct.org/meherbaba/Book_Files/Wayfarers_1.pdf., p.65.

2. The date was actually April 8th, 1932, when he said, "My coming to the West is not with the object of establishing new creeds and spiritual societies and organizations, but it is intended to make people understand religion in its true sense. True religion consists in developing that attitude of mind, which would ultimately result in seeing one Infinite Existence prevailing throughout the universe; when one could live in the world and yet be not of it, and at the same time, be in harmony with everyone and everything; when one could attend to all worldly duties and affairs, and yet feel completely detached from all their results; when one could see the same divinity in art and science, and experience the highest consciousness and indivisible bliss in everyday life... I intend bringing together all religions and cults like beads on one string and revitalize them for individual and collective needs. This is my mission to the West. The peace and harmony that I shall talk of and that will settle on the face of this worried world is not far off." (from *Lord Meher*, by V.S. Bhau Kalchuri, p. 1554).

3. The quote Don reads is from *God Speaks*, by Meher Baba (Walnut Creek: Sufism Reoriented, 1955, 1973) facing page 1: "I am not come to establish any cult, society or organization; nor even to establish a new religion. The religion that I shall give teaches the Knowledge of the One behind the many. The book that I shall make people read is the book of the heart that holds the key to the mystery of life. I shall bring about a happy blending of the head and the heart. I shall revitalize all religions and cults, and bring them together like beads on one string."

4. Meaning Kailash Temple at the Ellora Caves.

5. Don's visit to Kailash Temple alone at Baba's order, with Eruch as guard, was in the 1960s whereas this return to the temple was in 2004, approximately 40 years later, with over 30 people from America, England, Europe and India.

6. It was actually motion pictures with a Kodak Browning 8mm movie camera.

7. Meher Baba was clear that the Avatar, upon being unveiled to His Divinity, doesn't actually "meditate" per se, but does Universal Work, with a Universal Mind. It is doubtful that Baba would have described His work in these locations as meditation to anyone. — LW.

8. At Dilwara with Don, in 2004, we asked the Caretaker of the Dilwara Temples to show us that step which Baba slept upon. He explained to us that since Baba had slept there the temple entrance had been redesigned and that step was no longer available. My memory is that the step was now inside another part of the temple complex, and no longer part of the entrance (as if it was now inside a newer building). — LW.

9. According to Meher Baba, Shivaji, the great Hindu hero warrior of Maharasthra, was in fact a "minor incarnation" of the Avatar. See *Lord Meher*, Volume 2, p. 356, also Volume 3, p. 883, and p. 971, also Volume 4, p. 1306. See also, *Love Alone Prevails* by Kitty Davy, p. 320.

10. For more about the Moghal Empire see: http://en.wikipedia.org/wiki/Mughal_Empire.

11. Most likely the third minor incarnation Baba mentioned to Don was that of Shankaracharya, the great Hindu sage. See *Lord Meher*, Volume 8, p.2348-2358. See also *Love Alone Prevails* p. 258, and *Glimpses of the God Man*, by Bal Natu, p. 33-34. - LW

12. The quote that Don mentions about worry is from *Discourses*, "Qualifications of the Aspirant: Part II" (Volume III, p. 121), bold font from editors: "Moral courage and self-confidence should be accompanied by freedom from worry. **There are very few things in the mind which eat up as much energy as worry. It is one of the most difficult things not to worry about anything**. Worry is experienced when things go wrong, but in relation to past happenings it is idle merely to wish that they might have been otherwise. The frozen past is what it is, and no amount of worrying is going to make it other than what it has been. But the limited ego-mind identifies itself with its past, gets entangled with it and keeps alive the pangs of frustrated desires. Thus worry continues to grow into the mental life of man until the ego-mind is burdened by the past. Worry is also

experienced in relation to the future when this future is expected to be disagreeable in some way. In this case it seeks to justify itself as a necessary part of the attempt to prepare for coping with the anticipated situations. But, things can never be helped merely by worrying. Besides, many of the things which are anticipated never turn up, or if they do occur, they turn out to be much more acceptable than they were expected to be. Worry is the product of feverish imagination working under the stimulus of desires. It is a living through of sufferings which are mostly our own creation. Worry has never done anyone any good, and it is very much worse than mere dissipation of psychic energy, for it substantially curtails the joy and fullness of life."

13. The Balkans is actually a peninsula in Southeastern Europe, and is composed in full or part by the following countries: Albania, Bosnia and Herzegovina, Bulgaria, Greece, Kosovo, Macedonia, Montenegro, Croatia, and Serbia, as well as three other countries which are mostly outside the peninsula.

14. Laurent's attempt to practice exactly what Don suggests here can be found in Part II of to this volume: Forgiveness at Meherabad.

15. Cote d'Azur is known as the French Riviera, being the Mediterranean coastline of the Southeastern area of France.

Sunday Afternoon: The Glory of Companionship

Don: Well, should we spring into activity? Just a light spring. Anybody do any reflecting at lunch time that brought up amazing results?

Jamshid: Don't know about amazing, but I have something to share. At thirteen, in Iran, I cut off with religion, as a whole ... experience of Islam ... done with that. And experienced some searching, soul searching for some years. At about eighteen, I felt social justice was the ideal worthy of living for and dying for, for that matter, and gave another twenty years of my life to it. Thirty different groups existed who were searching for justice and so forth, in Iran, and each one of them could not work with and tolerate the other. There was such a deep division, and even hatred, and unhealthy competition, and then supposedly they are working for democracy, and love and justice, and equality and so forth. I barely escaped execution by the Islamic Republic in 1983, made it to the states, so wounded by the many divisions and sects that existed in that search for, "Truth and Justice."

Something that has separated me, constantly and continuously, from the Baba community has been a sense of separation from the sufferings of being on the planet ... and I have heard this, and I will be honest with you, I have resented hearing it. I have heard over and over that Baba said we shouldn't be involved with the "P-word" — politics. What I was hearing wasn't 'politics', *it was a negation of a sense of responsibility, and compassionate love, for all beings on this planet and beyond.* And that hurt me, and I felt – the one place that I thought I found people who get it, aren't getting it! It's almost like we do care to talk about things that don't really require giving. Yes, talk about love, and being this and that, and pure in the heart, and pure in the mind, and so on, but when it comes to getting out there and giving something, we put the brakes on because, "Baba said" – I am not saying I researched every word that Baba had said, but

I haven't found where Baba said, you know, the quotation that everyone uses, "not to get involved with politics." And I don't care for politics whatsoever. The first time that I heard, ever, something that put me on fire, was yesterday here ... Don's comments about forgiveness and the example he came up with, the Balkan states in Eastern Europe. And I thought – how refreshing, because this is being in the world. Now here's a test, can we be in the world but not of it? Can we be out there, be compassionate, be giving ... and not be in the righteousness of it. So, I can understand if Baba said something that probably meant – that's my understanding of it — that it's a dangerous way because we can easily become righteous and get polluted. I can understand that. But I cannot understand that Baba would have said something that would translate into inaction and indifference, and suffering of all forms of life, and even non-living. I can't understand that.

Meher Baba said, "Although I am in everyone and in everything, and my work is for the spiritual awakening of all mankind, I am always aloof from politics of any kind. My disciples and devotees should continue as before to abstain from taking part in political activities or discussion." (January 1st, 1949 via circular, in the context of fighting between India and Pakistan, from *Lord Meher*, p. 33˙8) – LW

Danny: Baba said that to Gandhi, yeah ... but you're making a distinction between politics and helping [those who are] suffering, and that's an important distinction.

Sevn: And even someone who says that, how do you know that these people that did say it weren't involved in something that was actually helping the world, in everyday life? How can you tell, in a group, what they do outside in their everyday life?

Jamshid: I am not put in a judgment seat about anybody else. I am saying that a conversation that happened here yesterday, coming from Don Stevens, not from someone maybe less exposed to – and less knowledgeable of Baba ... It seems I heard something totally different from Don yesterday.

Danny: ... the conversation about selfless service.

Doug: You know, Baba said that if you live a life of love for God and live it honestly, then that life can change things. And in that sense, even if you aren't a Mother Theresa, you can live by example and show by example a better way, through compassion and acceptance of others. In this way such attributes can be caught by others. They become contagious. Ultimately, this will be of great help to the world. And in this sense, then one's life is not separate. That's the way I look at it. It is a little more indirect than going out into the world and providing direct service to others, but to live a life such as this is also helping.

Danny: ... saying that I believe that in the course of our normal daily life, like Don said at lunch [during the first YPG meeting] a few years ago, every situation is an opportunity to love. Whatever you're doing, in the grocery store, wherever. I don't want to take anything at all from what you're saying, but I do believe acts of love have a beneficial effect on the world exponentially. That smile you give to the cashier can have a ripple effect that will have a much [more] positive effect...Baba [said it could have] a much bigger effect than we ever imagined. But at the same time, Baba did talk about service, and selfless service. And that is ... an important aspect of the Path. And something that we would do well to aspire to also.

And you know he talks about the discourse on "The Task for Spiritual Workers." And there's a lot of things to keep in mind, and because there's such a danger for the ego to get involved in a lot of going out and doing work for the world, that Baba has some really good wisdom for us to consider ... involved in that.

Marnie: The issue of social justice... I think it's a very powerful issue, and in my experience among Baba lovers I do not see us as a group culturally being active in social justice. My intuitive sense is, part of what you're running into, especially here among all of us... middle-class Americans is that our lives have been so comfortable. We are expressing our love for God through the culture in which we live and it's not a culture of going out there and fighting...of social justice. I have no judgment about it but part of what you run into among us is the culture in which we come from.

The whole idea of active forgiveness, Don, that you're bringing to our minds, may be a way we can actively start to know how to be socially active in a way that doesn't foster the ego. They're profound questions....

Doug: During the Indonesia tsunami many, many people died. You know, the American people were all over that event. Many who could least afford to give money emptied their pocketbooks to support the people over there. You know, we were leading the world in that relief effort. Its not like we were simply saying selfishly, "oh that happened over there." Americans really did come up to the plate and helped. Since it was a natural disaster, no one could blame anyone. Unfortunately, during manmade disasters, politics begins to play a part and the generosity of a given group of people may become compromised.

Marnie {to Doug}: We were talking about the Baba community.

Doug: Oh, I thought that we were talking about the world.

Jamshid: Nowhere in anything I said issue of nationalism…we are aware that the older mindset…that belongs to a couple centuries ago and has a function and a reason to that …really…a way for progressive thought more evolved state of consciousness. It's not the way to look at life, through division.

Marnie: Right.

Jamshid: I definitely wasn't insinuating that at all. I was only saying something that I heard…joy. Excitement and energy….that's what I'm sharing with you. That it is the first breakage from the mold that I had perceived badly — badly – because I felt an affinity with ... that I haven't experienced with some of my own brothers. With Payam and so forth and so on and with many other Baba lovers. And I saw then a separation because I wasn't seeing it translated into wider compassionate living.

Marnie: Mm-hmm.

Jamshid: And I am not talking about this plan or that plan or ... But here came my example, and something from Don that ... I felt a completely different understanding.

Payam: I think each of us has a unique talent that Baba has given us. Or multiple, many talents I should say. How to express that in the world is part of our discoverance. And some of us have tapped into it already. Some of us are still discovering it. And knowing you, Jamshid, I know that social justice is...a part of that ...however you discovered for yourself that...in action...being part of...that's going to be part of your discoverance, and maybe this is it. Maybe what Don has brought up is another avenue somehow which brings that into the world in a different way that uniquely taps into your talents...and you have the talent for that ... forgiveness ... and you have the ... mind ... is kind of calling ... you can't quantify it, but it's there. And so it has to express itself somehow. And I think what Don is asking is, is this ringing true for you? And maybe we don't know how it's going to manifest. And for me it rings very much true, because everything that I'm doing, I'm grateful to Baba for providing for me, but I've always felt there's more.

So what you said about forgiveness, whether I want to accept it or not, with the L.A. Center, I've been somehow pulled into many situations now where I have to...I don't know what you call it... be a peacemaker. I resisted it at the beginning, but now I—as challenging as this has been, it's also been immensely rewarding. So I know going into it, whatever form it takes, it's not necessarily going to be easy—actually quite challenging. But that's Baba, you know ...

Laurent: So I came to Baba in 1986, and....

¶ Don: In 1806?

Laurent: '86.

{Laughter.}

¶ Don: Excuse me.

Payam: You're an awfully young looking old guy.

Laurent: That was my last lifetime. I'm talking about this lifetime! I went to the Meher Spiritual Center almost straight away that first summer. And it's one of the first things I heard, is Baba said, "Don't get involved in politics." Almost immediately. And they said be careful that you don't have any political discussions here at the Meher Spiritual Center, because Baba didn't want that. So I mean, I can certainly acknowledge that that was drummed into me over the years many, many times. And I read quotes where Baba said even in more detail to people, that the problem is when you get involved in political work and political parties, unfortunately it tends to be more divisive and separative than it is helpful. He told people about that, for sure. But what I got all excited about, also with Jamshid, about this forgiveness, and I'd seen many of these before, because Don has many of these forgiveness intuitions – forgiveness is a spiritual solution that far transcends political boundaries. And these political stalemates, that really are — I mean, the best minds in the world still scratch their heads about Israel and Palestine, and Uganda, and Darfur and all this. And how do you get any movement?

¶ Don: And Kosovo.

Laurent: And Kosovo. The list goes on and on. And it's such a simple, brilliant solution. It's not even a new solution, right? It's an old solution of forgiveness, but the way it's being revisited now is very exciting for me. I don't even know why. I feel like Payam. I don't know how it will manifest or evolve. But I feel that inner calling, and percolating, of excitement for sure. I think it's wonderful and fantastic.

Glenn: I know that while Baba was in the body ... I believe he had one disciple ... who would go out in the world (and be) politically active, held a political office. But he didn't tell him not to be politically active, that was his choice, and then so Baba gave him, instructions, saying if you are going to do this and pursue this then, similar to the Sufi absolute honesty vow, Baba had different limitations that he placed on that individual. And he gave different examples of extraordinary politicians or leaders such that there wouldn't be anyone in the world of comparable ability to navigate those political waters for like another 700 years (i.e. India's first prime minister, Nehru).

But it isn't that no one should be involved in politics, but it's just such a murky water and such a dangerous path to tread ... the focus I believe with the spiritual path is an individual one rather than a collective focus, per se. I mean when you really focus on approaching the healing of whatever you want to do in the world and everything else by going within...whatever else and *surprisingly* somehow the world is a better place as your world is a better place within yourself. Baba did stress that inactivity or passivity in the presence of injustice is a weakness. So he didn't advocate nonviolence per se ... or you know, even taking up arms or doing whatever if it was what was appropriate. The violence / nonviolence chapter in *Discourses* refers to the weakness involved in not taking action in the face of something which clearly requires that you have to set things correct. But that's different than leading a movement, and I think when you have a group of people, each has their own individual spiritual path ... We don't all necessarily have the same karma or have the same need to pursue something in the world I think. And also whatever we do, the group reflects upon what someone may perceive as Baba's message rather than their own individual spiritual path. And so I think being involved in something like social justice, I don't think the spiritual path necessarily precludes it in any way. The group dynamic needs to be a process where individuals look to their Center, or what we do as a group as a model for their own spiritual walk with Baba....

Sevn: Well I think there are different paths of approach. If you go back to the three different yogas, which apply to many different traditions, there's the path of action, the way of Knowledge, and the way of devotion. I think it's all of them, as Baba says, as Krishna says, as Jesus said, they all lead to the same place. So I don't necessarily think the ascetic is in the wrong by going into seclusion, if that's what his path is. I believe that his actions will lead to the same place, although Baba did suggest that living in the world is a superior approach in this age. I have found that the little things in life sometimes send ripples that are incredible. The little interactions with the people in your life represent the silent workings of people around the world. Not necessarily Baba people, but everybody. The little acts of loving-kindness can send major ripples throughout the world. They often go unnoticed because there's no way to trace it back to one individual. Peace has to start inside a single person. Who they are, what they become will ripple out from there. People will be attracted to them and elevate them to the position that they belong. I don't necessarily think that's any different than the person who silently works as a teller at the grocery store. I think that qualitatively it's just as beautiful and affects the world in the same way as a person participating in larger projects.

Danny: There's something someone said yesterday in terms of this kind of work. And it was, "Don't support the illusions of others." And I feel like so much of spiritual work has to do that. Not encouraging that sense of separation. And I think that's where a lot of Baba's warnings about politics come in, because he didn't want any kind of divisiveness, which is illusion, being encouraged. Perhaps we can do that work, and bring oneness into it instead of reminding people of barriers. And of course that's where, obviously, the forgiveness comes up. {Laughs.} I mean forgiveness, that just knocks the barrier right down, that separation.

Sevn: I don't think there's a way to measure the effects of the power of a lover of God in the world. I mean, I think that monk that chants a thousand [mantras] every day, can have such a pivotal influence on the entire world, the very fabric of it, that it changes everything. You know, much more so than George Bush. And I really believe that.

{Moment of silence.}

Glenn: Baba ran World War II. I don't know to what extent, you know he said he didn't do miracles ... And yet he was doing all kinds of seclusions ... but my sense is he did most of the things I would imagine required running the affairs of the Earth and somehow getting it all done with his human form alone. Using the Mandali, playing games ... moving around ... whatever. I don't know what the heck he was doing or how he did it or what extent involved, whatever, but of course with the use of universal knowledge – using this mast Baba would connect with souls that way ... connect to the invisible radio waves in such a way during seclusion with masts...

to manifest the thinking presence of divinity in a human form. But whatever he did, you know let alone all the other things, you know for so many years ... like our individual human actions, whatever, that reverberate through the entire universe, while we are in human form on the earth. I can only imagine ... those who chant sincerely, or do whatever they do sincerely, run a grocery store or sweep the streets, equally impact the earth ... that's karma yoga.

Danny: I like Payam's point though about us each having our own gifts.

Marnie: ... That's what's so beautiful ... forgiveness. No matter what our gifts are, forgiveness is a means to grow more spiritually and to be more active, even if it's an apparently inactive way in the world.

Doug: You know that eighty million people died during the Second World War, and billions more suffered horribly. We all know this. We have no idea why God allowed this to happen or set it in motion in the first place. The suffering which he allowed is so gargantuan, in fact, that our minds are unable to fathom it, yet it exists as a historical fact. He actually fueled this conflagration and yet we have no idea what he was doing. We think of such suffering and we feel lost, but when we feel this lost, then we have to accept, through our faith, that he knows what he's doing. If he wanted everything to be tripping through the tulips, then that's what it would be, but life seems to be necessarily a series of oppositions, which it has to be in order for souls to progress. So for me I just have to turn away sometimes and wring my hands because I have no idea. This does not mean that I'm not going to help when I can, but if I get too upset about what is happening or has happened, then I'd be like many of the Northern Europeans after the war ... I'd be an atheist. I know many of these people. They say that there couldn't possibly be a God because if there was, he never would have allowed such suffering to take place. A loving God? There is no such thing.

¶ Don: Can I go back to part of what Glenn was saying so it doesn't get false? Just to be very specific, you mentioned you don't know what Baba was doing in all of the seclusions and so on. Actually I had a tremendously important conversation, for me, with Eruch on this, because by that time I'd gotten to know Eruch well enough to appear bonehead stupid without any embarrassment. And so I was very impressed by how many times, when I was under Baba's thumb, placed there by Murshida Martin, then later on meeting him personally, and being very conscious of the addition of the weeks and months that Baba spent in seclusion, sometimes to the extent that he ... refused to catch sight even of the person who brought a dish of food to him, to his funny little enclosure every day.

So to me it was rather earthshaking, because by that time I'd met Baba and I trusted him, so I knew that these seclusions had to be for a very pertinent reason. But from a businessman standpoint, I thought – that's a hell of a way to have to run the railroad.

So I said, "Why is it that Baba – more than any other spiritual figure I've ever even heard of (though I'm not an authority), has ever spent even a fraction of the time in seclusion that Baba did?" You know people bring up, well Jesus Christ was alone in the desert for so and so many weeks. Yeah, but that was once, and I don't know much of anybody else who has spent time [in seclusion]. And then he said a very simple thing that suited my financial bookkeeping mind in the petroleum industry. And he said, "Well, Don, you know, Baba's the last Avatar in this avataric cycle." And I had to admit that I hadn't read that. And so he said, "It's something like a corporate entity which is coming to an end. And before the balance sheets and the closure are formally and legally stated, there has to be a balancing of the accounts. And Baba is the ultimate bookkeeper in Creation, and so when the corporation for the avataric cycles comes to an end, he's got to balance the books. And even for the Avatar that means really a lot of work."

So Baba explained, I guess to Eruch and maybe two or three others — I had never heard it before — that these seclusions that Baba went into were related to that. And I just want to point out that in my mind then that gradually separated very, very much from let's say the function of the New Life.

And although Eruch didn't put this into words, I'm sure a number of you have heard me say that when I finished listening to Eruch's description of the New Life, which he had promised to give me, and did (and we taped it for almost two solid days), and then the women Mandali gave their side of the story, and that was another half a day. And at the end of all of this work, Eruch said, "Well, what do you think of all this?"

And I said, "Well, Eruch, I think it's a fabulous story, but goodness, really I just have to say, how was it possible that you people found the guts and the stamina to stick it out, with all of these things happening, crises and hardships all of the time?"

> The New Life was when Meher Baba set aside his divinity. Don seems to be contrasting that period with Baba's seclusion work where he definitely embodied his divine power and role. – KM

> These tape recordings became the book, *Tales from the New Life with Meher Baba* (Oakland: Beguine Library, 1976).

Eruch just looked at me absolutely flabbergasted, and said, "Well, Don, I failed you then." (And to have Eruch say that to me—I'm sorry if I'm repeating this story for the tenth time, but I hope I'm around to repeat it one day for the hundredth time.)

I said, "Eruch, I do apologize, I chose my words badly, it's not what I meant at all."

And he interrupted me and said, "No, Don, I mean it. I have obviously failed you, because I have failed to give you a real, real feeling of the glory of companionship with the Avatar." And when he said that, I was ashamed of myself that I hadn't picked that up. And secondly, I also felt – good heavens, here in just a simple nutshell, is Eruch, Baba's chief Mandali, giving the essence of what he felt the New Life to be: true, true, deep internal companionship. And then, through the next several months my mind began to put together more and more, and I just had to come to the conclusion that the New Life lived with those choice Mandali was setting down the forms, the ways in the new cycle of cycles, by which humanity would progress and manifest latent consciousness.

And it was such a completely new period that completely new forms were having to be put into place. I've referred to it on occasion rather playfully, but I think very graphically, by saying it was a new homesteading of a new territory of God's infinite consciousness. And I think that is accurate.

> When Don says "setting down the forms" he means archetypally. – LW

So certainly to me, let us say the seclusions of Baba himself were for a rather actually boring settling up of accounts, a very trying period. But then the new cycle, Baba was also responsible for the basics there. And it was just a plain new form. And Eruch had given, as far as I'm concerned, and I think it's dead right, and I think it is tremendously important, that the essence, the key note, of the New Life, of the New Age, of the New Humanity, is based upon really inner-links, real companionship. And for heaven's sake, if you haven't read it, go back and read the last message on the alphabet board.[1]

In that Baba did not speak of companionship but called it inner links – I mean to form inner links with you. I have now formed those links. And they eternally will not go away. My body can go away, but those inner links are there – and boy I know that is true, because I've experienced it again and again and again since Baba dropped the body. It is so indelibly, extraordinarily there, there can be no question of it. And it's I think the most delightful thing I've ever experienced in life – those inner links that remain there.

> Don paraphrases Baba's quote about inner-links. We give the entire message in the end notes.

Then Baba went on to say, "..now it's time for you to form them (inner links) among yourselves in a chain."

And boy, that is a tremendously important statement. So really it goes way, way back to some of the feeling and thinking of Eruch on the New Life, and the glory of companionship and inner links, that I feel

> Meher Baba had tremendous affinity with various Sufi orders, especially the Chishti Order of India and Pakistan. One major concept within all Sufi orders is the 'silsila' (Ar.), (literally) *chain* of spiritual connection, transmission, and power, from teacher to student, going all the way back to Caliph Ali and the Prophet Muhammad (pbuh). – KM

the whole possibility of people now using forgiveness. *And in the long run, forgiveness has to be made on the basis of rediscovering the glory of companionship, even with one's enemy, or the guy who has really cut you up.*

Could I introduce one other word, because I don't think we've had enough challenges today, have we? I think it has to be, for me, an even more fundamental word than forgiveness. Forgiveness is a toughie. But the other word that keeps coming back to my mind ... rather specific event, which I'll describe to you, if you let me have that much time. The word is "tenderness." And I don't know if you have ever felt that tenderness comes into the spiritual equation, or what it has to do with the Path or anything of that sort. I think probably most people think of tenderness simply [as] a mother and her baby. So I'll tell you the specific thing that brought that up so terribly importantly in my own personal experience. And I can't even perhaps give it the dignity of saying it was so and so such and such a time, in the company of so-and-so on such and such a date ... I don't know whether or I was having a simple dream, or whether I was in a semi-awake state, but I found myself in a long, long white hall.[2] No sign of any sort of illumination. No lights. But it was just beautifully, tenderly, simply white. And Baba was to my right. And he was holding my right hand with his left hand. And we were walking down the long white hall. And at the end of it, I didn't ask myself well how'd he get there, how'd I get here with him, what's this all about? I just knew that something important was happening. We walked along. And at the end of this long white hall, on the left hand side, I saw an open door. And as I saw that open door, I knew, in that room, God is sitting. And Baba is going to take me to see God.

As I walked along the corridor with Baba, and started coming reasonably close to the door, it was just like a tsunami. An absolutely incredible wave completely knocked my whole being into a flip of tenderness. And for some reason or another, I could even identify what that tenderness was all about. *And it was tenderness for the human who had to desert the beauty of Oneness and peace and Reality in order to go into this tremendously trying thing of Creation for the sake of God to be able to love.* Because that demanded what Baba has said to us: For love there has to be a lover and a Beloved. And if God is the lover, or if I am the lover, then there has to be separation for love to express itself.

So doesn't it seem crazy, I even realize at the moment it's impossible to understand why infinitude would have to go through

> Meher Baba said, "God is Love. And Love must love. And to love there must be a Beloved. But since God is Existence infinite and eternal there is no one for Him to love but Himself. And in order to love Himself He must imagine Himself as the Beloved whom He as the Lover imagines He loves." (Beacon Hill: Meher House Pub., 1963) p. 1.

sort of a play act of imagination. But it seemed just so real, and I knew that the tenderness of God for the human being, for asking them to go through what was necessary, so that God could love and be loved. And it was a tremendous experience. And I knew from that, that for some reason or another I'd been given a glimpse, really a wallop of an experience, because tenderness was going to be of such tremendous importance in the new age, with the New Humanity, and the New Life. And for some reason, when I began to think of forgiveness, I just knew deep in my bones, that underlying forgiveness, for it to be real, and to have any real impact, must be built upon a sense of real tenderness. End of story. Tenderness for everything. Particularly for one's fellow man. It's even deeper than friendship, companionship. And you might say it's the bones, and the blood of love.

I seriously recommend that you write down the word "tenderness" and the word "forgiveness" and just put some sort of something that links them together, because I think they are absolutely necessary. The one filling out and giving the support to the other. We've got to find forgiveness. But how you experience tenderness is just so terribly important. And again, I would say let's start at home. How many people can you say, when I think of that person I feel tender about them? And I know, when I can say that, that is a very, very, very special relationship. It goes so far beyond so many things that I've always thought were desirable or needful. But tenderness is totally, totally selfless. There's not even room for the concept of an ego in it.

I think it's – I'm ashamed of myself that I've lived so much of my life knowing the word, and yet having absolutely no concept of it. It wasn't till Baba led me by the hand to God's door. (He didn't introduce me to God by the way, just in case you're wondering.) But boy, I really got some essence of something that I think is one of the most important things of my life. And it's never left. I can never be around a human being again without having that relationship transformed by that experience. Just human being together was totally different after that. So, just a small suggestion.

{A long silence.}

¶ Don: Well, I hope I haven't busted up the party here. I've never heard a silence like that before in this group.

Laurent: It's good stuff, Don.

{Silence.}

☙

Sevn: I've noticed that people in my life that I really love, but that I don't have a real tender relationship with, and the fact that there's some difference there.

¶ Don: It's terribly important. When you just think for a moment, reflect on the word, tenderness, usually you know when it occurs. It occurs in a sentence, and you know what tenderness is, and so on. But then if you just say, well I wonder if it has some sort of even deeper, perhaps key importance in life going ahead. Then all of a sudden it hits you, I think when you really stop for a moment, and just calmly, sweetly, tenderly reflect on the word tenderness. Boy, it really hits you with a sock.

Danny: I was telling one or two people recently I was struggling to forgive my parents for some old family issues. And I was really struck by talking to them on the phone, somehow I was able to find within myself a certain amount of calmness and patience with which to deal with them. I don't know if you could quite call it tenderness. But it was certainly a lot more tender than I thought I was going to be able to muster. And it seemed like infinitely more progress was made very quickly in terms of bringing about peace just by being able to project that through my voice over the phone. Suddenly all the ways in which they felt threatened or defensive towards me just disappeared because I was able to bring that sense ... into it. So I wonder how many of these hostile statements that go back and forth between different countries could be avoided if they put the {laughs to himself} right people on the phone. So they don't react that way with each other, or could stop reacting.

Doug: I can remember watching Alan Wagner at the Pilgrim Center in 1983 dressing down one of the Indian workers in the kitchen. I was shocked by what I perceived as a performance which bordered on cruelty. The man simply stood in front of Alan and hung his head. But I spoke with some of the other Western residents there, and they all told me that if one is not that firm, these people simply do not do the work. Alan was not attacking this man on a personal level. He was, rather, attempting to teach this man what was expected of him in his job. I did not know Alan very well and I was frankly embarrassed. We were in their country! But, you know, the explanations which I received from everyone were almost identical.

Laurent: I have a good version of that from Heather Nadel, who I almost worship over there. She's unbelievable. And I was hanging out on the porch of the Pilgrim Center, and some taxi guy pulls up like half-an-hour late for picking somebody up, you know. She came out cursing at him in Marathi, just like taking him to pieces, about – "How could you be late?" and all that. And I was really interested in this, because I was probably nineteen years old and thinking – this is good. And I could tell something wasn't quite the way it appeared to be. And Heather would look at me every now and then and smile, and then go back to doing this. And then afterwards I knew what was going on. She had to play this role for him, you know? And she would ask him, "Why are you late?" And he said, "I left late, I don't have any good excuse," you know, "I just was too late." And she said, "Well next time you can't be late." And he said, "But at least I didn't make up some lie." You know, that's what he was saying to her. "I just told you." And she was playing a role without feeling angry. *She was acting angry.*

Doug: I think Alan was probably doing the same thing.

Danny: Don, we talked about this at the Neskowin meeting – I remember when you were a teacher, you said you learned the difference between the play anger and the real anger, and how, (correct me if I'm wrong), but I think you said, when it was the play anger, it didn't have any kind of negative effect later on, because somehow the children sensed it was not real, or whatever; it didn't have the same reaction with people. You could go right back to the healthy interaction. But with the real anger, then it just becomes more problematic later.

¶ Don: Yeah, I learned a lot about emotions, how they show, and what effects they have, [while] teaching.

Ellie: I just wanted to add that you know we have two cats in the house and I seem to have this overwhelming sense of tenderness towards animals and I have this emotion, this desire to be tender to them because I see such innocence in them. They couldn't hurt me. And although I can say I have a lot of love for…people, I think that I hold back from also bringing in tenderness; instead I love someone and have the expectation that they should want to love me in return. And because human beings as we are, we're a package of things; with animals, it's such a spontaneous flowing of love where actually the ego's not there.

¶ Don: Totally missing. No reservations.

Ellie: Right. This always stops the elements of loving from going to the next stage, which is bringing in the tenderness. Because there's maybe an expectation that when I give this tenderness to this person that it should evoke a…response ..an affirmation in me, my ego, and this is why sometimes maybe I hold back, or I'm too aware of me, so that that beautiful flow doesn't come out, even when I'm loving somebody.

¶ Don: Ellie, I'd like to suggest there is another possibility at least to reflect on, and that is when you are tender, you have absolutely no defenses.

Ellie: Mm-hmm.

¶ Don: Absolutely no defenses. And something within you knows that. And if this is not something that you have done before and found that it did not bring situations where you should have kept some reserves of defenses: unless you have that experience, something way down deeply inside tends to hold back as a safety measure. I think we've got a big supply of tenderness that, by God it is very, very wary about sticking its head out.

Laurent: But that's a fascinating thing that you're saying. That helped me a lot what you just said, by the way. Because if you think about God being behind the door, (and I've thought about that quite a bit since you shared that), God being infinite, and all the qualities we associate with God, has no need to defend itself in any way.

¶ Don: None at all.

Laurent: It's totally confident in its loving tenderness because there's nothing that can harm it. It's pure knowledge of being unable to be harmed in the slightest by anything.

¶ Don: Omnipotent.

Laurent: Omnipotent, omnipresent, everything. So there's no need for defensiveness, and yet in our ignorance, or I should just make it personal, in my ignorance, I keep defenses up. The few times I can think of pure tenderness, like you said, it's with Cyprus, with Aspen, sometimes with my wife, but sometimes not ... {Danny laughs.} So the ego and the defenses definitely come. But why would they ever come with a baby? It doesn't make any sense to be defensive with a baby.

Doug: But you know, with a dog or a cat, you know that you're not making yourself vulnerable by being tender because these little animals are not threatening to us in any way. And you know that Baba did say that fear occurs in the absence of love. There's a little part of us that holds back our tenderness because we're afraid to make ourselves vulnerable, because we don't know if the other person is going to turn around and hurt us. So we hold back, but people are people. Its kind of funny. We actually feel more free to be wholeheartedly tender with a dog or cat than with our fellow humans.

Sevn: The worthiness of receiving our tenderness. ...with a cat is innocent. Even close friends ...you know their little intricacies and dark areas. It's sometimes more difficult.

¶ Don: You know, really to be honest with ourselves, and I realize that it's tough enough to suggest to people to forgive unconditionally, but it's even tougher to support it with real tenderness. So it's a combination of almost impossibles, but I think that's what Baba's lined up for us. And if he has lined it up, it means that the way is there. That someway, he knows what is necessary, and he puts the necessary in place.

Laurent: Well, he's demonstrated it.

¶ Don: Sure, he's demonstrated it.

Payam: ...that's what the Mandali were constantly witnessing ... tenderness.

¶ Don: Mm-hmm.

Payam: The glory of that Companionship – hardship wouldn't matter because Baba was present with so much tenderness all the time.

¶ Don: Yeah.

{The group is silent.}

☙

¶ Don: Well, now forgive me, but let's go back to today's practical challenge, and that is if you were to try to figure out how you would start somewhere with the world's problems that demand some way at least a trial application of forgiveness, where and how would you go about it? And really this is the thing that I want to pose to the group right here and now. And from now until the next time we meet, use your intuitions, and reflect, and write down some of the things that come to you intuitively. How would I go about it, where? Would I take two or three people and say look, let's try to work out a project? Or would you go find a peace committee, somewhere or another, and say I'd like to join up with you, and reflect on what they're doing, and have your own experience of whether you think they're going about things in a helpful, constructive manner. Or whether maybe they haven't even gotten to first base. And it may possibly be that you find nobody in the whole peace committee has ever really done an act of forgiveness. And then maybe what you've got to do is to say – "Hey lookee, I think maybe we're trying to run even before we've even started to walk, or crawl ..." {Audio tape was changed so we lost a sentence} ... inventory of enmity and anger, and tried to come to grips with it. And maybe found to your astonishment, like that kid down in Marseilles did, my God, all of a sudden I see things totally different. And I can do it. And in the space apparently of a few minutes, he changed from total, hopeless opposition, to total, ecstatic acceptance. Now isn't that amazing? You know there's where you see the magic of, what should I say – avataric design and investment. You know they work, an Avatar – I've been around Baba enough to know he worked like hell.

Marnie: You know, Don, in response to your question – for me the world stage ...it doesn't feel authentic. It feels to me, the authentic part, number one, is just cleaning my own house.

¶ Don: Of course. I know that has to be. It has to be. It's where you start.

Marnie: ... I know I can get careless or sloppy in terms of falling into social conversations of wanting to have another person like me, for example ... I'll say something that I know kind of strokes their ego. And I think that's not helpful in terms of just what we're talking about. And so I think that for me the next step is developing that kind of interpersonal honesty, but without judgment. And with really practicing tenderness as the foundation, and trusting that Baba's going to take care of me, even when it's really scary. That's so hard, feeling vulnerable ... but I can deal by understanding that it's coming from God, so really there is no vulnerability ... My expectation is that Baba will create all sorts of opportunities for having to really live it which is really ... to integrate it.

¶ Don: So you take it from the personal to the natural circle close around you, naturally existing. And that's the second stage of the development. I think this is an awfully good suggestion.

Doug: Community.

Sevn: I went through everybody I could think of in my life, and think of who could challenge me to forgive? Or who's going through this process that…And I had to be honest. I really couldn't find anybody that I hadn't come to a fairly decent resolution about, right? And what I did find is that it shifted to this constant experience in my life of recognizing my shortcomings, the things that I do every day that will throw my life into turmoil. And how upset I get when I carry out this habit, or take a certain course of thought or action. And I really realized one of the most challenges for me in my life is forgiving myself for my own imperfections. And I always remember [Hafiz] saying that, you know, we have to learn to "forgive the dream."[3] And I think that's one thing that is difficult for me in my life.

Doug: Yeah, I guess that before it is possible to forgive others, one needs to begin by forgiving one's self.

Sevn: I think it's harder. I think if it's somebody else, it's their fault. {Laughing.}But you know, when it's my fault, it's much harder for me to reconcile.

¶ Don: Sevn, just do a bit of daydreaming with me for a couple of minutes. What do you think might happen if you said to yourself, okay, all right, I've already tried to look around and see maybe two or three or four trial cases where I feel indignant and wronged and so on. And actually after fairly legitimate and careful work, I just can't find one where I know there are problems, but where I haven't already done quite a good deal of facing up and working things out with them. What would happen then if you said to yourself, all right, so I find there's more forgiving that I have to do to myself for let's say the way I handle crises, and kick myself for not being better. And that's probably going to be a lifetime of work. But maybe I'll try an experiment then, of just jumping over into an existing social organization dedicated to some sort of a peacemaking in a wronged situation. Volunteer, and see what happens. What my experience [is] at that level ... your awareness that your own home base is still a very, very active field for forgiveness. Try a two-pronged attack, with the middle part already pretty well under control—the middle part that Marnie had been suggesting, which seems logical in many cases. In other words, to get the project moving. And I think this is a legitimate experiment to try.

Sevn: Yeah, you're right. I think perhaps sometimes…with an independent process, it has no reference. And I think having a point of reference, community experience (would be) very helpful.

¶ Don: Yeah.

{Silence.}

¶ Don: Are there — let's see, we've got now the hope that everybody continues the *God Speaks* intuition project — open ended, to work on. And then we've also got this business of the possibility of suggestions, concrete suggestions when, where and how, to start an actual pushing project for forgiveness. And by implication also a lot of reflection of tenderness, and what is its role, and how real is tenderness in my own life? Or is Stevens on a romantic kick, and that can best be sort of forgotten for now? Does that sound like reasonable homework?

Female Participant: Did you have some ideas about the next time we get together?

¶ Don: Well, by let's say, habit it would be somewhere on the East Coast in roughly six months. Or should we change the rules?

Male Participant: We had two East Coasts last time, so….

¶ Don: Oh, you think by balance two West Coast.

Sevn: No, but you're gonna wanna be on the East Coast, probably.

¶ Don: Well, it's easier for me, I must admit.

Laurent: Well, I know the Griffins were pained that they couldn't join us. And I think Marnie got a card. We came up with an idea that since they had made plans and taken time off from work, and everybody in the Griffin home was greatly looking forward to joining us in Portland, and then when the dates got shifted they couldn't come. It was very sad for them. We had the idea that if we got a card and all signed it and sent it to them with love—

¶ Don: Mmm-hmm.

Laurent: — it might help ease the pain of that. Is that a tender thing to do?

¶ Don: It might ease our pain.

Marnie: It's not a great card. I'm sorry.

Laurent: It's the thought that counts.

Sevn: Can we take a picture and print it out real quick?

Laurent: They can plug it into Mahmoud's printer, yeah. Great.

¶ Don: Golly. …graphics….

Laurent: They're not amateurs. We've got Doug here.

¶ Don: Oh, well, now we've got one of the world's authorities.

Marnie: {To Laurent.} You need to be in the picture.

Laurent: {fake Indian accent} I don't need to be in the picture.

{Group photo is taken.}

~

Marnie: So we might meet in Myrtle Beach the next time, or?

¶ Don: Well, that seems to be a favorite spot.

Danny: I think Salem was an awesome spot.

¶ Don: It has a lot to offer for it. But after all, the last time on the East Coast was Salem.

Danny: No, the last time was Myrtle Beach.

¶ Don: Oh yes, that's right, it was in the Spring after the operation.

Sevn: Everybody could stay at my place, so we'd have plenty of housing.

☙

¶ Don: Well, I think I'm going to pronounce the magic phrase "plumbing department" and disappear for a moment.

Laurent: We have to end on a better note than that.

¶ Don: This is not ending!

Laurent: Oh.

¶ Don: I assume that you're working out details of the next meeting—well, we went a half an hour over at the lunch period, so this would just be evening it up at this point. And we do have a crowded schedule to get through dinner and to the Center.

{Logistics of getting to the Avatar Meher Baba Center in Los Angeles are discussed.}

¶ Don: Well if I leave now ... well, let's have the silence first – shall we?

{Laurent whispers in Don's ear.}

Don {To the group}: Oh boy, such enthusiasm.

{Silence.}

¶ Don: Dearly Beloved Baba, as always it's been a glorious time with you. Thank you. Amen.

~ END OF SUNDAY AFTERNOON ~

Sunday Afternoon Notes:

1. On October 7, 1954 Meher Baba gave his last message on the alphabet board:

"There is no reason at all for any of you to worry. Baba was, Baba is and Baba will also be eternally existent. Severance of external relations does not mean the termination of internal links. It was only for establishing the internal connection that external contacts had been maintained until now. The time has now come for being bound in the chain of internal connections. Hence, external contact is no longer necessary. It is possible to establish the internal link by obeying Baba's orders. I give you all my blessings for strengthening these internal links.

"I am always with you and I am not away from you. I was, am and will remain eternally with you, and it is for promoting this realization that I have severed external contact. This will enable all persons to realize Truth by being bound to each other with internal links.

"Oh my lovers, I love you all! It is only because of my love for my creation that I have descended on Earth. Let not your hearts be torn asunder by my declarations concerning the dropping of my body. On the contrary, accept my Divine Will cheerfully. You can never escape from me. Even if you try to escape from me, it is not possible to get rid of me. Therefore, have courage and be brave.

"If you thus lose your hearts, how will it be possible for you to fulfill the great task which I have entrusted to you? Be brave and spread my message of love far and wide to all quarters, in order to fulfill my Divine Will. Let the words, Baba, Baba, Baba, come forth from the mouth of every child, and let their ignorance be reduced to ashes by the burning flame of my love.

"Come together in order to fulfill my will by taking your stand on Truth, Love and Honesty, and be worthy of participating in my task.

"I give you all my blessings for spreading my message of love."

From *Practical Spirituality with Meher Baba*, by John Grant (Merwan Pub., 1987), p. 216.

2. Don first mentioned this experience with Baba in *Meher Baba's Word and His Three Bridges* (London: Companion Books, 2003).

3. Here is the poem by Hafiz which Sevn mentioned, from the Penguin publication, *The Gift*,

Poems by Hafiz The Great Sufi Master (p.125), copyright (c) 1999 Daniel Ladinsky and used with his permission:

Forgive the Dream

All your images of winter
I see against your sky.

I understand the wounds
That have not healed in you.

They exist
Because God and love
Have yet to become real enough

To allow you to forgive
The dream.

You still listen to an old alley song
That brings your body pain;

Now chain your ears
To His pacing drum and flute.

Fix your eyes upon
The magnificent arch of His brow

That supports
And allows this universe to expand.

Your hands, feet, and heart are wise
And want to know the warmth
Of a Perfect One's circle.

A true saint
Is an earth in eternal spring.

Inside the veins of a petal
On a blooming redbud tree

Are hidden worlds
Where Hafiz sometimes
Resides.

I will spread
A Persian carpet there
Woven with light.

We can drink wine
From a gourd I hollowed
And dried on the roof of my house.

I will bring bread I have kneaded
That contains my own
Divine genes

And cheese from a calf I raised.

My love for your Master is such
You can just lean back
And I will feed you
This truth:

Your wounds of love can only heal
When you can forgive
This dream.

Part II

Forgiveness Intuitions by Don E. Stevens
(Between 2001 and 2008)

This first "forgiveness intuition" was given to Laurent by Don Stevens, from a floppy disk known to Don as "God Speaks Disk 2," as a file titled simply: "Forgive," dated June 11, 2001 at 5:02pm. Italics from the editor.

Forgiveness

When I had the letter asking me if I would write something on the subject of forgiveness, I felt both relieved that someone else felt as I did that this word just had to come to the fore and be carefully considered, but also, I felt a very deep sense of fatigue, because I knew instinctively that this would pose the same sort of problems that the challenge to conscious forgetfulness that is detailed carefully by Dr. Ghani in the Supplement of *God Speaks*, both raises and promises. I use the word "promise," as Ghani gives great impetus to the effort to access and master forgetfulness in stating that it is absolutely necessary to add this attribute to our capabilities to make progress on the spiritual path, and that implies that, if we manage to do it, then a major assist on that tough road will have been accomplished.

Forgiveness for me falls instinctively into the domain of love and unity. It would be difficult to try to pair two more imposing keys to God and Creation than to put these two words side by side. After all, if infinite indivisible unity is a fundamental characteristic of God, and if we reflect that Baba has said very clearly that love is the high road of all roads to Realization, then it is evident that one has mated two horses that are almost bound to win the course. But I must not make the mistake of putting the two words side by side without giving some reason for doing so.

While the civilized world had managed to fight two of the most dreadful wars of all time within short years of one another in the first half of the twentieth century, not to mention all the really horrible massacres kindled in smaller conflagrations, one might be tempted to write off any chance of finding anything approaching unity within humankind, at least for the present. Still, the hopeless optimist is bound to search under the frequent horrors that seem to savage the surface of recorded history, for evidence that all this is in some manner necessary in order that God's Whim to know His divinity consciously might manifest. But even putting into words the challenge, makes clear that this will not be an easy job under any circumstance.

Perhaps one might take a beginning clue to the puzzle from the conditions necessary just to start the process of bringing latent consciousness into a state of manifest actuality. This is, that consciousness is very evidently enlivened by the tension created by opposition or contrast, whichever way one prefers to put it. This is not a lightly suggested definition of conditionality, but one supported by the apex of modern psychology, in addition to the common sense observation of the average you's and I's. A bit of honest reflection shows at once the manner that darkness is brought into a starkly creative role when it is compared to and contrasted with light. Something springs into being that had not been there a moment before, and this we call consciousness of the light state.

From here, it is an easy step to observe that when consciousness has been enlivened by contrast and opposition, then certainly, if unity is to be reestablished as a fundamental for Reality, then something has to fuse diversity back into oneness. And if there is any principle available, it has to be the essence of forgetfulness, deliberate and uncontested, combined immediately after its accomplishment, with forgiveness. The only way these two attributes could function honestly and sincerely would have to be through the rediscovery of love. Otherwise, they remain frozen into eternity in a static condition of immobility.

When the necessary work of contrast/opposition has been accomplished and consciousness manifested, the driving energy stored up in those events in turn has to be dissipated. That is not easy to do, and Baba has given us some very discouraging statistics on the number of reincarnations it takes each individual drop-soul even to get to the first step on the return path to the Reality of unity. But it is eventually started, and that is where deliberate effort can be of help. Forgiveness is certainly part of the secret process that can help immeasurably in doing the necessary.

> "Secrets revealed in Turkey revive Amenian identity: Amenia's sizable diaspora ... is alarmed that the warmth may be misused as an excuse to forgive and forget in Turkey, where even uttering the words Amenian genocide can be grounds for prosecution."
> — by D. Bilefsky in The New York Times 1.10.2010 — LW

Strange, though, that nowadays even the word forgiveness has fallen into a sort of disrepute, as it seems to be more a characteristic of what is called unrealism than of reality. There is certainly not the time nor the space for us to plumb this deep problem of interpretation here, but I am sure that an honest baring of the matter will eventually lead inevitably to the conclusion that there is a profound connection with reality in the act of forgiveness. It just happens to be the necessary precursor to finding the beginning traces again of love, without which oneness is left in the domain of pious theory.

Let me be very blunt, while contrast/opposition is the prerequisite to the enlivening of consciousness, it inevitably leaves a deep residue of the habit of opposition in our lives. And this has to be erased before there is any possibility of finding the road back to infinite oneness. There, Ghani's description of conscious forgetfulness has a key role to play, but even that can only be a non-productive and static state of even eternal waiting if it is not succeeded in some manner by the act of deliberate wiping out of the memory of division and opposition. This is nothing other than forgiveness.

I was astounded by the wisdom of a famous columnist in a leading newspaper when, in commenting on the future to be expected from the atrocities committed in recent wars in several Slavic countries, he gave his formula for any real progress. He said simply, forgiveness. There is no other way, and forgiveness has no logic of justification; It just has to be, and then life can move along once more. It is this same forgiveness that we have to be prepared to find and grant, to others first of all, but finally, to ourselves, for what we have done to ourselves over so many, many lifetimes.

This is from an email exchange between Don and Laurent in December 2004. "MVDBLB" is an acronym Don frequently uses to address Laurent, and "BB" is how Don signs off, which means "Big Bear":

Subject: Whew!
From: Don Stevens <merwan94@yahoo.co.uk>
Date: Wed, 8 Dec 2004 08:48:23 (GMT)
To: laurent@yadrakh.org

Forgiveness

Paris, 3:00am, December 8, 2004

The act of deep internal forgiveness is one of the most important acts in the final termination of deep karma. The essence of real and meaningful forgiveness is the final knowledge of the inexorable destiny of a drop-soul to make a personal individual contribution to the infinite individualized divine consciousness of God. It is the true meaning of the term "destiny," and the special function of the Perfect Ones is to know the destiny of each drop-soul, and in knowing that destiny, to help that drop-soul to complete that destiny. Forgiveness is found and offered from within the reality of oneness, that is often found even unexpectedly within the moment.

The destiny of each drop-soul is always complex and unique, and some parts of that destiny conform to what is interpreted as positive and good, and some parts correspond to what is considered bad and negative. But all the parts of the complex must be lived under the enlivening and creative push of the Whim functioning within the drop-soul, and eventually be freed from compulsion in the involutionary stage of the drop-soul's ongoing. It is here that the essential role is played by forgiveness, as with the mutual act of forgiveness is accomplished the dream of Creation, without which the drop-soul remains ensnarled in successive twists and turns of personal karma.

Herein lies the key to the redemptive act of forgiveness. Pfaff's insight that only forgiveness can free the karmic racial entanglements of the Balkans is a very great truth.

And yet, the final truth is that even the human horror of the Balkans had to be lived through within the infinite consciousness of God, as an inescapable part of Truth. It's redemption and final placement within God's infinite Bliss is through forgiveness.

> William Pfaff is an American author, and columnist for the International Herald Tribune, Don's favorite newspaper. He references Pfaff's editorial in his Prologue to this volume, paragraph one, and in the preceding intuitions. – LW

Your own repeated experiences of falsity and extreme expression of personal ego on the part of even those chosen by Baba to be in his company must similarly be balanced and redeemed finally by your own acts of complete and spontaneous forgiveness. It is only in this manner that you can truly be a true part of your beloved Baba's work. This is the counterpart of unconditional love. It was what you gave Balbeur within an instant, and which he recognized within the instant.

> Balbeur is an acquaintance of Don's in France.

The fact that it was precipitated by his physical reaction to his diabetes was inconsequential. You gave true forgiveness, although ultimately it was an illogical act. He received and benefited by that forgiveness, despite the lack of logical connection, as he had earned it within the accounting system of another part of his life. You must be prepared for such illogical acts of forgiveness in your participation in your Father's life.[1]

☙

MVDBLB: This one was real work and some of it pretty hard

digesting.

... Incidentally, I did not completely level with you on reading your introduction[2] to my big intuition, as when you had told me you always figured the Whim was the motive force in Creation because it was not satisfied with the answer given to "Who am I?", as your intuition on that did not satisfy me at the time at all and still does not, but it was an honest part of the story and I felt therefore should stand. One day we will perhaps have the opportunity to go into that one.

> An Apple Betty is an old fashioned dessert. It is essentially a baked pudding made with layers of sweetened and spiced apples and buttered bread crumbs, usually served with whipped cream. – LW

I think I would love to offer an Apple Betty bear hug today,

BB

☙

This is from a file given to us by Don titled, "Forgiveness 2" and dated: July 2, 2007 at 4:52pm:

Forgiveness cont ...

The fact of the infinitude of God, and therefore of the latency of His infinite individualized consciousness, and the very mechanism of the dream of consciousness existing within the aspects of time and space, results in an infinitude of drop-souls being constantly born through the Om Point[3] and carrying on their lives within all stages of the evolution and involution of consciousness. Thus there are always very young drop souls in the early stages of shaking the knots of sanskara/habit patterns accumulated in all earlier stages of evolution, and this inevitably results in cruel and selfish actions.

Such young drop-souls must be born for this process (of shakings) into some physical location and parentage. The first geographic location to emerge from this "appropriate" stage of space was India, and then the Middle East, and now others in the West, but even "spiritually advanced" areas have blind spots and parents and drop-souls being born within these early pre-involution stages. They can and do commit acts that are quite simply savage and devoid of reason. The only manner of dissipating the effects of these savage acts based on their primitive sanskaras is through forgiveness. This is the burden of the more "civilized." This is the essence of what I[4] said in my words to my Father "Forgive them Father for they know not what they do" for these acts take their birth in the automaticity of the expression of the knots of energy stored from early experience in states of consciousness prior to the birth of the conscious volition of the human stages. Such drop souls are drawn to Oneness and are among the true pilgrims to the sacred sanctuaries and they to leave a certain deposit and are in turned cleansed to a degree. It is this deposit that I have been removing by my journeys with Eruch and meditating[5] there. Also I have revitalized the worlds great religions in my seclusions as well as preparing the new form needed to manifest the new areas of God's latent consciousness throughout the new cycle of cycles. This is the aim of this Merwan lifetime lived in the dream of Creation and not to establish a new religion. I have entrusted a great part of this to you and Sevn and others to bring now to the conscious level of humanity through appropriate means of disseminating my words and finally creating the film on which I spent so much time and effort in early stages of its creation during the early years of my Merwan and Perfect Master stages.

Be true to the trust and added years[6] I have given you for this task and love well the helpers I have chosen to help in this task.

☙

This is from a file given to us by Don titled, "Forgiveness 3" dated September 14, 2007 at 8:30am:

Paris 14/09/07 8:30am

Forgiveness is the ultimate test of the ego. To condemn is the ultimate declaration of separateness. In this incarnation I have reserved for my true devotees the expression of complete forgiveness, first in their own lives, and then in the teaching to others of the example that they are qualified to make for others. Do not confuse my function in this lifetime with the activity I have included importantly in other lifetimes when my lovers have built religions around my words. As I told the Press in London on my first visit in the 30s, I have not come to establish a new religion in this lifetime, but to revivify the world's existing great religions and gather them together like beads on one string. With my repeated visits with Eruch, as he has recounted to you, and the lengthy work I have done repeatedly at those spots and through other means as well, I have cleansed these and other focal spots of great and sincere veneration from much of the residue of hate and competitiveness which has so encrusted them, and readied them to be placed side by side in the great fact of Oneness of all Truth.

> These "focal spots" are the locations Meher Baba directed Don to visit in India, and film for him, which form the itinerary of the India Beads on One String tour. There are other sites as well. – LW

This basic chore of the scouring of the filth of hate and condemnation, which has been such a constant heritage of the relationships so often rampant between religions, must be completed by my devotees and those others they bring to this central task which I have confided to them in this final period of the last cycle of avataric cycles. Let there be no mistake; the assignment I give my true devotees is not that of building more churches and receptacles for the bodies of new believers in Meher Baba nor Jesus Christ nor of the Avatars in still other incarnations, but in preparing through forgiveness of the base for true and complete harmony at the deepest levels of feeling and being.

This has never been done before and will take great insight and patience to accomplish. The problem, of course, is the old one that has existed since the beginning of time: that of the "I" and "me" and "mine" of the ego. Just as the great receptacle of the ego becomes that of feeling one has become religious, so the next great refuge so dangerous to the functioning of Truth in the new cycle of avataric cycles is that the ego will find its haven in the act of condemning those who have deviated in their opinion from the Path of Unity. Instead, they are to be forgiven to allow them their real opportunity to join the surge of true unity that I have made possible in my deep efforts in this direction during my lifetime as Meher Baba.

Do not be confused. True forgiveness is now absolutely necessary to clean out the last dregs of resistance to real Oneness between the great religions themselves, and the reality of this true forgiveness is now to be lived and practised in the world by my devotees as their act of love and devotion to me. There is no other task as central and important as this, which I am entrusting to them and embodying in these words to you.

☙

This is from a file given to us by Don titled, "SUICIDE Bombing" and internally it has written: "Morning Intuition, 2:00am, 25/09/07" and continues:

SUICIDE BOMBING

It is important to remember that Baba's discussion of principles governing the activities of human beings within Creation are intended not only for his devotees, but in almost all cases for the conduct of those who follow religions based on his words in previous incarnations as well. It has come as a surprise to you that the reminder of the danger of a possible fall to the stone stage applies equally to individuals devoted to the teacher's principles when he was incarnated as Mohammed, and they are subject to the same rules of conduct as given in the birth as Meher Baba. Thus, as was given as a specific example by Meher Baba that killing for lust would result in the drop-soul falling to the stone stage and having to repeat all the later incarnations, holds equally for a Muslim.

> In the spirit of truing an intuition from Don, that is not what Meher Baba said about murder for lust. The actual quote from Baba about this is given here: "Those who have acquired extremely bad sanskaras, resulting from deeds like murder for lust, or greed, after death go downwards, into the region of animal spirits, to await a suitable gross form for earthly life." In *Avatar* by Jean Adriel (Santa Barbara: J.F. Rowiny Press, 1947) p. 106. – LW

This becomes very pertinent in the present situations in which so many followers of Mohammed follow a line of reasoning given out by some so-called teachers of the faith in the Muslim sect, that results in their being human bombs and perish in the belief that they thereby earn the right to immediate entry into Paradise.

While such action does not in any manner result in such admission, it is not necessarily true that their motivation is necessarily such that they fall to the stone stage either. This depends on the depth to which they are motivated by deep hate. When this is of a deeply destructive nature, then the drop-soul can fall all the way to the stone stage and have to repeat all of evolution again from that point. However the simple fact of having caused carnage and great loss even of life, the motivation of the drop-soul who has just sacrificed his life is not necessarily of the type of hate nor to the depth which results in the fall to the stone state. But in all cases there is not a shadow of doubt that this act will not give the right to pass to a heaven. In fact, almost certain it is that this act has greatly complicated the further lives that drop-soul must undergo. It is a form of willful suicide, and this always complicates ensuing lives greatly.

This clarification is very important to be made for the sakes of a considerable number of sincere seekers of the Truth at this time, and it is especially important that Sufis, who owe so much to Mohammed, [Peace be upon him and his family.] should consider this a part of their present important responsibility.

༄

This is from a file given to us by Don titled, "Forgiveness 4" and internally it has written: "Intuition, London, 4:30, September 28, 2007" and continues:

Logic and Rationality

In your original presentations of this very key and timely subject of forgiveness you emphasized that it was an irrational act. This needs repetition and careful clarification. It is irrational, as the roots of an important subject such as this, that need the ultimate treatment of forgiveness, are lost in the shrouds of time in large part, and therefore are not subject to an unwinding in a logical manner. It is true that the historical fact of the occurrence that is being considered from the standpoint of forgiveness [is] all too frequently still known and subject to some form of "reparations," but this is very often only the superficial part of the problem. Very frequently the emotional impact of the remembered events is generated by what is often termed "unjustified means of attempting to handle the problem." Often downright cruelty is observed or believed to have been exercised, and from where did that come?

This then is the heart of the real problem which must in some manner be handled, and it is never easy. The real reason for this is that the birth of the cruelty which "needlessly" was brought into the event no doubt originated in the cave-man incarnations of the drop-soul, or even earlier. The instinctive fight for survival has been present in Creation for long ages, and its treasure of stored impressions has been formed and preserved by mechanisms as old as is Creation itself. This means inevitably that they are beyond the reach of factual memory, and only the presently conscious witnessing of their surging and expenditure in action is clear and vivid. The rest, inevitably, is lost in the cloak of time, which in this case is all but impenetrable.

If one pauses for a moment, this fact can give literal meaning to the words uttered by Christ in his agony on the cross: "Forgive them, O Lord, for they know not what they do!" And this does not refer to the physical act of lancing his ribs with a javelin, but rather the emotive energy which surged from a hidden reservoir of hate and rage and was the real source of the wounding thrust. Quite literally, Christ with his infinite store of All-Knowledge DID know the source, but also knew that the soldier did not have the slightest idea of whence came the explosive energy which had swung the wounding lance.

The enquiring mind of the one searching for the true bases of motivation, and also the moral truths of the matter under consideration for possible relevancy, is certainly thrown at this point into a serious moral disarray. Where does the real opposite energy then come from which would be needed to resolve once and for all this great "wrong" that has occurred, and for which we are proposing a possible blank check, but issued on whose account in Creation?

Meher Baba has explained the fundamental principles clearly by which Creation and its creatures function, and such a clear debt is not to evaporate into just clean air without justification and without real equalization in some manner. And we need to be honest on this basic account before going into the delicate enough problem of forgiveness which must be established on firm moral ground.

Meher Baba has described to you personally the mechanisms involved when on occasion he granted you what he called simply "his Grace." He added, to answer your questioning and slightly unbelieving look, "But Don, Baba would not have given you that Grace if you had not already earned it."

There you had it, almost, but there were still a few tricky maneuvers you sensed and had to straighten out eventually. One of these mainly was the question of identity of the "earning" actions. Did they have to be acts in the same area of human activity as those being balanced by the Grace? Or was there some miraculous transference between accounts that could be brought to bear?

Baba solved that one for you by putting before your eyes a statement he had made before an attentive scribe, that one of the capabilities of a Perfect One was that they could transfer values between different accounts, thus taking from an oversupplied account and balancing out an undersupplied account. This you saw at once as being one of the greatest boosts to going out and searching for an account balancer right away.

So obviously there is a manner of balancing out even of accounts completely hidden to the normal eye dating back even to the start of Creation, but it does require the involvement of a very special qualification, that of being Perfect, which is God-realized. But there are always several of them on hand, and no doubt one of their preoccupations must be that of balancing out of these even prehistoric accounts, without which the particular account under question can never be closed, and that clearly cannot be the case. Hence a pretty busy schedule for the Perfect Ones sitting at their desks in Creation.

All of this discussion of account balancing is only one aspect of the currently key importance of forgiveness and how it functions, and above all, what the present position may be in all this of the devotee of Meher Baba. There will necessarily be a number of intuition sessions devoted to this matter which is immediate in its importance to the Avatar.

☙

This is from a file given to us by Don titled, "Forgiveness 5" and internally it has written: "Intuition 8:30am September 29, 2007" and continues:

Forgiveness and the whim

As the subject of forgiveness has come up repeatedly in group meetings in recent times, you have been very much tempted to say whimsically that it has run through your mind that one has to be crazy to be tempted to forgive an important act that has occurred in one's life and not received any attention by way of apology or offer of reparations on the part of the doer. In fact, the act of forgiving is ultimately based on a decision which has a very large support which is buttressed by absolutely no logical process nor wish to do a balancing of good and bad. Usually such an act is open to being judged as irrational and therefore a bit or a very big bit crazy. Certainly one feels exposed to criticism by even good, trusting friends for making such a move.

While we have already traced through some of the ethical background of where the motivation and especially emotional energy comes from in many acts of great cruelty, still it would be rare that all this is worked through by a hurt individual before considering forgiveness as the next necessary step in dealing with the hurt or outrage present.

But to one who has been introduced to the fact of Oneness in Creation and human living and has experienced some beginning sense of its importance and above all of its power, it is not too great a price to pay for establishing Oneness in an important domain of one's relationships. There is a great sense of discomfort when separation is the chief flavor of the daily diet, and this is what dwelling on hurts produces. The individual finds the mind irretrievably attracted back to the source of the wrong that one feels has been done, and blame and even serious anger blaze up without any means evident of how to control or even live with them.

If one has any sense of what one may expect from life in the way of balance and good humor and human warmth, then finally one becomes discontented with one's own discontent and begins to search for an acceptable antidote to apply to the illness one feels.

Although it is extremely distasteful even to contemplate, an act of forgiveness soon suggests itself, usually only to be discarded at once, at least temporarily.

The usual course of action often is however to decide to try suggesting some rational compensation on the part of the evil one. More often than not, this is immediately refused by the negative actor in the drama. They justify their actions with solid distortions of the truth one knows so well exists at the base of all this nonsense. More often than not, the situation becomes greatly inflamed by this effort at resolution, and one may well retreat after delivering some resounding condemnations, which in turn become part of the whole enduring fracas.

Various attempts to be rational and find a "balancing" action that the evil one may be persuaded to make are often made, and usually a great deal of fruitless time is spent in which nothing in the way of progress is achieved. All this is carried out in the name of being honest and arriving at a solution in which the compensating price is willingly paid somehow by the wrongdoer. The risk of further explosions with attendant further harm to the already discarded Oneness goes on and quite often the ground is laid for a classic interfamily or international incident that is then expanded to others not originally concerned, but [who] come to feel their rights are also involved. These classic disputes can carry on over evening visits and speeches from the public forum for centuries, with absolutely no progress being made towards their resolution. Thus great stores of time, energy and happiness are consumed and hate and dissension spread far beyond the original participants.

Somewhere about now someone suggests a magic formula in which original rights are preserved, but the price paid by the wrongdoer is believed to be small enough to be acceptable to him. Negotiations are set up and time and energy are expended, too often again with no real progress. Or the magic formula might be accepted, but soon found within the wronged camp to be insufficient or mistakenly conceived originally as being sufficient unto the cause. This is the beginning of an endless play of trying to reconcile the varied opinions of the team players, and often the same factioning occurs on the opposing side also.

Sooner or later someone suggests the only way to proceed is to forget the whole thing and trust time and confidence building projects to reestablish the peace and harmony that used to reign in almost forgotten times. This is really the work of the Whim, for only sheer inventiveness based on no logic whatever could ever conceive such an action. But it is the time now to begin to recognize the presence in all of Creation of the Whim, usually latent in each drop-soul, but present nevertheless. It is capable of having such a whim, and even getting those completely tired in the head with all the effort and no progress for so long, to try something completely different.

Seriously, it is now the time to recognize the Whim, its presence, and its extraordinary capacity to suggest the non-rational and completely new, and make it stick. We have not taken the presence of the Whim as a fact, and a powerful tool to be used consciously in these intractable situations which have defied centuries of "time curing all." It is time now to contemplate the resource of the Whim that exists in all of us and test the results that flow unexpectedly from the totally non-rational in situations like this. And it is the Oneness that results that is the unexpected visitor who comes through the door, and IS HE WELCOME!!!

And forgiveness? It is very much like love, in that it is unconditional. Consult the Whim deliberately before plunging [in] with forgiveness, but if it says simply, this is a case for the application of forgiveness, then don't ask the Whim "why?" Just do it and enjoy the sense of Oneness that surges when it is released by the sincerity of your decision.

ல

This is from a file given to us by Don titled, "Forgiveness 6" and internally it has written: "Intuition, afternoon Saturday-Sunday morning, September 29-30, 2007" and continues:

Forgiveness - the Avatar

Brendan did you a great service in questioning so sharply as is his custom concerning the background of the source and the realism of the process of forgiveness which has so occupied the center of your attention for some weeks now. And your own impulse to plumb your memories of experiences with Baba which relate to the subject, of which there are a very great many spread over the years, is a daunting but quite possibly a very productive task to undertake. It is certainly abundantly clear to you by now that Meher Baba surrounded his own activity in this area to a control on news relating to it which was unusual even for Meher Baba. This should be an indication of the delicacy of the task you wish to undertake.

First, an inspection of your own resources and the manner of their use. The principal one of these has been the series of motion picture films that Baba himself planned in detail for you to take, but without giving you any clue to their ultimate purpose. None of the mandali were taken into Baba's confidence in this regard, even those such as Donkin and Adi Sr. whom Baba involved directly in your presence in the planning of these journeys.

The second resource and centrally important was Eruch's having revealed to you that those places Baba had you film were the same locations that Baba had Eruch take him to visit repeatedly, and completely anonymously, with none of the mandali being brought into the picture even by Eruch. He had never told anyone of these visits during which, repeatedly, as he said, Baba entered into deep meditation for hours, and then terminated without so much as a comment to Eruch about what he had been doing nor why. But it was Eruch's gift to your involvement in the process to confirm that they were the same sites that Baba had you film, also without the least hint of the purpose of the project.

The third and also key to understanding what was and had been going on was the second and third times Baba sent you to Kailas Temple in the Ellora Caves area. The first time had been with Adi Jr. and Francis Brabazon early in your visits to India. The second was with Eruch accompanying you as your guard at sunset, and you instructed by Baba to go to the main temple room which you knew well by then, and to sit quietly there until you felt you had finished. What you were to do, and what you might have finished, Baba gave you not the slightest hint, and it was only after the chest expansion and resulting pain you felt there had reached the limit of your tolerance that you left the temple room and returned to Eruch.

To his query of what had happened you recited the story of the gradually developing sense of pressure within your lung cage until it became unbearable, so you left. You had no sense of fright or threat to you personally, but only concern that you not undergo physical damage. Eruch had no comment at all, nor did Baba when he queried you the next day, nor did he ever return to that visit in conversation throughout the years until he dropped the body. It was an important experience, but the nature of which remained a complete mystery to you.

The third visit to Kailas was with the first pilgrimage[7] group as you called them, who were study group members, mostly from Europe, who had requested through the years to visit with you the various sites Baba had asked you to film. Their request was simply stated as that these sites obviously were important to Baba, and therefore they were important to Baba's devotees as well, and now they wanted finally to be taken to visit them.

This third visit to Kailas produced the key realization on your part that the force in your chest when Baba sent you there with Eruch was simply a more acute physical sense of a similar experience you had had on several occasions with Baba and he had done something during a visit he was making to a group and performed some act of a spiritual nature during which you felt physically the force of his Avataric power in action. By this time you had come to know this physical sensation well, and as you leaned against the pillar in Kailas while the majority of the pilgrims went on to the other caves in Ellora, you felt this similar sensation, mostly in your rib cage. On previous experiences with Baba you had felt it more generally throughout your body, but you recognized it as Baba's spiritual power in motion and felt great joy in having identified finally your experience of long years before with Eruch.

Your own fourth experience relating to these films Baba had you take occurred when you were leaving the Hammersmith Hospital in London after recovering from acute dehydration and also a Salmonella infection resulting from that first pilgrimage to Baba's filmed sites. Suddenly you recalled Baba's words to the Press in London on his first visit[8] there in the 30s. He told them that he had not come to found a new religion, but to make the truths of the existing great religions available to the worthy devotees by revivifying those religions, and gathering them together like beads on one string.

Your own relationship to this key concept of the common base of Truth in all religions goes back almost to your childhood and has been important and recurrent. You have always wondered what Baba might have done or intended to do, but perhaps had been prevented from doing in this incarnation. And now you knew from your own experiences with Baba that undoubtedly he had quietly done a tremendous amount of investing of Avataric power and time in just this very project. It was a moment of great power and importance for you, and your sense of joy was completely unique in your experience. And no wonder, for it was the culmination also for the Avatar of long reflection, observation and exercise of the Avataric Whim, to bring such a complex and important act so far in this lifetime. And it had to be a momentous moment in your life too.

Now it is time to leave the important subject of your personal resources to use in developing the logic of the story of the Avatar's creation of the framework within which the beads came to the stage of collection on one string in this Avataric era, and what of that job has been accomplished and what remains to be done now. This is the delicate part of this story, and you must set it completely truthfully and clearly in the realm of having been constructed in your mind on some important facts based directly in your involvement in the story by Baba himself. But it must also be completely clear that you are dependent for important parts of what must be the glue of your story, upon inferences you have made with your own very active and creative Whim, and not through some magic of occult transmission [from] the Beloved.

༄

This is from a file given to us by Don titled, "Forgiveness 7" and dated, October 1, 2007 at 5:44pm:

Forgiveness 7

The manner in which the Avatar enters into the functioning of Creation is one of the most important and delicate subjects one may deal with. It calls for careful reflection before doing so and the observance of a type of honesty which goes considerably beyond the normal ranges used or even achievable by the human being. What we will attempt to set out today will tax the capabilities of intuition and your own care in sensing what is completely honest, at least in its creative goal.

Meher Baba himself has laid out rather simply in words the origin of the Avatar and his continuing role within Creation. The Avatar is, as he has stated, the first drop-soul to achieve God-realisation within Creation, and he remains the Avatar throughout the duration of Creation and continues to take rebirth[9] in his role of supervising the rogress of the human race towards realisation of the Truth, which is God, throughout that reach of time and space.

All of the functioning of the Avatar is situated within what Meher Baba has also made very clear as being that Creation, which is not God, but is nevertheless contained as a dream within the infinitude of God. Having used that word, it is necessary at once to caution that, unlike a human dream in most circumstances, the dream of Creation fulfils the change of the latency within God into manifest aspects of His infinite consciousness. The mechanics and details of the manner in which the Avatar carries out this incredibly complex and necessary task are left to the creativeness of the Avatar, for which he is well-equipped through his own Whim. This is identical to God's Whim, as the Avatar, as is true of all else, is a facet of God.

The second great principle of the Avatar's functioning in Creation is that each facet of the dream, as it is only a dream and came from Nothing and therefore must return to Nothing, is that no part of Creation may be left in an unbalanced energy state, as energy also is Nothing and returns to Nothing.

Each time the Avatar is reborn into Creation it is to restore some aspect of Creation which has threatened to slip seriously out of balance. This would involve the process of Creation having to undergo a considerable and complex repair job which would seriously interfere with the productive functioning of Creation in manifesting God's latency into manifested and creatively functioning Being. When the Avatar sees some aspect of Creation threatening to slip into a serious problem, it is his job to institute repairs at once through the placing en route in physical Creation of the necessary adjustments.

One of the most important recent corrective actions has concerned the manner in which spiritual energy is used. Energy of course is not a reality but part of the dream, and a great deal of the energy within Creation is utilized in the mechanics by which latent consciousness is manifested and becomes as it were living consciousness. Another such important change within the dream of Creation is that which produces the complex situation in which the indivisible Unity that characterizes God is embellished in a manner in which Love may be expressed. This, as Baba has pointed out, requires that there be a lover and also a beloved, which risks an impossible fracturing of indivisible Oneness.

But that is another lengthy story, so let us return to energy associated with the modification of latent consciousness into manifested consciousness.

As the barriers to progress on the part of the human drop-soul are made up of impressed energy accumulated in lifetimes of existence of the drop-soul in Creation, to effect their disappearance necessitates large quantities of energy being applied in the involutionary[10] stages of life. When the Avatar finds that the energy necessary for this process is largely being wasted outside this goal, he institutes a device for correcting it.

You have been very conscious of one of these corrections which Meher Baba instituted during your lifetime, and which has been surprisingly effective. This is what is epitomised in his "Don't worry, be happy" slogan which gained such fame so rapidly, and has been singularly effective in restoring the energy balances required.

A second one of these corrective fixes of the Avatar has been aimed at the large proportion of devotional energy wasted in religious wars and guru competition. This is the essence of the "Beads on One String" project as you call it. The Avatar apparently noted that increasing amounts of devotional energy were being fruitlessly expended in religious wars and mistaken spiritual goals set up by quasi-authoritative divines. It appears that to correct this important diversion he spent large amounts of time in meditation at key locales involved in order to right the energy patterns, with only Eruch standing by to watch over him as he did this. The energy and form status of this correction is now in place and it is only necessary, as you and a few others have divined, that it be massively backed through a process of forgiveness for the thousands of atrocities committed through the centuries in the name of God.

☙

This is from a file given to us by Don titled, "Forgiveness 8" and internally it has written: "Intuition, continuing from October 2 until October 4, 2007, London" and continues:

When, Where and How

Don, when you wrote down those three words, When, Where and How when you realized there must be a break of several days in this series of intuitions on Forgiveness, you realised that exploring this part of the plan for Forgiveness would be equivalent to jumping into a complex new area of our use of our intuitive communication, and dealing with a complexity of interweaving matters that are only now beginning to be sufficiently established in modern thinking and formalizing processes. To put it very simply but in its stark basic form, to deal adequately with the subject of handling long centuries of religious animosities and attempting to use the little understood act of forgiveness as a principal method of treatment means a public education process such as has never been attempted on anything on a global scale such as would be required. Nor has an educational project of any size ever contemplated considering such newly introduced areas of thought as habit patterns in the context of the sanskaras in which Meher Baba has given them far greater form and understanding of their conservation and history in the individual human being.

Add to this the scope in time of the problem to be handled, which is at the very least some thousands of years, even millions of years, if one traces back into early evolutionary forms. Then, finally, imagine the complete lapse into the unknown of assessing the manner of treatment of this complex, largely hidden in the recesses of forgotten time, with a technique you label bravely "The power of cleansing of the Oneness released by the act of unconditional forgiveness," and you have something which, just to try to define and put it into words, boggles even the highly gifted mind.

Enough said on the scope and newness of what we are now about to launch into. But it had to be put in honest and clear words, as you owe it to your companions whom you involve confidently in such challenges to put the scope of this project in clear, honest terms, so they will have some idea of the challenge they face.

In this first intuitive session on the H(ow) W(hen) and W(here), the HWW of forgiveness and the base of Religious Unity, let us assume for now that public education worldwide is one of the essentials, but it must be based on WHAT?

Here there is no substitute for "Personal Experience," and that goes back to the first learning stage you have already put to several study groups in France, each time with stunned reactions of even complete revolt on the part of steadily calm and rational persons you have known for some years. This has been due to the fact that you have pointed out the honest fact that the origins of the actions to be forgiven are almost always lost in the centuries of time passed since the original events. Also, your very difficult to digest second point is that even if one can establish some of the originating facts, the really heart core of the emotional drive which motivates the actions often to such cruel dimensions are a product of ancient experiences dating at least to the cave-man era of the history of a drop-soul's evolution, and that is truly lost in the shadows of time and reincarnation.

This is the central point, as you clarified so tellingly for Christ's words on the cross, appealing that they be "forgiven, for they know not what they do." And the life and death cruelty of the battle for subsistence in the early events of the evolution of form of the drop-souls are truly lost, and it is only the retained force of the emotions of those events that remain etched and seared into the depths of the unconscious storage of the individual.

The reasoning mind of the modern individual is lost in front of such considerations. And yet, what is to be done? Does one stay paralyzed and motionless and let repeated cruelty repeat itself endlessly because a straight lineage of cause and effect is not available, and even if it were, not subject to a "reasonable" solution? This is the dilemma that clearly the Avatar decided must be smashed in some manner and its energy content translated or dissipated so that it will no longer remain endlessly boring away for long ages at the very structure of enlightened perfecting of consciousness, which had started, and was persisting despite all the clamor and destruction everywhere.

When one tries the totally illogical and unreasoned experiment to forgive, unconditionally, and experiences the unexpected and powerful results attendant on such action, this gives the base for a noble process of further and broader usage of this daringly new technique. This can at least be the beginning of a rationale of technique and refinement of procedure that can certainly be expected.

But this is only the tiniest beginning of development of an entire new field of social experimentation and discipline. The first thing needed is then a syllabus of experimentation to be applied, and then a technique of applying the results to the masses who have been infected with varying intensities of hate and rejection.

Not least among the operational unknowns is how is forgiveness to be applied, and then a stunning question, how practically are its effects to be judged? Is there a measurement that can be made or even devised for the effectiveness of the operation?

Even the asking of questions such as these can easily result in a paralysis which risks the grinding to a halt of the very process that has been started. Clearly, the start must be on a basis that forgiveness, in simple original actions, produced a result that is desirable, and that this must be followed by the very principles of investigation and efforts to find the measuring and effects achieved which will allow quantitative evaluation and judgment of the effects.

It seems quite clear that one may well be on the border of starting an entirely new area of human research, and in a field which is crying for effort to improve a deplorable thicket of important unresolved conditions in which so-called civilization must live for the present, but hopefully not indefinitely.

Let us leave the matter for now and return later to some of the clues that we may unwittingly have unearthed for effective progress in the technique of forgiving, in our dealings with other hints the present Avatar may have given to the modus operandi on Forgiveness and the fact of the Unity of Truth. These are indeed concepts which it is needful to investigate in order to judge whether it is the time to clear them of the inaction of centuries so that they may begin to breathe and live creatively.

There is a great deal of accumulating evidence that the Avatar himself spent quietly a great deal of time and energy on the bases of these precepts. If he has deemed it time to do so much, then it is not too much to ask of ourselves that we begin to apply real effort to the question of their When, Where and How?

☙

This is from a file given to us by Don titled, "Forgiveness 9" and internally it has written: "Forgiveness 9, All day October 5, 2007-10-05" and continues:

Forgiveness 9

It was sad to sense the dispirited manner in which you ended the intuition session yesterday, and this is very unusual for you, as even when the issues are daunting you take them as an exciting challenge normally. But on this occasion it was evident that the size and nature of the unknowns to be dealt with had reached a record for your experience. But think for a moment of the nature of situations the Avatar must face in his unique task, and often without any hint of anything comparable in past experience. Yet he must face them and find the inventiveness of his Whim nevertheless capable of handling the necessary.

Remember, although you do not have the responsibility of the Avatar, nevertheless you have exactly the same characteristics and resources available to you, but it is just that they have never yet been challenged to the extent that his have been for many thousands of years. Even so, he comments at times as you know that God has been pleased with what he, the Avatar, has done in an especially rough situation. Ask to borrow a bit of his courage!

Even as the scope of the unknowns began yesterday to become clear to you, it was good to see that nevertheless they stimulated you and you saw immediately that your contact with Baba and the tasks he gave you to handle under his direct supervision had uncovered methods and avenues for exploration that you felt could be very helpful in working on unconditional forgiveness, and when, where and how it is to be applied to the great complex of religious hatreds. Let us review for a few moments some of those signposts that have always fascinated you.

The first of course is your own adopted ability to follow Baba's advice to humanity rather late in his physical life to establish inner links with one's fellow seekers. When you reread this "Last Message on the Alphabet Board" after some years of not coming across it after your first early perusal of it, it felt like renewing a wonderful old friendship to you. By then you had become convinced of the cardinal importance of forming real inner ties to important people in your life.

Marriage of course is one of the oldest and best classical means of establishing true inner links and fighting to retain them when they are threatened, as they so often are by the crises of daily life. They are absolutely essential to establish the group insight and effort which is necessary for resolving both personal and group problems as they are experienced in every great goal that one encounters on the spiritual path.

The frequency with which Baba utilizes the word "individualized" in relation to life in Creation also came as a great discovery to you and has been central in your understanding of the contribution of each drop-soul during the long adventure each one leads in physical creation.

The irreplaceable and enormous importance of the contribution of the individualized experience of the separately functioning drop-soul in the dream of Creation, rather than being a tragedy and to be erased as soon as possible is to dwarf the true richness which is brought by the aspect of individualized functioning. True, it has a deep challenge involved also as in the midst of this activity there lurks the continuing problem of the ego, and this is not to be forgotten at all. Still, it can be handled, and meanwhile the dream of separation produces the richness of design and the functioning of love which were and are necessary to the completeness of God Himself.

The central importance of stores of energy and its proper conservation and use has been a constant theme in your life, and greatly emphasised by Baba as you carried out various projects for him. This has been brought to a crisis stage repeatedly, and the lessons you have learned will be used to the fullest for the enormous pits of emptiness which religious enmity and cruelty have opened up before humanity at every turn. They are not just to be avoided, but actually filled with creative energy and beauty for a real solution to the yawning caverns excavated by ego and then filled by hate in the bloody wars that the ego drive of the drop-soul has created so lavishly.

There is a great store of beauty yet lying unused and unappreciated, and it will be wonderful to see the beginning use of these stores in time and creativity allowed when freed from the demands of hate and misappropriation.

This is from a file given to us by Don titled, "forgiveness 10" and internally it has written: "Intuition, London, 04:30am October 6, 2007" and continues:

Hate, Revenge

Hate and revenge are two more of the key words involved inevitably in the process of forgiveness, and it is not possible to deal effectively with the mechanics and manner of applying forgiveness to human problems without an effort to understand how both hate and revenge arise. There is the very old saying, "An eye for an eye and a tooth for a tooth."

The implications are clear at once to any human being old enough to remember and observe and decide. If I lose an eye or a tooth or some similar member of my body or among my possessions, then in some manner I have the right, so it would seem, to exact a penalty of an eye or a tooth in recompense. This is considered basic justice, but it has, one must admit, become somewhat obscured or even confused by an increasing demand that the circumstances of the loss do have some bearing on the compensating rights.

The fundamental principle of karma is in fact very generally speaking based on a somewhat similar equation, in fact the very nature of Creation is poised on a similar concept that everything starts with the creation of equal quantities of opposites, and that essentially, over time, that balance is demanded through the very functioning of events surrounding each human being. Hence each experience and the values inherent in each happening are alternating; thus if I am killed in one lifetime I must effect a comparable killing in another lifetime. And if I am rich in one incarnation I must be poor in another.

Thus if I covet something in this lifetime and go so far as to steal it, then in another lifetime I must undergo being stolen from as a balancing karmic action.

In this sense, it is difficult to label the balancing karmic act as one of revenge, as the principal actor in the original stolen action and the balancing stealing operation are almost certain to be different persons altogether. However, this is not necessarily so, but just likely, considering the passage of time and space.

While karma is spent in this gross universal manner, it is obvious that there may be other events produced which will have further complex consequences. Thus revenge ends almost without exception to be very personalized and linked directly to a given personality, while hatred tends to be far more generalized, although often tied to a massive operation involving hundreds and thousands of individuals, such as in a war.

How then can forgiveness operate in such important sources of great expenditures of psychic energy and be prevented gradually from perpetrating further and still further great wastes of psychic energy?

The problems of balances and complex book-keeping involved no doubt would paralyze the very best mathematical mind in existence, and yet apparently such a system of accounts and balances exists naturally and functions automatically within Creation. The practical question then becomes one of what effective action can the conscientious seeker take to help right a situation which has gradually resulted in increasing waste of creative energy in wars, revengeful massacres, and hatred of a race? Or stubborn refusal to contribute towards a society that one feels to extract continually more from oneself than one gains by hard work and has to pay into society through various means of taxation?

Perhaps the first rule that might be suggested is that one not insist on seeing the direct line that connects oneself to the situation in need of rebalancing, but simply assume it is part of one's total social responsibility, and be prepared to make a payment in good faith. This calls for a considerable enlightenment, and is not by any means inevitable. When individuals extract in large numbers more from a social good than they contribute, then the society so to say becomes bankrupt and the mechanisms necessary for its continued existence fail. Gradually a degenerate social whole is produced which increasingly falls apart and produces an environment that is judged to be in need of anything up to armed revolt or further.

But all this is rather far from the far more narrow and identifiable wastage which Meher Baba is apparently aiming at in his collecting of the world's great religions like beads on one string. However it is a similar situation of imbalance of values and must be seen as part of the whole of social income and outgo.

Nevertheless, for each individual who cares about God and one's relationship to Him, it is very important to identify personal situations in which hate and revenge operate, as these are among the first priorities for starting the cleaning up in one's own back yard.

☙

This is from a file given to us by Don titled, "forgive counterpart" and internally it has written, "Paris 14 November 2007, 8:30am" and continues:

Forgiveness Counterpart[11]

It would not be possible for an act of cruelty to produce a problem if there were not a counterpart sanskaric knot[12] in the nature of the one on whom the cruel act is perpetrated. This fact runs almost completely contrary to the unconscious allocation of responsibility and blame that are made. The one who originates the cruel act is judged as clearly and totally guilty and the injured one as the recipient of a clear act of injustice. But the workings of karmic law [are] far more discerning and bring about a meeting of apparent doer and receiver which in truth are far more balanced in each of the central elements of an act which produces an event.

Human events are always the result of a complex of sanskaric forces and often these are almost impossible to identify even by those most intimately involved in the succession of events which are antecedent to the physical actions and results which become the history of the happening on which attention is then focused.

The most common retort when damaging action has occurred is that "I did not mean do that to you," or "I would not have done that to you if you had not pushed me into it, so it is as much your fault as it is perhaps mine."

From there the story can become long and complex, with each side seeking to justify its actions by demonstrating the other party as having been the real cause through their actions at an early date in the train of events associated into the relevant forces collected into a building structure of resentment. Attempting to trace, understand and assign just blame in almost any complex of human actions demands a wisdom and honesty that are all too rare, and also subject to rapid efforts to hide and forget one's own actions and motives to present a watertight case for one's own virtuous motives and behaviour.

However, this by no means exhausts the really pertinent causes of behaviour. Meher Baba has given a major new understanding of the nature of sanskaras and their storage mechanism in his writings in this incarnation, and the implications of the drop-soul's mental body storage facility reaching over thousands of incarnations present staggering implications for understanding the true extent through time and space of the historical background of even simple human decisions and action. Each drop-soul is provided with an incredible storehouse of form and energy situations which are awakened in circumstances similar to those in which the original memory was formed. And these can be stored and not erased or lost in the slightest through thousands of years, to be awakened as it were in a circumstance which suddenly finds itself energised in a completely unexpected manner and pushing to express itself in certain well defined manners which have nothing to do with any remembrable act in the individual's experience.

To give a scenarioed example, it is perfectly possible that if I hunt and kill a deer in the mountains and another hunter from another hunting party thinks a shot he has just fired at the same deer [has killed it], but unseen by me, then walks over and begins to haul off the deer I just shot, the anger I feel and the instant retaliation I take even by force is very likely to come from a long-dormant similar situation when I was a cave-man trying to bring home meat for my family from a desperate hunt in the middle of the winter. Then a neighbour caveman in similar desperate straits runs over and tries to snatch my deer.

Perhaps the scenario here may seem far fetched, but it can illustrate the manner in which stored form and energy can enter into events happening long after an original stored memory and still roll out as if it were the continuation of something that had happened just a few minutes ago. Visual memory is very unlikely to match and recur, but the emotional content is surprisingly vivid and rapid to express itself.

We are only now in a position to understand the degree to which our present actions are energised and pushed into physical action with an emotional content that seems to have been manufactured just at the present moment. Even if the person injured is a very highly developed modern product of long civilizing influences, their reactions are often powered by events experienced and stored long decades and even centuries before the present action. You have seen on several occasions how individuals you have known for decades and treasured for their spiritual understanding and actions, have on occasion suddenly done something unexpectedly which struck you as barbaric and totally inconsistent with your own long term knowledge of their character. It is sometimes termed "a blind spot" in the nature of a very "civilized" person, but in fact it is an ancient and very primitive sanskaric knot which has not yet been exposed to a similar environmental stimulation before, or at least, not often enough to have gone very far in exhausting the knot of stored energy.

This was the true content of Christ's call out to the Father when the agony of the javelin thrusts while nailed to the cross caused him to cry out, "Forgive them, O Father, for they know not what they do."

In truth, the memory of the event stored has long disappeared and only the awakened physical form of an act is powered by the energy stored at the original time of the forming incident. It is an unnerving event to witness oneself act in a manner that one recognizes as primitive, and without justification in terms of present circumstances, and yet one has done it and is accountable for the act.

༄

This is from a file given to us by Don titled, "Tenderness" and internally it has written, "Morning Intuition, Paris, November 16, 2007 12:30am" and continues:

Tenderness

In your next blog, describe God's tenderness for humanity for what they go through in the dream of Creation, and the agonies of separateness, in order to manifest the latency of love in the infinite individualized consciousness of God. I took you by the hand some years ago along the white hall leading to what you felt correctly to be the door to where God our Father was sitting, and you felt the intensity of this tenderness powerfully and have never forgotten that experience. Now it is time to see that all this I have anticipated long ago in the original Discourse on Love in the words, "Love is the reflection of God's unity in the world of duality. It constitutes the entire significance of Creation."

Now it is the time when these words can be continued. It is through the processes present in Creation that the latency of love in God can manifest and which then can be expressed within the principles of Creation as tenderness. In the past it has been assumed that it is the act of sex which is the means of expression of love as manifested in God's being. This was partially true in the past, even in the stages of involution of the drop-soul, but as the force of the energy of the act of sex is gradually diminished, the manner of the expression of love within the physical domain, while still physically expressed, becomes progressively centered in acts of tenderness.

This will be especially helpful for those consciously and deliberately on the Path, and has been anticipated by your intuitions of some months ago on "Tactual Sublimation." Now this can be understood more simply and clearly through the more central and accurate word of "tenderness."

Concurrent with the clarification and extensions now possible in the very important realm of love and its development and expression in Creation, it has become feasible as well to develop a strategy to preserve and utilize more productively the great forces developed in the devotional aspect of religions. This energy has long been wasted largely in animosities and wars between the various religious sects, and now is to be used for demolishing barriers on the Path of return to Oneness.

This, too, I foreshadowed in the press conference I gave in London in 1931 when I said I had not come to establish a new religion or sect, but to revivify the great existing religions and to gather them together like beads on one string.

You and others have now been able to piece together the great pains I have gone to in preparing the forms and the energy resources needed to put this great new chain of progress en route. The acts of my devotees you correctly see as central in placing the principle of unconditional forgiveness in a central role for this great process for the salvage of devotional energy for the future spiritual progress of humanity.

꼬

This is intuition was contained in an email from Don to a group of us, as follows:

From: "Don Stevens" <merwan94@yahoo.co.uk>
To: Deborah Sanchez, Sevn McAuley, Laurent Weichberger, Renate, Rob Ryder, Bruce Milburn, David Lee, Keith Ashton, Alfred and Marion Saunders
Sent: Thursday, January 24, 2008 8:57am
Subject: Today's Intuition

Dear Ones, Here is today's intuition, seems life has crowded them out lately and this one seemed rather testy to me as it unfolded. Maybe I'd better tend to business a bit better, but I thought I had done a pretty good job on forgiveness. Apparently not good enough.

Much love, Don

By the way, I am very intrigued by the first indication of locations of spots given, which supports Sevn's basic feeling on the subject.

Much love, Don

Intuition, London, 12:30 24 January 2008:

The Elements of Forgiveness

None of you have understood yet that I have given an entirely new dimension to forgiveness by staying in meditation at key points of great veneration and given both form (archetypes) and energy (avataric) at these physical locations. These are also available at other times and locations but their access and use is more readily handled by having made initial contact at various places which I have made known at various times and through various means of leaving important indications in the public records surrounding my activities, especially through Eruch and Don. As you touch this stored form and energy you will find resources available to you such as you had never dreamed existed in forgiveness before.

All you have to do is touch the door-knob and you will know what I have prepared for you to use.

༄

This intuition was contained in an email from Don to a group of us, as follows:

From: "Don Stevens" < merwan94@yahoo.co.uk>
To: Deborah Sanchez, Sevn McAuley, Laurent Weichberger, Bruce Milburn, David Lee
Sent: Sunday, January 27, 2008 10:44am
Subject: Today's Intuition

Uncompanionship

Of course no such word exists in the English language. In most instances, however, the opposite of a human trait or characteristic does exist, such as love and hate, true and false, but the opposite of companionship is a sheer blank in this regard. It is partly for this reason for instance that I chose the term inner links in place of companionship when I gave out my last message on the alphabet board. Inasmuch as a link is often a material object, as in a metal chain or a cord which ties two objects together, we have at once the sense that this tie can be broken or cut, and so the term "unlinked" has instant significance, whereas to uncompanion a relationship has no meaning and was not invented.

Nevertheless, circumstances do exist in life in which a deep relationship does cease to exist for one reason or another. Even, one is no doubt familiar with one or even several instances in which a very important human tie has been effectively disrupted, most commonly through the death of the other person involved. This is very simply resolved in conversation by speaking of the death of the party or disappearance, but often coupled with the remark that for some reason their presence seems to persist. This often calls for no further explanation and is very commonly left without comment.

Using this invented word of uncompanionship as an opposite for companionship, it is important for a few moments to examine the realities of the unlinking that occurred or perhaps always existed in this instance. The entire context here is that it is a rare and even distressing situation.

You have known one male and one female, both of whom are especially dear friends in your estimation, but for whom that relationship has always had certain odd characteristics, such as the unawareness of important circumstances causing pain, of which the friend seems to have no recognition, and consequently will say or act in a manner which you would automatically avoid or handle, if necessary, with extreme delicacy. On the other hand, each of these otherwise deeply loved and admired friends, plods without the least concern into subjects you would avoid or handle in a totally different manner. This has always puzzled you, as both are highly intelligent and in many ways deeply concerned about the welfare of their friends.

In each instance you are aware of an important relationship existing since childhood for these two individuals. In one instance the relationship was one of the greatest admiration and veneration, and in the other repulsion and rejection totally of feeling relationship. In each instance, the deep feeling involved, had become predominant in the manner in which later relationships were handled. In each instance one or even several important areas of human contact came to be paralysed and thus non-functioning, or rejected even, as unwanted or unsavoury. This always caused sooner or later sharp upsets in otherwise deep and fulfilling relationships, and so life continued with a somewhat limping gait evident from time to time, and at other times very valued and highly productive.

Compare this with the deep links formed with the Master. In this case the difference, especially in the case of the Perfect One, his relationship actually fosters the forming of links with other human beings, so the net effect is the reverse and need not be feared to risk severing of links except in instances of damaging possessiveness being involved in a prior existing relationship.

Uncompanionship is extremely difficult to resolve and requires an expert or some insight on the part of the one who is de-linked in certain situations. Such insight can on occasion be given by a very close companion who is greatly trusted, but unfortunately this damage is self-protecting and is often regarded by the wounded one as being a special heritage of the greatest value to them. Then it will perhaps require the grace of a ready perfect One.

☙

This is from a file given to us by Don titled, "pilgrimage" and internally it has written: "Morning Intuition, Paris, 18 February 2008, 2 :30am" and continues:

Pilgrimage 2008

... As the place of the Pilgrimage is being realized to be centrally important in Baba's scheme of bringing to reality his London prediction that he intended to revivify the great world religions and bring them together like beads on one string, the concept of the place and importance of these pilgrimages needs considerable expansion. They represent a very important part of the mechanics of erasing the hate and warfare that has accompanied the course of the great religions for so many hundreds of years. Responsible people at each pilgrimage site should be contacted and advised of the expected date of the visit of the pilgrimage group at their site of responsibility, and permission granted to the leaders of the pilgrimage group to film and photograph at complete liberty on that occasion. On the occasion of each visit the group should have studied the historical background of the construction of the temples and a theme for meditation agreed upon to parallel Baba's meditations when he accompanied Eruch to each of these points. Santosh might act as the librarian for the historical research. Also the fact of Meher Baba's visits with Eruch long ago and his meditation should be described and the fact that he made no effort to publicize these visits should be recounted. The composition of the pilgrim group should also be made clear and its role of assisting the mechanics of erasing hate and division emphasized. This should be very carefully handled so as to avoid any suggestion of taking matters into our hands and out of theirs ...

℘

This is from a file given to us by Don titled, "Synergy" and internally it has written, "Morning Intuition. Paris, February 20, 2008, 11:30am" and continues:

Synergy in Religion

(I have been reading a great deal in the newspapers about great buyouts and mergers of large companies in the expectation of important savings to be made by so doing, and also many reports over the years that the financial rewards expected did not materialize. Often a term used repeatedly is "synergy" expected between the two companies being combined. This morning a huge combination involving Microsoft and Yahoo was reported to be undergoing a good bit of negative speculation due to very different business philosophies between the two companies, making it very improbable that the "synergies" often expected would be very hard to uncover when two such divergent philosophies are present in the two groups negotiating. However, I have seen many other reports over time where synergies were discovered even beyond those expected, and the combination resulted in great benefits. Synergy struck me as being a concept in the business world which has been developed and anticipated positively by fusions and close cooperation, but is never encountered in connection with the relationships of different religions, where it would seem almost to be a repugnant possibility. I was struck by the difference between business and religions.)

Why is it that in large part the great religions, instead of producing a concept in practise of synergy, have tended more often to produce rejection, discord and, often, bloody wars? Have their basic principles of belief been misunderstood, and above all, been mismanaged? Should the world's great religions fire their CEOs and substitute managers trained in business principles instead? Would they develop an over-riding profit incentive that would result in a search and adoption of the synergies that must exist, in place of the incredibly wasteful religious wars that have so indelibly stamped the passing centuries of so-called blossoming of rational civilization?

Seriously, the spiritual heritage of humanity has been so seriously mismanaged for centuries by the "officially" responsible management of the formal accredited hierarchy that it would not be outside of rational expectation that one might, should, expect and look for corrective action from the spiritual hierarchy charged we are often reminded, with the surveillance of the ongoing of Creation.

And, in fact, you have been accumulating evidence, Don, that this has occurred through Meher Baba's preparations for the New Humanity living in the New Age in the New Cycle of avataric Cycles. The wastage of the force of spiritual devotion of true devotees through the centuries in misguided and bloody warfare has always been a disastrously high proportion of the total available. As the entire process of especially the involution of consciousness speeds up with the increasing age and complexity of Creation, an important resource of the psychic energy required in this stage is the store of energy related to devotion to the Master, the artistry of the particular ism, and also to the spiritual hierarchy.

The inherent need for energy to power involution can be largely satisfied through savings made in reducing the enormous drain into sheer cruelty and hate. To accomplish this, a new ethic in regard to racial and religious hatred offers a vast potential, of which the Avatar is completely aware. And what he is effecting in the present major cyclic change-over is a revolution in ancient habit patterns. Synergy in the true sense of the term is being introduced into the process for the first time.

(Next Intuition: Devotional Synergy)

This is from a file given to us by Don titled, "SynergyDevot" and internally it has written, "Today's Reflection. Paris, 21 February 2008, all morning" and continues:

Devotional Synergy

This is a succession of thoughts and recollections from a variety of sources, and importantly among other resources, Baba's own clear words to us concerning various principles he has explained especially concerning the birthplace of the Avatars and the environment into which the Avatar is born. As these thoughts began to come to me I became aware at once that the story of the births of the Avatar forms an importantly meaningful pattern of logic which is largely ignored, and little appreciated and utilized. This has been due to the confusion that has surrounded the grim facts of the competitive warring and hate created by followers who adhere tightly to the form and stories of the life and actions of the succession of births through which the Avatar has already passed. First of all, Baba is very clear that the levels of development spiritually of different areas of the earth's surface are very different, and the area in which that spiritual level first rose to that required to form and sustain the level of consciousness capable of the realization of God, was within the confines of present day India. Baba further clarified that this gradually expanded to surrounding sectors, only now having risen generally throughout the expanse of the continents of the earth so that in the future the Avatar's birth will take place in the West as well.

Then, next, the Avatar is born into a family capable of allowing him to develop to the spiritual level capable of knowing himself as God, and in an environment in which he can give out the message of spiritual Truth needed for the further development of the understanding of the function of Creation and the living forms that populate it. This can be called the Message Apt for the Time, and in the words that can be understood to express it. All this is chosen to the maximum capacity of the geographic location to suit the message to be given to humanity for the furthering of the manifestation of consciousness in the area destined for that period of Creation.

While the geographic location and the family, culture and timing of the birth of the Avatar are chosen with the best resources available being paramount, the use of the message of the Avatar is far less efficiently handled by those who receive and disseminate it. This is an inevitable tragedy of the result of the absolute freedom of chance prevailing in the necessary freedom of Creation and, in fact, in the very nature of God Himself. However, this freedom as the canvas for the painting of divine individualized consciousness does not in any way afflict the characteristics of God Himself. He has certain attributes which are the skeleton of His being, and they are maintained forever as His very nature. All that is manifested in the dream of Creation does and must adhere to these principles, despite the freedom of chance in the environment of Creation in which they are developed through the individual Whims of the infinite number of individual drop-souls which are born and perfected within their manifest consciousness. All conform finally to the characteristic skeleton of God's individual infinite nature, and this is absolutely assured through the final inspection made of each drop-soul – always by a Perfect One – as it passes from the sixth to the seventh plane of reunion into infinite God.

As all of Creation exists in time and space, and this allows love and consciousness to manifest, it is seen that age is a fact and has both assets and liabilities to offer within the process taking place. Complexity is inherent in the nature of creativity and creativity is necessary for creative beauty and the creation of individualized beauty. It also allows the process of the evolution and especially the involution of consciousness to speed up. And if this process is carefully handled, which is one of the principal responsibilities of the Avatar and the Spiritual Hierarchy, the speeding up can become far more effective and reduce also the pain factor considerably in the dream life-span of the individual drop-soul. Here is where what might be called the true synergy of religious devotion becomes critical, and it is this which the Avatar as Meher Baba took in hand for the first time in this Creation the needed resources and forms to allow the Truths of the various avataric teachings to be used harmoniously instead of in the largely destructive pattern of the war of ideals generated by uncontrolled allegiance to the form and personality of individual incarnations of the Avatar. Instead of preserving the harmony of the various forms established by the avataric incarnations, the followers in their excessive love and loyalty to the form of the given Avatar, manage to warp and modify the teachings to the point of causing them to contrast and seemingly contradict even the forms and teachings of other incarnations of the same one Avatar.

This is of course the reverse of Truth, and this is what uses up so much of the stock of the creative psychic energy of devotion.

Of course, each individual drop-soul eventually makes its way through this confusing barricade, but it both slows the rate of progress and it also decreases the net total of psychic energy which can be disposed of in the ongoing spiritual path of return to God. Correction of this necessitates first the neutralizing of existing hate patterns through finally effective forgiveness, which necessitates in turn considerable sophistication and application of directed energy. Meher Baba has done the first great job of developing the forms and energy supplies needed. It is his devotees who will carry the direction and protection necessary for this process to become effective. It is the greatest spiritual challenge that any group of spiritual devotees has been assigned to this point in Creation, and it is not expected that it be done perfectly and speedily, but Meher Baba has done a tremendous work with great creativeness and dedication, and he has also gathered around him the devotees of courage and capacity to do a tremendous job in this task.

‧

This is from a file given to us by Don titled, "Shivaji" and internally it has written, "Today's Intuition. Paris, all afternoon, February 25, 2008" and continues:

Shivaji: From Where, and To Where?

This has been a never before, and perhaps it will be a never again also. This question suddenly appeared in my head as I was reading the *Herald Tribune* after lunch and astonished me for many reasons. After I had tried futilely to answer the question of what esoterically were the antecedents of Shivaji, as a minor incarnation of the Avatar before he was born as Meher Baba, and what happened to the physical combination used by Shivaji during his lifetime, I went about other tasks in the apartment.

Then suddenly the question broke out in the forefront of my consciousness, why had this question never come to me during the long years between the time Baba first told me about his minor and veiled incarnation as Shivaji, and today? Am I such an imbecile that I could not see that this simple question was one of the most intriguing and fascinating puzzles I had ever encountered, and here it was dead in the center of something Baba himself had brought up so long ago, and I was so dull that I had never tumbled to its existence.

I disposed of that ego-destroying query by getting into the middle of another problem in the household, but then back another part of the puzzle came up and swamped my attention. Baba himself had made me greatly aware of the existence of sanskaras and their fundamental importance in the human being and the long, complex history of the antecedents of development of the personal collection of sanskaras and the unbroken chain of cause and effect and inheritance which characterized each human being's sanskaric heritage, and here I had been directly in front of one of the greatest mysteries that could be imagined: where did the sanskaras necessary for the production of Shivaji come from, and where did they go? Simply incredible I had not seen this fascinating question right in front of me, and how could it ever be reconciled in any case with what I thought I had gradually learned as it were at the feet of the Avatar Himself?

Part of the puzzle looked as if it could be handled by applying the same principle I had developed gradually to explain the readiness in each avataric advent of the drop-souls ready to assume the roles of the various disciples without having to accept the common assumption that Creation is a repeating story of the same general problems and the repeated use by the Avatar of sanskaras with the same characteristics and where there is never anything new finally but simply the same story repeating itself. And this just did not square with my observations of the Avatar I knew and how he worked with humanity. But he did have all Knowledge, so knew all the drop-souls in Creation and their characteristics, and so had the choice of selecting the ones most closely resembling the Johns and Peters and so on that had existed before and were required for certain characteristics that were needed in the general repetition of type problems, but each time essentially new in important aspects.

While this gave me a few moments of solace, again the incredible unknown of how all the newness of inserting a Shivaji into Creation when the five Perfect Ones demanded that sort of solution of the Avatar came back, and I had to admit that this, I think, is so big and so fundamental that I must place it in front of my companions and ask they make it a joint reflection and intuition project for perhaps several years, as it has all the air of demanding a rethinking and re-reflection and re-intuiting of a very great deal of what has seemed in place and sufficient unto the needs of Creation.

- Finis -

Endnotes Don's Forgiveness Intuitions:

1. Avatar Meher Baba, whom he refers to as his father. – LW.

2. This is a reference to the chapter "Sacred Mountains" by Don and Laurent in the book *Meher Baba's Gift of Intuition,* by Don E. Stevens and Companions (London: Companion Books, 2006). In this email from Don, the terms "MVDBLB" and "BB" mean, "My Very Dearly Beloved Little Bear,' and "Big Bear" respectively. – LW.

3. Regarding the Om Point, Meher Baba said, "Ultimately the aspirant has to realize that God is the only Reality and that he is really one with God. This implies that he should not be overpowered by the spectacle of the multiform universe. In fact, the whole universe is in the Self and springs into existence from the tiny point in the Self referred to as the Om Point. But the Self as the individualized soul has become habituated to gathering experiences through one medium or another, and therefore it comes to experience the universe as a formidable rival, other than itself. Those who have realized God constantly see the universe as springing from this Om Point, which is in everyone." In *Discourses* , by Meher Baba (Myrtle Beach: Sheriar Foundation, 1987), p.190. Copyright © 1987 Avatar Meher Baba Perpetual Public Charitable Trust, India.

4. Note how the tone of the intuitive voice has shifted from Don's intuitive voice to that of the Avataric tone, and as if Meher Baba is speaking. – LW.

5. Regarding Meher Baba's work of cleansing the sacred sites of the world, he spoke of this directly: "On one occasion, referring to the purpose of his visits to different shrines, tombs or dargahs of saints and Perfect Masters, Baba stated: 'By my living presence, I clean the tangled atmosphere of the shrines of the dead saints, Sadgurus and Qutubs. This complicated atmosphere is of the thought world. Thought force is really very strong and powerful. Chaitanya did not go to places of pilgrimage for the sake of pilgrimage, but for cleansing their atmosphere which were full of the sanskaras of thoughts of worldly people. For my work, a pilgrim on the third plane is more helpful than the place of a dead Master of the seventh plane; but a well-known dead saint or Master may have a strong influence due to the multitudes going to his tomb. That is why I thin down the effect of this complicated thought atmosphere by visiting such places.'" In *Lord Meher,* by Bhau Kalchuri, p. 2391, and on-line here: http://www.lordmeher.org/index.jsp?pageBase=page.jsp&nextPage=2391

6. The phrase, "added years I have given you," is a reference to the fact that Don died in the ambulance on the way to the hospital in Salem, MA after the YPG gathering there in September 2006. He was immediately resuscitated by the EMTs and put in the cardiology unit where he subsequently underwent heart surgery. – LW.

7. This first Beads on One String pilgrimage tour was in 2004.

8. It was actually Meher Baba's second visit to the West, April 1932, and the message about "Beads on One String" was delivered to Paramount Film Company (for a newsreel) April 8th in London. See *Lord Meher*, p. 1554 on-line here: http://www.lordmeher.org/index.jsp?pageBase=page.jsp&nextPage=1554

9. The incarnation (or advent) of the Avatar should not be confused with the reincarnation (or rebirth) of human beings. – LW.

10. Involution is a term coined by Meher Baba meaning the turning of human consciousness (and awareness) inward to experience successively the inner-planes of the spiritual path. For more on involution see *God Speaks*, by Meher Baba.

11. This intuition, and those after, occurred to Don after the YPG gathering recorded in this volume.
12. Sanskaric knot is a phrase used by Meher Baba to describe impressions in the mind of man. See *Discourses*, by Meher Baba, "The Formation and Function of Sanskaras."

Photo of Avatar Meher Baba (circa 1926) at Meherabad, India

Forgiveness at Meherabad

by Laurent Weichberger

> Who did it? They should come forward and acknowledge their guilt so that I may forgive them. They should not be afraid, because I am Infinite Forgiveness.[1]
> ~ Meher Baba

> The judges of the world bring guilt to the guilty and punish them. I bring guilt to the guilty and forgive them.[2]
> ~ Meher Baba

Background

Meher Baba's sister, Manija, explained that while he kept silence (and after he gave up using the alphabet board to communicate) Baba used hand gestures, and she elucidated the specific gesture Baba used for forgiveness[3]:

"One particular gesture which has always touched me, very deeply, there was one gesture for two words, there was one gesture for love and for forgiveness; same gesture. It was coming from the deeps; it's like welling up – it wells up.

"Love wells up from your heart, and so does forgiveness. And when Baba would make that gesture, Baba would say, **'I give my love'** or he would say, **'I forgive you.'** And when Baba would say 'I forgive you' it seemed like such an Oceanic gesture. "As if the Ocean waters have come over, and that wave has come over to the beach, and receded leaving not a trace, not a chicken track, on the sand.

"Total forgiveness."

Now, here is a short story about Meher Baba's relationship to forgiveness, and then I will share about how I took this talk of forgiveness to heart on a recent pilgrimage to Meherabad. This story[4] about Baba takes place in Jabalpur, India on December 31st, 1938. Papa Jessawala is Eruch's father. One of Baba's disciples, Jal, had played a joke on Papa, which upset him to the extent that Papa complained to Baba bitterly about it:

Smiling, Baba spelled out, **"I would not forgive Jal, but to forgive is my nature. If I don't forgive him, the world will collapse! Only by my forgiveness does the world continue, not otherwise!"**

It took some time for Baba to convince Papa to let go of the situation, as he didn't believe Jal should be forgiven. Ultimately, however, Baba prevailed upon Papa to open his heart:

"All right," motioned Baba. **"I won't forgive Jal, but you forgive him!"** Jal asked Papa's forgiveness, and finally, after hours of fuming, he forgave him.

PILGRIMAGE

In November 2007, I planned to visit India with my dear mother, Anne, and sister, Sarah. It would be their first trip to India. I made my first pilgrimage to that sacred land in 1988, and so I "know the ropes" already to some extent. I was set to fly on Monday, November 19 from Flagstaff, Arizona. Finally, the departure date came and I had not one or two, but four flights to take in order to reach India: Flagstaff > Phoenix > Los Angeles > Frankfurt, Germany > New Delhi, India.

I spent the night in Delhi at an inexpensive bed and breakfast, waiting for my mother and sister to arrive the next evening. The next day, I went out to the International Airport with the driver of an Oberoi hotel car. The flight from Chicago bearing my kinfolk was delayed, so I explored the Delhi airport. I decided to buy them each a brightly colored fake flower garland. After all, how many times do you make your first trip to India? And then as I continued to wait, I got hungry and tired, so I found a stall that sold "Nescafe" (which is Hindi for coffee) and a veggie-roll-type-thing (think Knish with spiced vegetables).

In the back of my mind, since arriving in India, I couldn't help but feel -- "Oh Baba, all I want to do is come down from Delhi to you, but here I am waiting for them to come and then we plan to see the Taj Mahal, and other things, and I have to wait until Saturday ... " My deep yearning was just to be with Meher Baba at Meherabad, but I had agreed to show them some great sights first. As I waited in the line to order and then pay, a man directly in front of me had his shoulder partially blocking my vision of a sign on the back wall of the stall, which for some odd reason I was drawn to read. In its partially visible state it read:

"Management is not
 responsible for your
  longings."

When he paid and moved away, I saw the "**be**" and laughed. Baba was teasing me, and I felt his presence and love with me. Eventually my mom and sister arrived, and I garlanded them as they emerged from the immigration section. We soon were in the car to the many starred hotel and relatively early to sleep. After seeing sights in Delhi, we flew to Pune, where we visited Hazrat Babajan's tomb, and Meher Baba's family home, before the drive to Meherabad, the divine seat of Avatar Meher Baba.

I had set a few goals for myself on this journey, as follows:
1. Get my mother and sister to the threshold of Meher Baba's tomb (Samadhi) at Meherabad.

2. In so far as possible, with Baba in the Samadhi, forgive my father for his suicide.

3. Visit the "Pumpkin House Orphanage" which friends and family in Georgia have been instrumental in founding.

4. See about building a house on Meherabad land, where I wish to retire one day, Baba willing.

The second point, on forgiveness, was something that had been brewing in me for a long time. This process was brought home to me more recently during a weekend seminar in Los Angeles with Don Stevens, a longtime close disciple (Mandali) of Baba's, during which we focused on the topic of forgiveness. I had brought up my dilemma about not having my father present in my forgiveness process, which created this giant communications chasm, and the futility of trying to span it alone. How can one build such a bridge across a cavernous gorge?

In the end I decided that I would simply do my best with Baba, and leave the results to Him. Thank you, Don, for insisting on the importance of forgiveness on so many levels. This has helped me greatly.

On the way to Meherabad, I spotted a number of road-side flower-wallas, and suggested to mom and sister that we could get a nice garland to place on Baba's Samadhi, to which they agreed. I told our driver, Kailash, that we wanted to stop at the next garland-walla, to which he also agreed. We found our garland and paid for it, and I noticed a little hungry puppy, which I fed with some of our butter-biscuits (a biscuit in India, and England, is a sort of cookie for us in America).

Meherabad

Before long we were signing the register at the old Meher Pilgrim Centre (which is now the Trust Pilgrim office), and then up to Meher Baba's blessed Samadhi with our garland, still fresh. This being Anne and Sarah's very first time visiting Baba in India, I wanted it to be as special as possible, so we entered the Samadhi together, three-as-one, holding a giant rose and jasmine garland. I stepped up on the left side and with one opposite me, and one at Baba's feet, we three laid the garland down lovingly with a soft, "Avatar Meher Baba Ki Jai."

I prostrated myself at Baba's blessed feet and said a few words to Him, I don't remember what, before leaving them to have their own experience with Baba. Emerging from the tomb, I got my *prasad*, and sat down on the same wooden bench where Baba-lovers have been sitting for decades now. As soon as they came out and there was no one else wanting to enter the tomb, I rose and entered the tomb again, this time alone. It was on this second entry, that I consciously formed the intention to give my forgiveness to my father, Philipp, for his suicide.

My first girlfriend, Nisi, upon reading a draft of this chapter, challenged me to share more deeply about how forgiveness towards my father, in and of itself, is a "human challenge and universal battle." Let me say this: when Papi (as we called him in German) threw himself off the rooftop of our apartment building in 1985, I was thrust from being a teenager in high school to suddenly being "the man of the house." My mother and sister suffered tremendously at his loss, while I felt some sense of relief. Of course I was also sad, and probably angry, but I remember primarily being confused. To me, the immediate and practical considerations of caring for my family outweighed my own personal process, at least initially. So, I got a job and started going to college at night, while watching my mother and sister pick up the pieces of their own fractured psyches. Within a few months I came into contact with Meher Baba, and shortly after recognized him as my Master.

Now what exactly was there for me to forgive – the loss of adolescence? The abandonment by a father of his beloved son? This much I did know – if ever I would (or could) forgive, it would be because I was wholehearted about doing so, and not because I should. It would be in my time, in my own way, whatever that was. The fact of his being "here today and gone tomorrow" was immensely confusing and it made contemplation of the whole issue of forgiveness daunting – no, that is not true, for the first ten years afterwards it was inconceivable. Eventually I left New York, and got married to my beloved wife Lilly. Only as time continued to roll on, and we created our own family, did I start to get any real perspective. At some point, I believe, forgiveness is born out of compassion for the state in which any action (or thought, or word) is made. In other words, when I could get to the place in my own heart in which I could see even a shadow of that state of suffering which would cause a person to commit suicide, then I could begin the process of starting to complete the meaning of forgiving my father. The "how" to accomplish that came after about another ten years. I am reminded of a quote from Meher Baba's special message *Twelve Ways of Realizing Me*[5]:

> If you experience the desperation that causes a man to commit suicide and you feel that you cannot live without seeing Me, then you will see Me.

There has never been a doubt in my mind that my father was clinically depressed and experienced agonizing desperation. I am sure he honestly believed that he could escape to somewhere less painful, that death meant some type of freedom. Having known my own anguish, I was ready to embrace his decision, whether I approved it or not.

With my head at Baba's feet in the Samadhi, I told Philipp, "I forgive you," and said some other things as well. I asked Baba to help me, and my father, in this process. Without Baba I feel that I am helpless to reach across the chasm of death. With Baba, I was able to embrace the emotional leper that was my father. Surprisingly, this forgiveness was not difficult. I was not moved, it was totally non-dramatic and gently uplifting. It just felt right, and timely, and good — like a silent dove flapping gently away from open hands. I shared more with Baba, and then in that timelessness of Baba's Samadhi eventually I rose up again, and departed.

Knowing me, I probably got in the line at the Samadhi a third time. I will just say that time at Meherabad slowly slips away as the fragrance of the Master's engaging love overpowers the senses, and one realizes what is truly important -- loving the Lord of Love. Most of what captivates our western minds is utterly meaningless. After the flight down from Delhi, then Baba's family home, Hazrat Babajan's tomb and now our arrival at Meherabad, you can bet we were totally spent. Upon finding our rooms at the new Meher Pilgrim Retreat, I think mother and sister realized, "There is a God, and She is Horizontal."

I told them, as lovingly as possible, that they are safe now, and that as I am also tired, I may or may not see them at breakfast in the morning (I have long felt that missing a meal in order to sleep a little is worth it) ... And that tomorrow, Sunday, is a "Meherazad-day" and so I would be riding the special bus that takes Baba-lovers to Baba's home. In trying to explain all this to Sarah on the way to India, I said the easy way to remember the difference between Meherabad (where we slept at the centre) and Meherazad is this:

Meher*abad* = Baba's Tomb, as he is buried here with his close disciples (Mandali).
Meher*azad* = Baba's Room, as he lived the last years of his life there with his Mandali.

In Persian, Meherazad means Meher is Free (meaning unbound), whereas Meherabad means Meher is Flourishing. I wrote an essay about what the name Meher itself means, so I will not get into that here, except to say of course it is Baba's first name which can be translated as Compassionate. We can link forgiveness to compassion for sure. To be honest, his given name was Merwan S. Irani, and the name Meher Baba was given to him by his early circle of disciples.

I think it was Sunday night during dinner at Meherabad that I met the group of Persian students that were studying in Pune, but had all come from Iran. In any case, they were delightful, and as I sat with them we shared about Persian poets, and culture. I believe it was "Rose" that recited a few lines of Rumi in Farsi (the Persian language), and I asked her to tell me the meaning in English. She said the lines were from a famous poem by Rumi which he spoke to his son, Sultan Veled, while he lay dying on his deathbed, and it was his last poem for his son (maybe his last poem period, I don't know).

The title is literally *On the Deathbed*, and I was deeply moved by it. I guess Rose was sufficiently aware of my sincere interest in Rumi and this poem, as the next day, Monday, she appeared standing before me at the outdoor seating area of the centre dining area, holding out a piece of paper printed with a poem towards my receiving hands.

As I read the poem in English I was deeply touched by Rose's care for me, that she would go through the trouble to find a computer (near Meherabad), search online for this poem, and print it out for me. Then I saw that below the English text in the lower right was the Farsi original from which the translation was made. This also made me happy as I could refer to it later if I had any questions on the meaning of the translation. It was clear that the translation was made by someone fluent in Farsi but perhaps not an English poet themselves. I decided to work on it a little, and bring it into good shape so that I could better appreciate what Rumi was sharing with his beloved son. Rose sat with me outside on a bench as we went over the English line by line, and when I questioned a word, she could refer to the Farsi herself and tell me the word Rumi used. I know a tiny bit of Farsi, and so I knew what Rumi meant in one case as soon as I heard the word.

Upon return to the states, I decided I would rewrite the poem where needed, when I wrote my *Journey to India* story, so as to keep the majestic poetic nature of Rumi as intact as possible, while adhering to the meaning of the translation I was given. This poem follows now. If I have strayed from the Master's intended meaning, it is due to my ignorance, while if it is aligned with his intent, it is due to the grace of my beloved Master, Meher Baba:

On the Deathbed[6]

Go, lay your head on a pillow, and leave me alone.
Leave this ruined, night-wandering, love-afflicted one, alone.

We are with the wave of love, from nightfall until dawn, alone.
If you want, come and forgive me, or else be cruel and go.

Run away from me, so you too won't fall into danger,
Choose the safe path, leave this treacherous path behind.

We have crawled, with our tears, into this corner of grief.
Grind 100 acres of wheat, at the mill house, with the waterfall of our tears.

We have a ruthless killer with a heart of hard stone.
When he kills, no one says to him, "Now find a way to pay the blood-money!"

The King of All that is Beautiful and Good doesn't have to be faithful.

Oh pale lover, be patient and remain loyal.

There exists no cure for this anguish except to die.
So how can I tell you to cure this pain?

In my dream, last night, I saw a Saint[7] on the path of love,
Beckoning to me with his hand, encouraging me to come near.

If there is a dragon on your path, love is like an emerald.
From the sparkle of the emerald banish the dragon.

Enough! Because I am useless and you are a spiritual artist.
Narrate the deeds of Bu Ali,[8] kill me just like they killed Bol Ala.[9]

~ Rumi

It was not until I was on my return home from India that I contemplated more deeply the way this poem came to me from Rose. I had not told her or any of her Persian companions at the Baba centre that I was in the process of forgiving my father for his suicide more than twenty years previously. I never shared with anyone during the trip that this was going on, or that one of the most difficult aspects of my process was not being able to achieve any type of real closure — as my father was so totally out of reach. And yet here was a poem from Rumi to his own son, on his deathbed, and so many lines of this wondrous poetry remind me of my own father's poems and style. So, it was somewhere between India and home that it dawned on me that Baba Himself had found a way to let me know that He heard my prayer and was present as I forgave my father, and this was His Way of letting me know that He is with me in my process. Now, re-writing it in late December 2007 for this chapter in *The Doorbell of Forgiveness*, I notice for the first time the line:
"If you want, come and forgive me, or else be cruel and go."

As I re-read this, I feel Baba's confirmation; His ways are vital and alive, and He is most present.

Thank you, Baba.

On our last day at Meherabad, I know at least two things happened, because I wrote them down in my journal. I had gone to the morning arti, when Baba's lovers not only bow down to Baba, and surrender themselves to Him, but they delight in singing their hearts out to Baba on the porch in front of His grave. That morning, my old friend Elaine sang a ghazal that Meher Baba had composed Himself, and I was tremendously happy at hearing my Divine Master's words. When I saw her again at breakfast, I asked if I could please copy down the translation which she had read out before singing it to Baba. She agreed, and here is a version of Baba's ghazal, based on what Elaine allowed me to copy from her personal songbook. This ghazal has no title:

When in my heart I saw the form of my Beloved,
Wherever my glance fell I only saw God Almighty.

He is that matchless one that appears in matchless forms.
I myself saw that unknown one manifested in thousands of forms.

Not only this entire material world,
But my honor and my religion I sacrifice to Thee.

My heart and the richest blood in my body, my very soul and the life of my soul,
And everything else within me I scatter at Your Feet.

It was early this afternoon when I bumped into dear Eric Solibakke, an American poet who lives in Oslo, Norway, and now also

Meherabad. I love this man! He makes my wearing of purple pants look like a pinstriped suit. His colorful attire and soulful countenance make my day brighter whenever I come into his gentle contact. We spoke about many things that afternoon, including the "Perfect Master of Greece," the role of intuition, and many other uplifting subjects. Later, he handed me a printed paper which contained Baba's holy words from a discourse which reminded Eric of our conversation regarding intuition. I record here below exactly what Eric printed for me as it is a pivotal part of that discourse (compare this to what Baba's ghazal says above). Isn't it fascinating how everything is so interlinked:

Once the aspirant has the bliss of the *darshana* of a Master, that sight gets carved on his mind, and even when he is unable to establish frequent personal contact, his mind turns to the Master again and again in an effort to understand his significance.

This process of establishing mental contact with the Master is essentially different from merely imaginative revival of past incidents. In the ordinary play of imagination, the recall of past incidents is not necessarily animated by a definite purpose, whereas in establishing mental contact there is a definite purpose. Owing to the directive power of purpose, imagination ceases to be a mere revolving of ideas and reaches out to the Master through the inner planes and establishes contact with him.

Such mental contact with the Master is often as fruitful and effective as his physical darshana. The inward repetition of such mental contacts is like constructing a channel between Master and aspirant, who becomes thereby the recipient of the grace, love and light which are constantly flowing from the Master in spite of the apparent distance between them. Thus, the help of the Master goes out not only to those who happen to be in his physical presence but also to others who establish mental contact with him.[10]

After such a full and rich day, I had to end it with a visit to Baba's blessed Samadhi, our last chance before an early morning departure. What can be said about the love that flows between the lover and the Beloved?

Things that are real are given and received in silence.

~ Meher Baba[11]

HOME

Shortly after returning home from India, my (twelve year old) daughter Aspen went out to a musical evening in Flagstaff with our dear friend Skye, where the featured performer was Jean Paul Samputu. He also spoke that night about the power of forgiveness, as he was a survivor of the 1994 Rwandan genocide, and is now an Ambassador for peace and forgiveness. Aspen was visibly moved by his words when she shared with me the next day about what he told the audience. I was inspired and succeeded in doing a phone interview with him a few days later which we published[12] in the summer of 2008.

Of the many profound and spiritual things he shared, the most stunning was that he was able to forgive his old "friend" who participated in the genocide. As Jean Paul explained during the interview, " ... my mother, father, three brothers and a sister were murdered by one of our best friends. He was our neighbor, and he was such a good friend. And that's what happened in genocide, brothers killed brothers, friends killed friends, even husbands killed their wives."

When I heard Jean Paul's story, from his own mouth to God's ear, and that after the genocide God instructed him to forgive this murdering friend, I knew this was exactly the type of work Don Stevens had shared with us as being so vital to the spiritual progress of the New Humanity. Forgiveness is the only real way forward for some conflicts which seem impossible to resolve. Now I am certain that Jean Paul, Don, and many others will take up the mantle of encouraging this forgiveness effort globally. For some, this spiritual endeavor will be under the guidance of Avatar Meher Baba, present within each one. May it be so.

Rejuvenation

During December 2010, on a special visit to the Meher Spiritual Center, some more clarifications and confirmations came to me in the context of forgiveness, which I feel inspired to share here in closing. My ride from the airport to the center upon arrival in Myrtle Beach was Donna Stewart, whom I have known for many years. In the few minutes we shared in her car, as she drove me to my cabin, she asked what was going on in my life. I responded that I was creating this book with Don and the YPG. When she heard the title we had chosen, she shared a stunning quote from Baba about forgiveness which I had never heard. I asked her if she could find it and send it to me, so we could have it accurately for this publication, which she later did.[13]

> Without love, none can cultivate the noble habit of forgetting and forgiving. You forgive a wrong done to you in the same measure in which you love the wrong-doer ... Forgiveness follows love.
> ~ Meher Baba

Lastly, I have been contemplating the nature of Meher Baba's prayer, "O Parvardigar" (sometimes titled *The Master's Prayer*). In this prayer, Baba starts each new stanza with "You are ... " and proceeds to divulge the nature of God. For example:

> You are without beginning and without end. Non-dual, beyond comparison, and none can measure You.

However, when I was considering the ramifications of this prayer recently, I definitely felt that Baba was also explaining that it is actually our own true nature, as individual souls. This is the fact of the existence of the soul, independent of impressions. In conversation with Joan Agin (during the same visit to Myrtle Beach), we both felt Baba was imploring us to see His detailed portrayal of God as an indication of our own latent divinity. Therefore, we can intentionally look beyond the falsity (or illusion) of the shadow play of impressions, and see that forgiveness must be tied (in some way) to these descriptions from Baba regarding the nature of God, Reality and the soul. Meher Baba speaks eloquently to this position when He states[14]:

I can forgive; I have come to forgive. Forgiveness is the highest thing for those who are forgiven. It is not a great thing to me to forgive. In fact, in reality there is nothing to be forgiven, for there is really nothing like good and bad. *You* find them so, and they *are* there in duality, due to your own bindings in duality.

In the bondage of duality there is good and there is bad, but in reality everything but God is zero. *Maya*, which causes you to mistake illusion for reality, is present for you but not for me. *For me, only I am, and nothing else exists.* It therefore means nothing for me to forgive, and everything for you to be forgiven.

Forgiveness consists in loosening the bindings of duality in *maya*, which makes you feel and find the One as many. Therefore 'I forgive you' amounts to the loosening of your bindings.

Although it takes a lot of time to build a big stack of hay, a single lighted match can burn all of it in no time at all. Similarly, regardless of the accumulated dirt and refuse of sins, divine forgiveness burns them away in no time.

While I started writing this rejuvenation section here now, the song "Take My Life and Let it Be"[15] came on my Pandora (internet radio). I used to sing this hymn frequently to Him when I first "came to Baba," as I knew He was well aware of it, saying it was the *Bhagavad-Gita* in a nutshell. I will take this as a hint from Him as the best way to conclude this chapter:

Take my life and let it be
Consecrated, Lord, to Thee.

Take my moments and my days,
Let them flow in endless praise.

Take my hands and let them move
At the impulse of Thy love.

Take my feet and let them be
Swift and beautiful for Thee.

Take my voice and let me sing,
Always, only, for my King.

Take my lips and let them be
Filled with messages from Thee.

Take my silver and my gold,
Not a mite would I withhold.

Take my intellect and use
Every power as Thou shalt choose.
Take my will and make it Thine,
It shall be no longer mine.

Take my heart, it is Thine own,
It shall be Thy royal throne.

Take my love, my Lord, I pour
At Thy feet its treasure store.

Take myself and I will be
Ever, only, all for Thee.

Forgiveness at Meherabad, Endnotes:

1. From *It So Happened*, by William Le Page, p. 59.
2. From *Lord Meher*, by V.S. Bhau Kalcuri, Vol 15, p. 5304, (source lordmeher.org accessed September 29, 2010).
3. Mani S. Irani on Meher Baba's forgiveness gesture, from the film, *Eternal Beloved*, (at 12:30 into the film), copyright (c) Meher Prasad (Myrtle Beach, SC).
4. From *Lord Meher* Volume 7, p. 2353 (source lordmeher.org accessed January 11, 2010).
5. From *Twelve Ways of Realizing Me*, at http://www.ambppct.org/meherbaba/12-ways-of-realizing-me.php (accessed February 4, 2010).
6. English translation of Rumi poem by Fereshteh Azad and Laurent Weichberger, with consultation from Reza Abrahimzadeh.
7. Rumi uses the word "Pir" which Meher Baba defined in *God Speaks*: Pir is a 6th plane Master; Satpurush in Vedantic.
8. Abu Ali Sina — Avicenna — a prominent Persian scientist and philosopher, also known as the father of modern medicine.
9. He was killed by Fadayan.
10. From *Discourses*, by Meher Baba, "The Place of Occultism in the Spiritual Life: Part II" (6th edition) pp. 97-98.
11. From *Lord Meher*, p. 1932.
12. See: "Jean Paul Samputu and the Power of Forgiveness," by Laurent Weichberger, (April 13, 2008), *OmPoint International Circular* (issue #2) pp. 18 – 22, at http://www.ompoint.com/OmPoint_Circular_2.pdf.
13. From an email to Laurent from Donna, December 15, 2010, subject: "Hi from Donna found the quote." She stated, "This is the Baba quote I picked out of the basket last New Years Eve at the Center.
   I do not know the source."
14. From *Listen, Humanity*, by Meher Baba (edited by Don E. Stevens) p. 68. Available on-line here http://ambppct.org/meherbaba/Book_Files/LISTEN,%20HUMANITY.pdf (accessed February 2011).
15. Hymn by Frances R. Havergal (1874).

Epilogue

Looking for a way to begin — a chance to start without knowing how — I take a 'fāl' (Persian: 'omen') or *sortes* (Latin: 'drawing lots') from the poetry of Hafiz. My finger finds this line:

When there is no purity, one are the Ka'ba and the idol-house.[1]

Encountering these words immediately suggests two insights central to the variegated conversations recorded in this volume. First, that forgiveness is a work of purification on which rests the very possibility of authentic religion, that is, religion as the practical love of Reality as opposed to the mere veneration of self-projected idols, what Meher Baba defines as the *religion of life*.

"The Religion of Life is not fettered by mechanically repeated formulae of the unenlightened, purblind and limited intellect. It is dynamically energized by the assimilation of Truth, grasped through lucid and unerring intuition, which never falters and never fails, because it has emerged out of the fusion of head and heart, intellect and love."[2]

Second, that the work of forgiveness, for all of its difficulty and seeming impossibility, proceeds paradoxically, not unlike the act of taking a 'fāl' from a text, through the freedom of an essentially negative condition, in the midst of the experience of *not* knowing, *not* remembering, *not* worrying.[3] Real forgiveness is necessarily on the way to forgetfulness, a state of being that, rather than leading to oblivion, proceeds by the mind's own perception *that* there exists an infinitely important unknown *what* at once beyond and essential to itself. As Meher Baba explains, such forgetful forgiveness arrives at real remembering.

"[W]hen the same mind tells him that there is *something* which may be called God, and, further, when it prompts him to search for God that he may see Him face to face, he begins to forget himself and to forgive others for whatever he has suffered from them. And when he has forgiven everyone and has completely forgotten himself, he finds that God has forgiven him everything, and he remembers Who, in reality, he is." [4]

As the image of the title suggests, *The Doorbell of Forgiveness* is fundamentally about the relation between these two dimensions of forgiveness, between what it is and how it is. Its focus is on the *act* of forgiveness, or better, on the necessary identity of forgiveness and its act. Though some attention is given by the contributors to forgiveness as project, to what can be materially accomplished by means of it, what matters here above all is *that* one forgives, regardless of the result. This is the deeper meaning of the doorbell image which, more than offering a comforting allegory of what forgiveness achieves, places priority on the imperative *to* forgive, to the lovely and risky impulse to ring the bell. The external power of forgiveness, its ability to open ways out of intractable individual and collective problems, rests wholly within its intrinsic value, in its being its own 'reward'. This means that forgiveness is not simply a virtue or something good to do, but a *true value* in the sense elaborated by Meher Baba.

"Mistakes in valuation arise owing to the influence of subjective desires or wants. True values are values which belong to things in their own right. They are intrinsic, and because they are intrinsic, they are absolute and permanent and are not liable to change from time to time or from person to person. False values are derived from desires or wants; they are dependent upon subjective factors, and being dependent upon subjective factors, they are relative and impermanent and are liable to change from time to time and from person to person." [5]

So forgiveness demonstrates the truth of its value by virtue of being itself an exercise in freedom from subjective factors. In these terms, the impulse to forgive is to be understood as something different than a desire or will *for* something. Instead, forgiveness is ordered toward the actualization of its own truth, the making real of its own potential to be. One forgives, not so much by aiming at some concrete end, such that one could definitively arrive at the success or completion of forgiveness, but rather by *staying within* the truth of forgiveness, by not transgressing the imperative to forgive. Thinking of forgiveness in this way, as the activity of remaining inwardly free from (and not necessarily rid of) the forces that cannot forgive, helps to clarify the deep relationship between forgiveness, spontaneity, and forgetfulness. Meher Baba's words on this relationship are inextricably linked with the idea of freedom from results. With regard to the practice of forgiveness as a kind of good work, we find the general principle that service or work bound to the objective good of others, though "of immense spiritual importance," is from the perspective of the goal of life, a kind of interminable dead-end.

"[A]s long as the idea of service is ... tied to the idea of results, it is inevitably fraught with a sense of incompleteness. There can be no realisation of Infinity through the pursuit of a never-ending series of consequences. Those who aim at sure and definite results through a life of service have an eternal burden on their minds."[6]

The principle of freedom from results is defined more absolutely in Meher Baba's description of the purposelessness of divine, infinite existence, our arrival at which is the very goal, or purpose, of everything.

"Reality is Existence infinite and eternal. Existence has no purpose by virtue of its being real, infinite and eternal. Existence exists. Being Existence it *has* to exist. Hence Existence, the Reality, cannot have any purpose. It just is. It is self-existing. Everything — the things and the beings — *in* Existence has a purpose. All things and beings have a purpose and must have a purpose, or else they cannot *be* in existence as what they are. Their very being in existence proves their purpose; and their *sole purpose* in existing is to become shed of purpose, i.e., to become purposeless. Purposelessness is of Reality; to have a purpose is to be lost in falseness. Everything exists only because it has a purpose. The moment that purpose has been accomplished, everything disappears and Existence is manifested as self-existing Self. Purpose presumes a direction and since Existence, being everything and everywhere, cannot have any direction, directions must always be in nothing and lead nowhere. Hence to have a purpose is to create a false goal. Love alone is devoid of all purpose and a spark of Divine Love sets fire to all purposes. The Goal of Life in Creation is to arrive at purposelessness, which is the state of Reality." [7]

Forgiveness enters this purpose-enflaming fire. Rupturing the chain of never-ending consequences, it relieves beings from the burden of results and opens the way into actually living within the inherent purposelessness of Reality. Far from fleeing life, forgiveness gives life back to itself as the very place of freedom.

"This realisation must and does take place only in the midst of life, for it is only in the midst of life that limitation can be experienced and transcended, and that subsequent freedom from limitation can be enjoyed." [8]

Felt from the perspective of this goal, forgiveness is less a duty or responsibility than the radical activation of the seemingly passive power of not-worrying, a very difficult and profoundly enjoyable exercise in the freedom of one's inherent divinity. The exercise of forgiveness accordingly has a spontaneous character or style. Practicing it might be called a form of immediate cooperation between the impasse of experience and the ultimate independence of reality.

"[B]y virtue of being absolutely independent it is but natural for God to exercise His infinite whim to experience and enjoy His own infinity. To exercise a whim is always the mark of an independent nature, because it is whimsicality that always colours the independent nature." [9]

Meher Baba thus places forgiveness within the broader category of *positive forgetfulness*, a happy state combining awareness of and non-reaction to both adverse and favorable circumstances that flowers in conspicuous creativity.

"Positive forgetfulness ... and its steady cultivation develops in man that balance of mind which enables him to express such noble traits as charity, forgiveness, tolerance, selflessness and service to others. ... Positive forgetfulness, although it lies at the very root of happiness, is by no means easy to acquire. Once a man attains this state of mind, however, he rises above pain and pleasure; he is master of himself. This forgetfulness, to be fully effective for the spiritual life, must become permanent, and such permanence is only acquired through constant practice during many lives. Some people, as a result of efforts towards forgetfulness in past lives, get spontaneous and temporary flashes of it in a later life, and it is such people who give to the world the best in poetry, art and philosophy, and who make the greatest discoveries in science." [10]

The practical crux of positive forgetfulness lies in this developmental relation between steady cultivation and spontaneity, in the fostering of an impulse not to react that bears abiding and unforeseeable fruit, what Meher Baba calls "manifestations of genuine spontaneity of forgetfulness."[11] The doing of forgiveness resides in dynamic relation to the inevitable unfolding of perfect, universal individuality.

"The limited individuality, which is the creation of ignorance, is transformed into the divine individuality which is unlimited. The illimitable consciousness of the Universal Soul becomes individualised in this focus without giving rise to any form of illusion. The person is free from all self-centred desires and he becomes the medium of the spontaneous flow of the supreme and universal will which expresses divinity. Individuality becomes limitless by the disappearance of ignorance." [12]

The imperative to forgive must thus be understood in the broader phenomenal context of the paradoxical correlation between habit and freedom. Forgiveness is spontaneous, but its free exercise is a development of habitual practice, the liberating result of ongoing intentional action.

"The life of true values can be spontaneous only when the mind has developed the unbroken habit of choosing the right value." [13]

The crucial distinction to be drawn, the distinction across which the decision to forgive operates, is thus between habits that bind and habits that set free, between, on the one hand, actions whose impressions [*sanskaras*] limit life and intensify separateness and ignorance, and, on the other, actions whose impressions liberate life and generate knowledge and enjoyment of its inherent unity—a spontaneous state of being also known as *love*.

"In love ... there is no sense of effort because it is spontaneous. Spontaneity is of the essence of true spirituality. The highest state of consciousness, in which the mind is completely merged in the Truth, is known as *Sahajawastha,* the state of unlimited spontaneity in which there is uninterrupted *Self-knowledge*." [14]

The core of this distinction (between binding and liberating actions) lies in the inevitable deconstruction of the ego, "the false nucleus of consolidated *sanskaras*."[15] The restrictive and ultimately eroding ego is the recurring obstacle on the path of experience, the imprisoning framework that each and every action works to reinforce or destroy.

"Any action which expresses the true values of life contributes towards the disintegration of the ego, which is a product of ages of ignorant action. Life cannot be permanently imprisoned within the cage of the ego. It must at some time strive towards the Truth." [16]

As a mode of relation to this inevitable disintegration or decay of the limited ego — limited because it persists only in ignorance and active denial of the inviolable unity of all life — forgiveness is definable as a movement of giving experience over to the unitive gravity of spiritual reality. Taking direct action against the very constraints of action, against the psychic chains that would determine it as re-action, against the interminable self-condemnations encapsulated in the separative rallying cry of *never forget!*, forgiveness forcefully and non-violently asserts the absolute spontaneity of reality, the inescapable freedom of which the pseudo-whims of personal interest are a pale shadow.

"At the pre-spiritual level, man is engulfed in unrelieved ignorance concerning the goal of infinite freedom; and though he is far from being happy and contented, he identifies so deeply with *sanskaric interests* that he experiences gratification in their furtherance. But the pleasure of his pursuits is conditional and transitory, and the *spontaneity which he experiences in them is illusory* because, through all his pursuits, his mind is working under limitations. The mind is capable of genuine freedom and spontaneity of action only when it is completely free from *sanskaric* ties and interests." [17]

Forgiveness is an act of relinquishing interest, not for the sake of becoming disinterested, but on behalf of a deeper interest that absolutely exceeds the framework of determined interests. The one who forgives is not uninterested in the particular problem that forgiveness addresses. The one who forgives is instead *hyper-interested* in the problem, interested to a degree that is totally uncontainable by the relation to the problem as object of worry or negative concern. Forgiveness puts into play a profound need to relate to reality in a non-reactive way, to become more intimate with it precisely by remaining *outside* the confining and ultimately uninteresting patterns of self-interest. Forgiveness thus partakes of the "divinely human life" embodied in the Avatar whose appearance, like the advent of forgiveness itself, takes place in the middle of seemingly terminal conflict:

"The *Avatar* appears in different forms, under different names, at different times, in different parts of the world. As his appearance always coincides with the spiritual birth of man, so the period immediately preceding his manifestation is always one in which humanity suffers from the pangs of the approaching birth ... There seems to be no possibility of stemming the tide of destruction. At this moment the *Avatar* appears. Being the total manifestation of God in human form, he is like a gauge against which man can measure what he is and what he may become. He trues the standard of human values by interpreting them in terms of a divinely human life. *He is interested in everything but not concerned about anything.* The slightest mishap may command his sympathy; the greatest tragedy will not upset him ... He is only concerned about concern." [18]

This does not at all mean, however, that forgiveness should be conceived as a solely individual process of human spiritual self-development. Like the unseen work of the God-Man that occurs on all levels of being and is only partially perceivable to humans, the mystery of forgiveness is that it is radically for the other and the world itself. One does not ring the doorbell only for oneself, for the ringing of it effects a real alteration in the objective world, in oneself *and* others. This fact is essential to the meaning of Meher Baba's description of the "charity of forgiveness":

People ask God for forgiveness. But since God is everything and everyone, who is there for Him to forgive? Forgiveness of the created was already there in His act of creation. But still people ask God's forgiveness, and He forgives them. But they, instead of forgetting that for which they asked forgiveness, forget that God has forgiven them, and, instead, remember the things they were forgiven — and so nourish the seed of wrongdoing, and it bears its fruit again. Again and again they plead for forgiveness, and again and again the Master says, I forgive.

"But it is impossible for men to forget their wrongdoings and the wrongs done to them by others. And since they cannot forget, they find it hard to forgive. But forgiveness is the best charity. (It is easy to give the poor money and goods when one has plenty, but to forgive is hard; but it is the best thing if one can do it.)"

"Instead of men trying to forgive one another they fight. Once they fought with their hands and with clubs. Then with spears and bows and arrows. Then with guns and cannon. Then they invented bombs and carriers for them. Now they have developed missiles that can destroy millions of other men thousands of miles away, and they are prepared to use them. The weapons used change, but the aggressive pattern of man remains the same."

"Now men are planning to go to the moon. And the first to get there will plant his nation's flag on it, and that nation will say, It is mine. But another nation will dispute the claim and they will fight here on this earth for possession of that moon. And whoever goes there, what will he find? Nothing but himself. And if people go on to Venus they will still find nothing but themselves. Whether men soar to outer space or dive to the bottom of the deepest ocean they will find themselves as they are, unchanged, because they will not have forgotten themselves nor remembered to exercise the charity of forgiveness." [19]

"Forgiveness is *charity*, not only because it expresses divine love, but because it actually *gives* something to the other, something better than all other possible gifts. What does forgiveness give? Much of the discourse in this book is trying to answer this question, which is why it is continually concerned with the question of *sanskaras* or impressions, the very of medium of conscious experience."

"There are two aspects of human experience — the subjective and objective. On the one hand there are mental processes which constitute essential ingredients of human experience, and on the other hand there are things and objects to which they refer. The mental processes are partly dependent upon the immediately given objective situation, and partly dependent upon the functioning of accumulated *sanskaras* or impressions of previous experience. The human mind thus finds itself between a sea of past *sanskaras* on the one side and the whole extensive objective world on the other." [20]

The answer that *The Doorbell of Forgiveness* arrives towards is that forgiveness gives a *new past*. The patient and forgiving reader will here discover many ways of recognizing how this is not only a metaphor, but a literal and actual fact. Forgiveness effects a real and palpable alteration in the stuff through which the limitations of past actions remain operative in the present. It accelerates the decay of dead forms and clears new pathways to "the Present, which is ever beautiful and stretches away beyond the limits of the past and the future."[21] Much more so than the violence and suffering to which it conspicuously responds, forgiveness participates in and attests to the struggle of life itself.

"All life is an effort to attain freedom from self-created entanglement. It is a desperate struggle to undo what has been done under ignorance, to throw away the accumulated burden of the past, to find rescue from the debris left by a series of temporary achievements and failures. Life seeks to *unwind the limiting sanskaras of the past* and to obtain release from the mazes of its own making, so that its further creations may spring directly from the heart of eternity and bear the stamp of unhampered freedom and intrinsic richness of being which knows no limitation." [22]

Nicola Masciandaro, Brooklyn, NY 2011

Endnotes

1. *The Divan-i-Hafiz*, trans. Wilberforce Clarke (London: Octagon Press, 1974), 216.3.
2. From a message sent by Meher Baba to Mildred Kyle in 1948, published in Seattle by Warren Healey, in Bal Natu, *Glimpses of the God-Man*, Volume VI: March 1954-April 1955 (Myrtle Beach: Sheriar Foundation, 1994), 87.
3. Such a relation between forgiveness and unknowing is suggested by Jesus's "Father, forgive them; for they know not what they do" (Luke 23:34).
4. Meher Baba, *The Everything and the Nothing* (Beacon Hill, Australia: Meher House Publications, 1963), 69-70.
5. Meher Baba, *Discourses*, 6th ed., 3 vols. (San Francisco: Sufism Reoriented, 1967), 3.139, original italics elided.
6. Ibid, 1.133. Cf.
7. Meher Baba, *The Everything and the Nothing*, 62.
8. Meher Baba, *Discourses*, III.12.
9. Meher Baba, *God Speaks*, 83.
10. Ibid, 213-214.
11. Ibid, 214.
12. Meher Baba, *Discourses*, I.41, original italics elided.
13. Meher Baba, *Discourses*, II.64.
14. Ibid, 192.
15. Ibid, 66.
16. Ibid, 65.
17. Ibid, 162.
18. Meher Baba, *Discourses*, III.15, my italics.
19. Meher Baba, *The Everything and the Nothing*, 69.
20. Meher Baba, *Discourses*, I.54.
21. Meher Baba, in Bhau Kalchuri, *Lord Meher*, 5809, <http://www.lordmeher.org>.
22. Meher Baba, *Discourses*, I.113, original italics elided, my emphasis.

Don Stevens

Don Stevens used principles of fostering companionship and paying attention to the opportunities presented by daily life as a most vital and important venue for spiritual development. Although he was never grandiose, he always seemed equally aware of a larger purpose or even a grand design as well as the seemingly minor details. To this end, his personal life habits of cooking and cleaning would be given quiet, methodical attention in the same measure as a careful explanation of projects as large scaled as the "Beads on One String" pilgrimages. He was a true artist at living.

Don Stevens was fun to be with. In the kitchen he would enjoy demonstrating the value of properly "chambre´-ing", or, bringing to room temperature, food, particularly meat, before cooking it, and, he would invariably take the time to be present and attentive to the process of preparation both to the food itself, and to those with him participating in the culinary adventure. His attention would extend from care of preparation through care of eating – always careful to watch the amount he ate, and to appreciate what was being consumed. For most of his life red wine accompanied two meals a day, though in his later years he would just have wine before eating for health reasons, and he would theoretically limit himself to one glass a day. The care of being present to those with whom he was dining also made the meal a special, sweet occasion.

The ability of Laurent Weichberger to simply publish transcripts of Don's meetings testifies to the clarity of Don's thought and speech. On reading over or listening to a recording of what Don would say on a given occasion, one will be struck by the care and completeness with which he would articulate his thoughts. A typical device of Don's was to start discussing a subject with a question. That would often mean that Don also had, in his mind, an approach to the solution that was sometimes quite surprising to what those with him were anticipating. Don demonstrated a unique combination of methodical clarity with adventurousness in his thinking and intuiting process. He was frequently venturing forth into new theatres of exploration; in fact this manuscript is a prime example. At the same time the very structure of his thought was clearly rooted in his personal relationship with Meher Baba and in Baba's words - words that Don worked with so closely both with his translation activity, writings, and group work.

At the time of this writing, Don has just recently passed away, on April 26th at the age of 92. His tireless work culminated with the final German translation of *Listen, Humanity* being completed just one month before his passing. Don had triumphantly completed all the translations and publishing tasks that Baba had put before him forty years ago – of *God Speaks*, the *Discourses* and *Listen, Humanity* into the three major European languages. Again, Don exercised the same attentive care with these translations as he did with everything else in his life, making sure he had just the right experts and editors in place for the various tasks at hand, and that the resulting product was as true to the original as possible – just as Meher Baba would have wanted it.

Don maintained a balance between energetic work and an active appreciation of life. For this reason he could not be said to be obsessive or compulsive. He relaxed when his body or mind needed relaxation, but he was an expert in time and energy management. The result of this was that he set a superb example as an effective worker who never lost the joy of his very productive activity. The work schedule that he had started as an international oil executive continued into his retirement with an enormous program of world travel that took him across both Eastern and Western Hemispheres at least twice annually, and often a yearly trip would be added to the Southern Hemisphere as well. While at home in Europe, he would seldom stay in any one place for more than two weeks at a time, making rounds to visit his important Meher Baba groups in Paris, London, Duneau, Marseilles, Cagnes-sur-Mer, and Le Mans. Later Don would establish important connections in Italy and the former Yugoslavia. The wider international trips were also taken with the purpose of visiting Baba groups worldwide – from India to Argentina, to all corners of the United States, to Mexico, and to Australia – just to name a few.

Don's preferred method of meeting was interactive. Unless there was a very large crowd, he gravitated toward the sharing of ideas in a small group setting over giving a lecture. Don enjoyed meeting regularly with a number of small groups and encouraged that these groups commit to a regular meeting process thereby forming circles of spiritual companionship. In his London group's book, *The Inner Path in the New Life* (London: Companion Books, 1989), a way of approaching group work deeply investigated the purpose of this companionship in spiritual development. Following the publishing of that book there was a rise in interest in companionship-oriented group activity. One offshoot was the Young Peoples Group (YPG) that was founded by Don and Laurent in the USA. One of the original purposes of the group was to enable Don to pass along his lifetime of experience with Meher Baba to a younger generation.

Different topics would be on the agenda at each YPG meeting which would typically span a two day weekend of morning and afternoon sessions. The *Doorbell of Forgiveness* is the product of one such group meeting. This transcript is a prime example of the style and substance of Don Steven's group activity. There is the give and take conversation among the companions, the honest feedback to one another's thoughts, feelings, and concerns, the mutual sense of support [and respect], reflections on the challenges of daily life, and a good sense of humor. As Meher Baba has said, "When five or more are gathered in my name, I am there."

Don Stevens made the most of this invitation.

Cynthia and Richard Griffin
June 5, 2011 – Salem, MA

Acknowledgements by Laurent

First and foremost, to Don Stevens, for sharing so generously, and deeply, and frequently over the last seven years of his love, his hard earned wisdom and his intuitions so that a torch could indeed be passed by him, and Meher Baba, to the younger generation. Your life itself is a colossal monument of love for Baba.

Love to the "God Parents" chosen by Don to host our gatherings. Without you we would not have been able to listen, and share, so comfortably.

I bow to the young people's group for showing up. My computer actually contains 165 files in 31 folders under the folder: C:\OmPoint\MeherBaba\DonStevens\YPG. Alison, Ben, Betty, Cynthia, Danny, Doug, Ed, Ellie, Glenn, Heather, Jamshid, Kira, Payam, Leslie, Mahmoud, Marlena, Marnie, Nasrin, Nicola, Richard, Ryan, Sam, and Sevn, you are each now carrying a very special torch.

Much appreciation for Daniel J. Sanders, for his huge contribution in both transcribing and editing over three years, and also to Karl Moeller, for stepping up to the editing work as Don requested. Thank you for meeting me in the middle on EMDR.

We are grateful to Payam Russ, Marnie Frank, and Nicola Masciandaro for the Preface, Introduction, and Epilogue respectively.

Many thanks, to Ralph Schmid at Third i Design for such a great job on the layout and design of the book. You do fine work, brother. You are a wunder-mensch.

To Danny Ladinsky for allowing us to reprint the splendid poem, "Forgive the Dream" from *The Gift*, a remarkable poetry book reflecting the spiritual purity of Hafiz. I got kin in that body!

A million hugs to Fereshteh Azad and Reza Abrahimzadeh for helping me to rewrite "On the Deathbed" by Rumi for this publication. Without your native Farsi, I would have no chance.

A wholehearted Jai Baba to Elaine Cox for allowing me to steal Baba's precious words from her personal songbook while at Meherabad.

Love to Joanie Agin and Donna Stewart, in Myrtle Beach, for sharing exactly what Baba wanted me to hear about forgiveness while on retreat at the Meher Spiritual Center.

Special thanks to Douglas Frank for the use of his photos of Don in Neskowin and elsewhere.

We recognize the work of David Fenster at Meher Nazar Publications. Thanks for the use of the image of Meher Baba at Meherabad. Your continued work to preserve Meher Baba's images and words, in a way befitting the Avatar, is most inspiring.

Kisses to my beloved wife Lilly (I choose you!) And to my precious children, Aspen and Cyprus, thanks for being so supportive of all my work with Baba over the years. He knows, and I couldn't do it without your love.

And to all the wondrous people at Companion Books: Deborah Sanchez, Wayne Smith, and Sevn McAuley. Thank you for believing in this book project, and for manifesting it with me now.

Also from Companion Books

Some Results, by Don E. Stevens (1995). Paperback: 113 pages. ISBN-13: 978-0952509714.

Meher Baba's Word and His Three Bridges, by Don E. Stevens with Norah Moore and Laurent Weichberger (2003). Paperback: 234 pages. ISBN-13: 978-0952509745.

Mandali Email, by Don E. Stevens and Bhau Kalchuri (2005). Paperback: 79 pages. ISBN-13: 978-0952509738.

Meher Baba's Gift of Intuition, by Don E. Stevens and Companions (2006). Paperback: 197 pages. ISBN-13: 978-0952509769.

Sexuality on the Spiritual Path, by Don E. Stevens, Charles Haynes, David Carter, et al (2007). Paperback: 206 pages. ISBN-13: 978-0952509776.

Celebrating Divine Presence: Journeys into God, by Laurent Weichberger, Yaakov Weintraub, Thomas Knoles, Karl Moeller, et al (2008). Paperback: 392 pages. ISBN-13: 978-0952509790.

These books are all available at Amazon books: www.amazon.com.

www.ingramcontent.com/pod-product-compliance
Lightning Source LLC
Chambersburg PA
CBHW061603110426
42742CB00039B/2670